Beyond Othering

Syracuse Studies on Peace and Conflict Resolution
Robert A. Rubinstein and Çerağ Esra Çuhadar, *Series Editors*

Select Titles from Syracuse Studies on Peace and Conflict Resolution

Back Channel Negotiations: Secrets in the Middle East Peace Process
Anthony Wanis-St. John

Civil Society, Conflict Resolution, and Democracy in Nigeria
Darren Kew

Making Peace with Referendums: Cyprus and Northern Ireland
Joana Amaral

The Paradox of Repression and Nonviolent Movements
Lester R. Kurtz and Lee A. Smithey, eds.

Peacekeeping in South Lebanon: Credibility and Local Cooperation
Vanessa F. Newby

People's Peace: Prospects for a Human Future
Yasmin Saikia and Chad Haines, eds.

Western Sahara: War, Nationalism, and Conflict Irresolution, Second Edition
Stephen Zunes and Jacob Mundy

Youth Encounter Programs in Israel: Pedagogy, Identity, and Social Change
Karen Ross

For a full list of titles in this series,
visit https://press.syr.edu/supressbook-series
/syracuse-studies-on-peace-and-conflict-resolution/.

Beyond Othering

A Gandhian Approach to Conflict
Resolution in India and Pakistan

Debidatta Aurobinda Mahapatra
& Seema Shekhawat

Syracuse University Press

First Edition 2023

23   24   25   26   27   28   6   5   4   3   2   1

∞ The paper used in this publication meets the minimum requirements
of the American National Standard for Information Sciences—Permanence
of Paper for Printed Library Materials, ANSI Z39.48-1992.

For a listing of books published and distributed by Syracuse University Press,
visit https://press.syr.edu.

ISBN: 978-0-8156-3817-9 (hardcover)
        978-0-8156-3810-0 (paperback)
        978-0-8156-5692-0 (e-book)

Library of Congress Cataloging-in-Publication Data

Names: Mahapatra, Debidatta Aurobinda, author. | Shekhawat, Seema, author.
Title: Beyond othering : a Gandhian approach to conflict resolution in India
     and Pakistan / Debidatta Aurobinda Mahapatra, Seema Shekhawat.
Other titles: Gandhian approach to conflict resolution in South Asia,
     the India-Pakistan context
Description: First edition. | Syracuse, New York : Syracuse University Press, 2023. |
     Series: Syracuse studies on peace and conflict resolution | Includes bibliographical
     references and index.
Identifiers: LCCN 2023006421 (print) | LCCN 2023006422 (ebook) |
     ISBN 9780815638179 (hardcover) | ISBN 9780815638100 (paperback) |
     ISBN 9780815656920 (ebook)
Subjects: LCSH: Gandhi, Mahatma, 1869–1948—Influence. | Conflict management—
     South Asia. | India—History—Partition, 1947—Influence. | Other (Philosophy) |
     Belonging (Social psychology)
Classification: LCC JZ5584.S65 M35 2023 (print) | LCC JZ5584.S65 (ebook) |
     DDC 954.04/5—dc23/eng/20230421
LC record available at https://lccn.loc.gov/2023006421
LC ebook record available at https://lccn.loc.gov/2023006422

Manufactured in the United States of America

Contents

Preface

The killing of George Floyd in 2020 led to protests across the United States and the world. The incident ignited a raging debate, which can be viewed through the lens of "othering," a recurring theme in the study of human interactions and cultures. From a broad perspective, othering can be interpreted as a recognition of different identities through mutual understanding and appreciation. Multicultural societies thrive as different groups live in harmony and do not perceive each other in hostile terms. In its narrow and rigid dimension, othering is based on the perception that cultural distinctions are separate and rigid. This view leads to the clash of cultural identities, reflected in conflicts involving race, color, language, geographic locations, and even indiscernible markers of distinction.

We examine this rigid aspect of othering while exploring pathways for conflict resolution. We do not suggest reductionist solutions based on exclusivist ideas and practices. Instead, we scrutinize these ideas from a broader, more inclusive, perspective, with a focus on the India-Pakistan conflict in South Asia. We also examine ideas that promote, or have the potential for, belonging. Such an examination helps to illustrate how reductive, narrowly conceived othering runs counter to the idea of belonging and peaceful coexistence. In the context of twentieth-century South Asia, we attempt to reconcile the thesis of othering and the antithesis of belonging via the framework of Gandhian conflict resolution. We do not argue that violent othering will be resolved completely anytime soon, or that differences need to be eliminated, as peaceful and nonviolent differences are hallmarks of healthy cultural relativism. We argue that these differences need not necessitate distancing, wars, and violence.

We apply a Gandhian critical framework to bear upon othering and make a case for a peaceful South Asia, and world, through inclusiveness and appreciation for the differences that, in sum, characterize belonging. We do not claim that the Gandhian critique holds solutions to all such problems, but believe that it can provide an alternate approach, yet under-explored, to addressing the violent conflict in the South Asian region. This alternate approach is useful for examining conflicts rooted in othering at multiple levels—interpersonal, national, regional, or global. Through this forward-looking approach, we explore peaceful solutions and make a case that our study is instructive for understanding conflicts in other places such as the Russia-Ukraine conflict in which the two neighbors are engaged in a war.

Gandhi's inclusive ideas and practices helped him to appreciate humanity beyond constructed divisions of race, class, religion, and culture. He practiced nonviolent philosophy to work for peace at all levels in all possible ways. Differences in religion, identity, or ideology notwithstanding, the Gandhian nonviolence imperative effortlessly dictates an all-embracing nonviolent and transformative worldview. The healing power of Gandhian "soul-force" is context free and universal, and Gandhi argued that if it can work in one place (such as South Asia), it can work at any other place or time. The Gandhian worldview recognizes no enemies but acknowledges differing opinions, values, and identities. It rejects rigid othering as tantamount to both physical and psychological violence and encourages us to pause and think: Are violent methods of conflict resolution, which originate in rigid othering, effective to realize sustainable peace? Have media circulated images of George Floyd's killing, or of children drowning in the Mediterranean, or of people unbelievably surviving air bombings in Syria, Yemen, and Ukraine not jolted our shared conscience into recognizing the connection between these inhumane situations and the rigid othering?

To promote belonging, we argue, new narratives must be cultivated, and genuine attempts must be initiated to counter rigid othering and promote engagement, whether in South Asia or in any other conflict situation. Mere formation of a political organization, media coverage, or crafting policy for the appeasement of a particular political constituency would be a repudiation of Gandhian engagement. It is difficult to have genuine engagement in any larger sense unless it is based on psychological understanding and harmony. Psychological engagement is more important than economic and political engagement for addressing deep-rooted othering, which may amplify with each act of violence. Gandhian ideology favors a more creative nonviolent approach to resolving conflicts that promotes belonging. Gandhian *Sarvodaya* (well-being of all) is relevant here, as it is based on the premise that peace is incompatible with othering. Through an examination of the partition of the Indian subcontinent and the complex politics involved in it, we argue though it is not possible to effect conciliatory belonging in the region overnight, or to reverse the destructive psychology of othering anytime soon, it is nonetheless necessary to realize that new ideas and practices must be conceived and implemented to promote peace in the subcontinent.

The research for this project was built on our earlier research on conflict resolution and peace building. Seema's location in Kashmir for more than two decades and Debidatta's location in the region for about three years proved useful for this research. Our doctoral and postdoctoral research examined different facets of conflicts in South Asia. While conducting field studies in South Asia, we witnessed firsthand the suffering because of violent othering. In our earlier research, we did not bring Gandhi or the concept of othering and belonging to bear upon conflict and peace in South Asia. Nor have we come across any such study. This work is the first of its kind in applying theories of othering and belonging to conflict resolution in South Asia. This study is also one of the first to apply Gandhian conflict resolution to the region. We argue that the application of Gandhian ideas to othering and belonging is relevant not only as a theoretical exercise but also as a call for nonviolent social praxis to promote belonging. We emphasize the necessity of crafting policies that prioritize the intersectionality of nonviolence and inclusive and sustainable peace. We believe that our work will pave the way for breaking othering-generated stereotypes and create sensitivity toward mutual understanding, empathy, respect and dignity, and a yearning for belonging and heart-to-heart engagement.

We are thankful to all who collaborated with us directly or indirectly in our research. We are grateful for every opportunity that came our way to understand the conflict and its various facets. Our formal and informal interactions with Indian and Pakistani friends provided insights for research. We are thankful to them. We are thankful to the library staff of Florida State College at Jacksonville, University of Central Florida, University of Massachusetts–Boston, Rollins College, Kashmir University, Jammu University, and Jawaharlal Nehru University for facilitating our research. Our teaching at academic institutions in India and the United States provided new perspectives. Teaching courses on human rights, peace studies, Asian politics, and gender provided the opportunity to delve deep into various issues of relevance. The interactions with the students provided fresh insights on othering and belonging. Without all the fascinating interactions and a common affinity for peace by peaceful means this work could not have been possible. We are thankful to our friend and colleague Richard Grego for going through the manuscript and offering valuable suggestions. We are grateful to our families and friends for their encouragement and support. Finally, we are thankful to Deborah Manion of Syracuse University Press for encouraging us to continue our work with passion and peace of mind.

Beyond Othering

Introduction

Partition, South Asian Conflict, and Gandhi

In this study we examine one of the momentous events in human history, partition of British India in 1947, to argue that the psychology that led to partition has not abated. It continues to manifest itself in multiple reoccurring ways, including, but not limited to, interstate wars and communal violence. This psychology, the psychology of othering,[1] permeates not only politics at a higher level but also everyday life. Observing an India-Pakistan cricket match, the most popular outdoor game in South Asia, provides a sense of this psychology on a popular level. The mass hysteria generated by this game on both sides exudes the visceral feeling of a live war. A win leads to celebrations with nationalist slogans, distribution of sweets, and fireworks. A loss leads to mourning and a promise of revenge. In exploring social-political partition and post-partition developments in South Asia in this interdisciplinary work, we examine the psychology of othering to make an argument that there is a need for undoing psychological partition to resolve India-Pakistan conflict and that, toward this end, Gandhian ideas are relevant. We study a historical event, the partition, its psychological and ideological wellsprings and consequences, and explore Gandhian principles to address the most prominent conflict in South Asia.

The partition of British India created the two independent states of India and Pakistan. M. K. Gandhi opposed the partition. One of the major factors behind his opposition was the apprehension that the partition politics, rooted in the psychology of othering, might turn South Asia into a near-permanent conflict zone. His apprehension was not without basis. The post-partition violent wars and communal carnage recall memories

1

of partition, the stories of which are passed from generation to generation through multiple, and often contradictory, narratives. Therefore, examining partition is akin to reliving it or, to use the Comtean phrase, "living dead men's lives,"[2] at least at a psychological level. In this work, we examine possible linkages between many contemporary developments and the psychology that shaped similar events in the past. We focus on the India-Pakistan conflict while arguing that internal and external politics in South Asia cannot be delinked, since they operate in the same social milieu. We argue that the partition genie never returned to the lamp, and though geographical partition was accepted, howsoever reluctantly or readily, the psychological partition continues to persist and shape politics in South Asia. The geographical partition is not reversible but psychological partition needs to be addressed.

Neither scholars of nationalism nor scholars of British India have found a comprehensive explanation for partition in their narratives. There are several scholarly explanations of the event.[3] For some, it centered primarily on the failure of colonial rule, reflecting an unpleasant transition from colonial rule to the postcolonial world. For others, it was the impact of colonialism on the transition to nationalism and modernity. One explanation is particularly relevant to this work. Gilmartin explores the "high politics" and "low politics" of partition and examines how their intersection galvanized identity politics and partition.[4] High politics is politics at a higher level. It describes how leaders at the top shape events at the grassroots. The lower side of the political spectrum describes the stories from the ground, involving people who experienced and suffered partition. For our research, big ideas that shaped identity politics and the psychology of partition in British India and that continue to shape events in South Asia, within and between states, are relevant. We argue that one must go to the core of these big ideas, unravel their key elements, to understand partition. We also contend that both "high politics" and "low politics" of partition reinforce each other. Understanding this linkage helps to clarify the acrimony shared by post-partition states of India and Pakistan and the communal divide within these states.

The partition gave physical life to the psychology of othering, which, in the post-partition scenario, engulfed the politics of South Asia. It continues to sustain and nourish itself with each act of violence, whether at a small scale or a large scale. This work is interested in addressing the psychology of othering and exploring pathways for peace to address the post-partition conflictual politics of South Asia. Toward this end, we do not suggest the reductionist solution of rolling back history and undoing geographical partition, nor do we make an argument in recidivism for partitioning the subcontinent further. We examine these ideas to expose their underlying motivations and elaborate on how they run counter to the idea of peaceful conflict resolution. In this sense, we analyze several ideas—those that prompted partition and continue to shape the post-partition developments and those with the potential to promote peace in South Asia. We attempt a dialogue between the elements of othering and the elements of peaceful belonging. Such an exercise, we argue, will help elucidate how some ideas promote othering and other ideas promote peace or at least are worth considering for peace.

This work transcends the search for a partition narrative. Even though we examine big ideas and their role in partition, the goal is not to make a postmortem of the past but rather to explore pathways for peace. Toward this goal, we refrain from any "thick description" of partition events, the communal killings, refugee situation, and displacement of millions of people. There is a plethora of literature on various aspects of partition, focusing, among other things, on the actual event of the partition and its multiple aspects, including the communal carnage, and the refugee and displacement situation. While not denying their significance, and even using some of that description from the events in the history and politics of partition, we explore solutions. We examine the psychology of othering and juxtapose it with Gandhian ideas to explore conflict resolution in South Asia. To put it another way, by applying a Gandhian framework, we offer a counter idea to the idea of othering for conflict transformation in South Asia. We argue that the idea of othering, which focuses on homogenous states, is problematic for modern times. The ideology of a homogenous state—for example, an Islamic state, or a Hindu state, or a Christian state, or a Buddhist state, or any state based on a homogenous identity such as religion, color, or race—runs counter to the ideology and practice of globalization. Though radical ideologies and their patrons such as the

Islamic State of Iraq and Syria, much weakened now, adhere to the ideas of homogenous states and extend support to such movements worldwide, these ideas and practices run counter to the idea and construction of modern states. Back in 1972, Connor made a study of 132 states and found that only 12 of them could be described essentially homogeneous from an ethnic viewpoint.[5] Not "moral monism," which we explain later, but multiculturalism and pluralism have become credos of the post–Cold War globalized world. South Asia, and India and Pakistan—the beleaguered offspring of partition—cannot escape this global trend. There is an urgent need to explore solutions to their conflictual relations via alternative ideas and practices.

Significant capital has been devoted to resolve the India-Pakistan conflict without desired outcomes. Against this backdrop, we argue that the Gandhian ideas for conflict resolution are worth exploring. We do not claim that Gandhi holds solutions to all problems in South Asia or the world, but such an exercise will highlight an alternative approach, yet unexplored, to address conflicts rooted in the psychology of othering. Though we apply this alternative approach to South Asia, particularly to the India-Pakistan conflict, we argue that such an approach is useful in addressing conflicts at multiple levels, whether interpersonal, national, regional, or global.

Ideology, Identity, and Partition

In South Asia the psychology of othering took the shape of a political project in the form of the two-nation ideology. Though the ideology factored Hindus and Muslims in British India as two nations, it could be applied to other contexts. It mainly referred to religious identities, but one could include identities such as race, color, language, and other markers of separateness in the definition of identity. The notion of groups with different identities coexisting within the boundary of a state, and forming a single nation, is considered impossible from this perspective. Cultural identity understood in this way is not the sense of identity as articulated by Emile Durkheim in his analysis of national identity,[6] in which multiple identities could embrace common symbols such as national anthem or national flag as symbols of national solidarity. In a multiethnic and pluralistic state, two-nation ideology suggests, minorities would be marginalized. As it is unlikely that groups with different identities would have equal numbers to balance each other's influence in a modern state, the two-nation ideology predicts ceaseless conflict in multiethnic nations. The two-nation solution, put simply, is "one distinct group, one state." There is significant literature on partition in different contexts and on its beneficial and harmful impacts.[7] Broadly, two lines of argument can be identified. First, conflicting ethnic aspirations can be addressed through federal governance and crafting policies to address the aspirations of ethnic minorities. Second, partition is a viable solution to long hostilities and violent relations between ethnic communities. The partition of Ethiopia in 1993 and the partition of Sudan in 2011 inspired some of these studies, as well as recent debates on ethnic communities and their aspirations in countries such as Cyprus and Iraq.

The assumption that group identities clash requires critical examination. Tajfel and Turner define a group as "a collection of individuals who perceive themselves to be members of the same social category, share some emotional involvement in this common definition of themselves, and achieve some degree of social consensus about the evaluation of their group and of their membership in it."[8] The essential criterion for group membership, hence, is that the individuals consider themselves and are considered by others as members of a group with a specific identity. As most modern societies are multiethnic and multicultural, it is possible, Burton argues, "there would be problems of frustration and lack of participation and identity. Most, as a consequence, have high levels of alienation, leading to conflict situations of many kinds that affect the whole of a society and, indirectly, the world society."[9] The question is: Does the existence of multiple groups necessarily lead to conflicts? Burton in his study of "deep-rooted conflict" argues that deep-rooted conflicts involve deep feelings.[10] For Lederach, conflict emerges and develops based on "the meaning and interpretation people involved attach to action and events."[11] A conflict, thereby, is not merely about separate identities and cultures, but how members of a group perceive members of other groups. Agnew argues, "In the process of social interaction groups form geographically and differentiate themselves from one another. In this process, certain patterns of behavior and systems of symbols are selected as identifying markers to distinguish 'we' from 'they' as clearly as possible. Though sharing a large number of cultural characteristics, groups celebrate their uniqueness in terms of contrasting cultural elements and promote these elements as to exemplify difference rather than similarity."[12] When groups perceive their identity as conflictual vis-à-vis other identities and mobilize, a conflict ensues. The first author has elaborated on this argument in an earlier work.[13] In the Indian subcontinent, Hindus and Muslims as two different groups existed for centuries. The Muslim appearance in India happened in the medieval period, but there was no major clash as decisive and violent as the partition. There were wars between Hindu and Muslim kingdoms, but those wars could be explained in terms of territorial expansion, ambition, and resources, not purely in terms of a clash of identities. Though the differences existed until the twentieth century, those differences were not articulated in terms of othering.

How did the idea of othering and two-nation ideology gain roots in British India? While examining this question, we focus on big ideas, which shaped the politics of partition. Considerable literature is available on Muhammad Ali Jinnah, the political founder of Pakistan. There is relatively less literature available on Muhammad Iqbal, considered the spiritual father of Pakistan. In 1904, Iqbal wrote a song in Urdu, titled "Taranah-e-Hindi" (Anthem of the People of Hindustan). The first line of the song reads, "Sare Jahan Se Accha Hindustan Hamara." It can be translated as "Our land Hind-land [or Indian subcontinent] is better than the entire world." Another stanza of the poem translates, "Religion does not teach us animosity. We are all 'Hindi' [a reference to inhabitants of the Indian subcontinent], and we all belong to Hindustan."

Iqbal's increasing familiarity with Islamic thought and literature and visits to Egypt, Turkey, and Iran changed his worldview. In 1931 he claimed to have a dream about a "new movement in Islamic countries."[14] Notably, the movements for Islamic consolation in Europe and other parts of the world were taking place in the nineteenth and early twentieth centuries. Schimmel traces the period of the 1850s, in which the Sepoy revolt against the British rule took place in India, as a "period in India as well as in other parts of the world a time of preparation for new consolidation of Islamic ideals."[15] As Iqbal's poem, written in 1904, demonstrates, he was not initially influenced by this idea of Islamic consolidation. In this sense, one can identify two phases in Iqbal's philosophy and activism: while the earlier phase was characterized by the acceptance of the multireligious identity of India, the later phase gravitated toward religious consolidation and demand for a religious state.

Iqbal later questioned the separation of church and state, or, by extension, religion and state, which was a foundational principle of modern states since the Treaty of Westphalia (1648). He considered such separation a mistake. In a letter in 1937, he wrote, "The biggest blunder made by Europe was the separation of Church and State. This deprived their culture of moral soul and diverted it to the atheistic materialism. . . . The European war of 1914 was an outcome of the aforesaid mistakes made by the European nations in the separation of the Church and the State." Influenced by Sa'id Halim Pasha, the grand vizier of the Ottoman Empire (1913–17), Iqbal argued, "Islam is a harmony of idealism and positivism," and it is a "unity of the eternal verities of freedom, equality, and solidarity."[16] Iqbal's argument reflected a religious worldview, with Islam at the center. He believed that only an Islamic legal system, based on Islamic principles, could provide justice to Muslims. Any other system, drawing from secularized modern principles of jurisprudence, lacked that competence. This view of life and the world could be explained by his sense of "moral monism," in which, as articulated by Bhikhu Parekh:

> only one way of life is fully human, true, or the best, and that all others are defective to the extent that they fall short of it. Since every way of life necessarily embodies several values, moral monism either argues that one value is the highest and others merely a means to or conditions of it, more plausibly and commonly that although all values are equally important or some more than others, there is only one best or truly rational way to combine them. For the monist evil, like error, can take many forms, but the good, like truth, is inherently singular or uniform in nature. Even as the same proposition cannot be true in one place or false in another, the same way of life cannot be good for one person or society and bad for another. Although the monist considers only one

way of life to be truly human, he is not committed to the view that all human beings or societies ought to live by it. He might believe that since they are unequally endowed intellectually or morally, those unable to lead the truly human life should be left free to live such inferior ways of life as are best suited to them. What he cannot concede is that the good life can be lived in several more or less equally worthwhile ways.[17]

Iqbal was keen to apply his vision to the Indian subcontinent. He conceived the idea of carving out an Islamic state from British India, particularly from its northwest, where Muslims were in the majority. In his presidential address to the Indian Muslim League at Allahabad in 1930, while formally introducing the two-nation theory, he argued, "The formation of a consolidated North-West Indian Muslim State appears to be the final destiny of the Muslims, at least of North West India. . . . [T]he life of Islam as a cultural force in this country very largely depends on its centralization in a specified territory."[18]

Phillips Talbot, an American journalist and diplomat who reported on the freedom struggle in India during the 1940s, explored how the ideology of two nations—that Muslims are not minorities, but a separate community, in need of a separate nation-state—was cultivated. Sir Abdul Qadir, a prominent journalist from British India, during a meeting with Talbot, elaborated the justification behind his support for partition. First, Muslims will get no fair deal under Hindus; second, the Congress party is communal, not nationalist; and third, Muslims are not a minority but a separate community.[19] While the first concern emerged owing to democratic politics (which is, to put it simply, rule of majority and underrepresentation of minority interests), the second and third concerns reflected the idea of othering.

Othering was intensified with the rise of Hindu nationalism in the early twentieth century. According to Kulke and Rothermund, the Muslims were suspicious of Neo-Hinduism, which emerged in the late nineteenth and early twentieth centuries, and even "distrusted its profession of religious universalism. The emphasis on the equality of all religions was seen as a particularly subtle threat to Islamic identity."[20] The electoral politics and the taste of power and privilege contributed to this sharpening of identity politics. The Hindu-majority political regime, which took over power in the late 1930s, contributed to the idea of othering. Talbot elaborated: "The preponderantly Hindu regimes of the Indian National Congress between 1937 and 1939 brought new life to the Muslim League, because Muslims could unite in opposing ministries which they thought were ruling according to a philosophy of life entirely different from their own. Political activity, then, has made Muslims more conscious of being brothers in Islam."[21]

One line of the argument suggests that the British policy to divide Bengal along religious lines in 1905 was a precursor to the partition, which happened four decades later. According to Kulke and Rothermund, "Lord Curzon did not hesitate to point out to the Muslims of eastern Bengal that he conceived of this province as Muslim. The Bengali Hindus, on the other hand, noted with dismay that they were in a minority in the new province of Bengal."[22] The partition of Bengal and creation of communal electorates under the Morley-Minto reforms of 1909 further sharpened the communal cleavages. The idea of separate religious identities was consciously used and mobilized for political purposes. British writer Leonard Woolf, who was a civil servant in Ceylon (Sri Lanka) in the early years of the twentieth century, argued that, had the British transferred power in 1940, partition could have been avoided. He wrote, "I have no doubt that if British governments had been prepared to grant in . . . 1940 what they refused in 1940 but granted in 1947—then nine-tenths of the misery, hatred, and violence, the imprisonings and terrorism, the murders, flogging, shootings, assassinations, even the racial massacres would have been avoided; the transference of power might well have been accomplished peacefully, even possibly without Partition."[23]

Though Woolf's assertion might appear an exaggeration, we argue that the British policies played a role in contributing to the psychology of othering and giving it a political shape. The All-India Muslim League was founded in the East Bengal capital, Dacca (Dhaka), as a pan-Indian Muslim organization, merely after a year of the partition of Bengal, in 1906. This organization later spearheaded partition under the leadership of Jinnah, who argued that the idea of coexistence of Hindus and Muslims is an impossibility. During his presidential speech at the Muslim League conference at Lahore in 1940, in which the league formally announced Pakistan, Jinnah elaborated:

> It is extremely difficult to appreciate why our Hindu friends fail to understand the real nature of Islam and Hinduism. They are not religions in the strict sense of the word, but are, in fact, different and distinct social orders, and it is a dream that the Hindus and Muslims can ever evolve a common nationality, and this misconception of one Indian nation has troubles and will lead India to destruction if we fail to revise our notions in time. The Hindus and Muslims belong to two different religious philosophies, social customs, and literatures. They neither intermarry nor interdine together and, indeed, they belong to two different civilizations which are based mainly on conflicting ideas and conceptions. Their aspect on life and of life are different. It is quite clear that Hindus and Mussalmans derive their inspiration from different sources of history. They have different epics, different heroes, and different episodes. Very often the hero of one is a foe of the other and, likewise, their victories and defeats overlap. To yoke together two such nations under a single state, one as a numerical minority and the other as a majority, must lead to growing discontent and final destruction of any fabric that may be so built for the government of such a state.[24]

Indian National Congress leaders, including Gandhi, Nehru, and Ambedkar, countered this argument. While acknowledging the differences between the two cultural systems, they argued that there exist common grounds to develop a common national identity. Ambedkar wrote:

> Isn't there enough that is common to both Hindus and Musalmans [Muslims], which if developed, is capable of moulding them into one people? Nobody can deny that there are many modes, manners, rites and customs which are common to both. Nobody can deny that there are rites, customs and usages based on religion which do divide Hindus and Musalmans. The question is, which of these should be emphasized. If the emphasis is laid on things that are common, there need be no two nations in India. If the emphasis is laid on points of difference, it will no doubt give rise to two nations. . . . If the Hindus and Musalmans agree to emphasize the things that bind them and forget those that separate

them, there is no reason why in course of time they should not grow into a nation. . . . Is it right for the Muslim League to emphasize only differences, and ignore altogether the forces that bind?[25]

Nehru argued, "Though outwardly there was diversity and infinite variety among our people, everywhere there was tremendous impress of oneness, which had held us together for ages past, whatever political fate or misfortune had befallen us."[26]

This perceptional difference, argues Josef Korbel, chairman of the first United Nations Commission on India and Pakistan,[27] was fundamental to partition.[28] Gupta adopts a similar approach and argues that "intrinsically antithetical ideological commitments" of the Indian National Congress and the Muslim League, the two major political parties, played a critical role in partition.[29] The antithetical ideological commitments have not ceased to exist; they have assumed new forms and provided momentum to acrimonious politics in post-partition South Asia. The partition, projected as a solution to minimize a direct clash between communities by separating them, and post-partition developments in South Asia raise some relevant questions: Is the partition idea useful to address the conflict in South Asia or elsewhere? Or, from a long-range perspective, can partitioning communities and minimizing scopes of direct interaction provide a lasting solution to conflicts in the increasingly globalized world characterized by multiculturalism and pluralism?

Post-partition South Asia

South Asia is a fluid concept without a universally accepted definition.[30] It emerged as a postcolonial political construct, comprising eight states: India, Pakistan, Bangladesh, Sri Lanka, Nepal, Bhutan, Maldives, and Afghanistan. While the states in the region share certain characteristics, the term does not fully capture the region's diversity in terms of the history, culture, fusions, and transformations happening since the ancient period. We do not explore in detail the geographical, and even sociocultural, dynamics of the South Asian region, as this study does not necessitate such an elaboration. We position the discourse on South Asia within the partition politics and social forces that led to one of the bloodiest events in the region's history, with implications for the present. Recognizing that South Asia is composed of several states, we focus on India and Pakistan, the two significant players who bore the brunt of partition, and argue that their conflictual relations dominate South Asian politics.

The image of South Asia, as generally portrayed in comparative politics and conflict resolution literature, is one of suffering, nation-building travails, and underdevelopment. For Goor, Rupesinghe, and Scarione, the states emerging out of colonial history have not "evolved gradually over a period of time but were (geographically) designed and created by outsiders. . . . As a result, in most developing countries traditional structures have remained intact."[31] This is apparent in the case of state formation in South Asia. The Radcliffe Commission, which was tasked with drawing a border between India and Pakistan, drew it within weeks, amid contested claims and complex geography inhabited by diverse populations spreading over thousands of miles. India and Pakistan, even while being burdened with abrupt border drawing, a colonial past, and entrenched traditional structures, remain obsessed with state security and consider each other to be major threats. The situation in the case of India and Pakistan remains compounded by twin factors: first, they share a colonial past and bloody history; second, their geographical proximity serves as a constant reminder of this acrimonious past and shapes their present relations. Among various factors that contribute to the complexity of nationalism and politics of South Asia, Connor argues, one is that "it is the minorities and not the dominant group who populate the border region." The other is the "pernicious" and "crazy-quilt" nature of ethnic composition of South Asia. He points out, "Rather than inhabiting a single, contiguous region, many ethnic groups are separated into a number of widely spread, tiny enclaves. This phenomenon greatly increases inter-ethnic contacts, thereby increasing political complexity."[32]

The partition aimed at resolving the communal conflict. The postcolonial history and politics of South Asia do not support such a claim. Persistent India-Pakistan rivalry is a crucial feature of South Asian history and politics. The Kashmir conflict is considered a major determinant of India-Pakistan relations. Going beyond a Kashmir-centric explanation of

India-Pakistan hostility, some scholars have offered other explanations of this rivalry. Cohen focuses on factors such as strategic importance and shared water and ecosystems.[33] For Paul, the "enduring rivalry" is simultaneously over territory, national identity, and power position in the region.[34] Others explore the role of external powers, domestic political and institutional structures, and culture that shape actions of leaders, color historical memories, and help build collective identities.[35] We argue that the India-Pakistan conflict is deep-rooted. It involves the very structure and operation of ideas, ideologies, and psychology that led to the creation of India and Pakistan. The conflict is not about territory or resources. Though these factors play a role in the conflict, they can be considered ancillary to a deeply embedded psychology of othering, the fundamental factor shaping the conflict. Some scholars take a similar position. Tracing the origin of Indo-Pak conflict to religion, Burke argues that Hinduism and Islam are two "closed systems" that lacked tolerance and understanding of each other. The hasty departure of the British from the subcontinent under a policy of "cut and run" prevented the smooth transfer of populations across newly formed boundaries, thus resulting in mass killings. This tragedy, he argues, provided fertile ground for the hostility between predominantly Hindu India and Muslim Pakistan.[36] For Ganguly, the two neighbors are engaged in "a relationship of unremitting hostility," mainly owing to the differing ideological commitments of the Congress and the Muslim League.[37] Virdee contends that the incompatible discourses, which shaped the partition, have subsequently impacted post-partition politics. For her, "The ideologically incompatible discourses arising from "divide and rule" and "two-nation theory" understandings of partition that followed from independence have been the framework upon which the relationship between India and Pakistan has evolved in the independent history of both nations."[38] While drawing on these studies to examine the South Asian conflict, we evaluate them mainly in terms of the psychology of othering, and, further, we explore the prospects for transformation of the conflictual relationship.

Looking for solutions is timely. The possession of nuclear weapons by India and Pakistan in 1998 added a new, and arguably dangerous, dimension to the conflict. The two states have not used nuclear weapons despite fighting a war in 1999 and engaging in multiple border clashes, but the reference to nuclear weapons by political leaders keeps fear of their prospective use influential in political relations.[39] A study estimates that an India-Pakistan nuclear war would result in the loss of 50 to 125 million lives, besides causing environmental disaster in the region that crisscrosses the Himalaya, Karakoram, and Hindukush mountain ranges; the Indus river system; and a host of other biodiverse systems.[40] Wolpert makes a pessimistic prognosis: "With their capitals and major cities less than ten ballistic missile-minutes from each other the two countries have become the world's most dangerous match for the potential ignition of a nuclear war that could decimate South Asia and poison every region on earth."[41] US president Bill Clinton's characterization of the region as the "most dangerous place on earth,"[42] in 2000, runs parallel to such a prognosis. The limited war in 1999, massive deployment of forces on the borders in 2001 and 2002, attacks on the Indian Parliament in 2001 and in Mumbai in 2008, intense border clashes in 2016 and 2019, and seemingly endless saber rattling are manifestations of this persistent rivalry. That the conflict is a stark reality after more than seven decades of the partition, that the region is no more peaceful than it was during the partition, and that the states live in fear of war and nuclear conflagration cannot be considered apart from the deeper psychology of othering. While bringing this point home, our task is exploring pathways for peace by applying Gandhian conflict resolution toward this end.

Factoring Gandhian Conflict Resolution

In 1949, after a year of the assassination of Gandhi, English novelist and thinker George Orwell wrote, "Saints should always be judged guilty until they are proved innocent, but the tests that have to be applied to them are not, of course, the same in all cases. In Gandhi's case the questions one feels inclined to ask are: to what extent was Gandhi moved by vanity—by the consciousness of himself as a humble, naked old man, sitting on a praying-mat and shaking empires by sheer spiritual power—and to what extent did he compromise his own principles by entering politics, which of their nature are inseparable from coercion and fraud? To give a definite answer one would have to study Gandhi's acts and writings in immense detail, for his whole life was a sort of pilgrimage in which every act was significant."[43] For Orwell, Gandhi represented the consummate and ideal saint and politician. There is an interesting literature on how Gandhi combined two aspects, the prophetic and the strategic, even though some scholars emphasize one or the other. John Lewis argues that Gandhi's rejection of violence was based on expediency. He contends Gandhi embraced nonviolence strategically, as an "effective way in which a disarmed and disorganized multitude can resist armed troops and police."[44] Mehta, on the other hand, argues, "Gandhi would have demurred at the idea that nonviolence was a strategy."[45] We argue that Gandhi combined idealism and realism, since his idealism was not devoid of real-life components and his realism was not devoid of idealistic moorings; rather, both reinforced each other within a holistic worldview. Gandhi's relational conception of social-political-spiritual cohesion undercuts the conventional distinction between idea and practice. Informed by the Vedanta ontology on which his ethics and politics were predicated, idea and act are not distinct dynamics but instead represent interdependent aspects of an ultimately unified continuum. His famous saying, "My life [the domain of practice] is my message [the domain of idea]," corroborates this point of view.

Until the partition became a reality, Gandhi thought it was avoidable. For him, India was the land of multiple religions and cultures, and its division would weaken its multicultural identity and undermine religious harmony and coexistence. He could not "tolerate any proposal for vivisecting the country" and wanted to be a "trustee of all the Hindus and Muslims, Sikhs and Parsis, Jains and Christians living in this country." Even when accepting the reality of partition, he argued, "The partition was indeed an error, but the leaders (not I) felt that it was unavoidable." As mentioned earlier, Gandhi opposed partition not merely as an idealist. He could foresee that the psychology that gave rise to it would not end with a onetime division. His concern was not merely with the partition but with its long-term implications. The pragmatist in him was worried that unless the deep roots of partition were addressed, South Asia might turn into a permanent conflict zone. He argued that physical partition might be a logically understandable development in history, but South Asia could not be peaceful unless its psychological partition was addressed. He argued, "We may take it that physical division of the country is now certain. If . . . our hearts are true we can behave as if they had not been partitioned." Further, "we should not let our hearts be sundered. We must save our hearts from being fragmented."[46]

Gandhi's hope for peace in post-partition South Asia did not materialize in his lifetime. Had Gandhi's wish to live until he was 125 been fulfilled,[47] he would have witnessed momentous developments, including the fall of the Berlin Wall and the end of the Cold War. Importantly, from the point of view of this work, he would have witnessed his apprehension—that psychological partition would not be satiated with onetime partition and its manifestation in many other violent incidents—turning into a reality. He would have witnessed the India-Pakistan wars of 1965 and 1971, the creation of Bangladesh, multiple border clashes, and many more incidents of explicit and implicit violence between these neighbors. Besides interstate violence, he would have witnessed the psychological divide manifesting in communal riots within the states. The saint in Gandhi would have been pained to see his ideals in tatters, but the politician in him would have worked for pathways to build peace. We explore these pathways later in this book.

Though Gandhi is a "profound conflict theorist," argues Weber, his ideas for conflict resolution have not been fully explored. He notes, "It is puzzling that links between Gandhian social philosophy and recent conflict resolution negotiation literature . . . have received so little scholarly attention. While there seems to be no direct causal link between the two bodies of knowledge, conflict resolution literature in the guise of modern problem-solving and win-win (as opposed to power-based and zero-sum) approaches leading to integrative conflict resolution (as opposed to mere compromise and distributive outcomes) strongly echoes Gandhi's own writings."[48] One explanation for this scholarly negligence could be that Gandhi's writings often appear to researchers as unorganized and even contradictory at times. This is misleading. Gandhi was not a theory builder. He was an individual of action, and his action birthed theories. At the same time, it would not help to accept Gandhi as an absolutist, infallible, or godlike, though some of his ardent followers might have held such views. His autobiography candidly elaborates his fallacies.[49] Some scholars, hence, rightly argue for a selective approach while engaging with Gandhi to exclude ideas that seem "idiosyncratic, provisional, outdated, and in need of radical revision or complete rejection."[50] This selective approach, we argue, does not obviate the relevance of Gandhian thoughts for resolving conflicts. In his study of associational life and communal peace in four cities of postcolonial India—Aligarh, Hyderabad, Surat, and Ahmedabad—Varshney found that Surat and Ahmedabad witnessed relative peace because of multiple factors, among which was the influence of Gandhi. He explained, "Making the argument that the fight against the British was not simply about winning independence but also about rebuilding Indian society, and by including Hindu-Muslim unity as a primary goal, Gandhi put in place arguments and inspiration for a cadre-based political party and a whole host of social and educational institutions, which sought to integrate Hindus and Muslims."[51]

This consideration brings us to these questions: What is the Gandhian approach to conflict resolution? How is Gandhian conflict resolution relevant to addressing the conflict in South Asia? Put simply, Gandhi's theory and practice of conflict resolution stem from his worldview, which can be summarized through three interrelated principles. First, there are certain universal moral principles that are context-free and that apply to all—individuals, groups, and larger organizations, including states. These principles must form bedrocks for peace among people, societies, and states. Among them, nonviolence is the foremost principle. Second, these universal principles are not something outside of the human self and their collectivities. These principles are embedded within. Third, the individual is at the center of the universe. Or, rather, the individual is the state and the world in miniature. Gandhi argued that the universal principles, valid across the multiplicity of contextual circumstances characterizing the human condition, must be governing principles of life and action for individuals, and, by extension, societies and politics, for peace.

Gandhi rejected violence as a method of conflict resolution not merely because it is "immoral." The practical Gandhi rejected violence as a crude and insufficient mechanism for peace. He argued, "It cannot be said that violence never achieves anything," but it is "absurd to say that violence has ever brought peace to mankind."[52] Boulding echoes Gandhi: "Violence . . . leads to the suppression rather than the resolution of conflict; it drives conflict underground but does little to eliminate it."[53] Gandhi forbade violence because the consequences are devastating. There is no shortage of literature or empirical research on how violence leads to destruction. And, in this era of global connectedness and instant information, one does not need specialized knowledge to understand the link between violence and destruction. Gandhi argued that violence, as a method of conflict resolution, could not be completely eradicated unless the root causes of conflicts were explored, understood, and appropriately resolved. For him, the pursuit of interests, whether individual or national, is not evil per se, but exclusiveness, and, by extension, othering, leads to conflicts.

The rejection of violent methods to resolve conflicts necessitates the urgency to look for alternate methods. In this context, nonviolence, considered one of the major universal principles for peace by Gandhi, requires exploration. Juergensmeyer argues, "Various forms of less militant response, including the methods of conflict resolution adopted by . . . Gandhi, deserve a second look."[54] For Sharp, "The quest for an alternative to war is now our common task in which Gandhi pioneered so significantly. Is it not now time that a full investigation into the potentialities of nonviolent action is both deserved and required?"[55] For Gandhi, nonviolence is a better alternative for resolving conflicts. He urged there must be faith in nonviolence before one can even think of putting it in practice. Among his contemporaries, which included figures like Lenin and Mao, Gandhi was a rare figure who launched a mission to bring desired change through nonviolence. Though some of his colleagues within his own political party were skeptical of these methods, Gandhi was unwavering in his approach to conflict resolution.

For Gandhi, nonviolence is not mere abstinence from violence or passive resistance; it is spiritual commitment. Nonviolence is a potent weapon to achieve desired changes "not only by rejecting and spurning violent courses of action but also by trying to build societies in which violence would not be cultivated and nurtured."[56] He argued, "I do justify entire non-violence and consider it possible . . . between . . . nations and nations."[57] We investigate this Gandhian approach and its potentials to achieve conflict resolution in South Asia. We also argue that the Gandhian approach can be applied to resolve similar conflicts in other parts of the globe.

The Organization

Is Gandhi relevant to a study of the partition? How did Gandhi respond to the psychology of othering and the partition? Does Gandhi provide an alternate framework to examine the conflicts originating from psychological othering? And by extension, how is the Gandhian approach relevant to the post-partition South Asia? These questions guide our research and inform our analysis. In this introductory chapter, we have provided an overview of the book and touched upon its essential claims. We have briefly explored the partition of the Indian subcontinent, examined the concept of South Asia, explained the complexity of the two-nation theory, and described the Gandhian approach to conflict resolution to contextualize our arguments. In the subsequent chapters, we elaborate on the arguments made in this chapter. In chapter 1, we explore Gandhian conflict resolution and its various facets. We explore the breadth and scope of conflict resolution literature in general, position Gandhian ideas and their relevance in this field, and then examine literature and practices shaped, or at least influenced, by the ideas of Gandhi. We find such an exercise useful as, by doing so, we attempt to reinterpret Gandhian principles by way of contemporary conflict and peace literature. We then examine the Gandhian theory of conflict resolution and its relevance to the psychology of othering. We also explore its potential for resolving the ongoing conflict in South Asia. Essentially, we raise the question of whether, if Gandhi was relevant in the twentieth century, we can examine his thoughts for the benefit of the twenty-first century. And in this exploration, South Asia—Gandhi's field of action—has figured prominently. In chapter 2, we revisit partition in an exercise to understand the current politics of South Asia. We elaborate on the ideology that led to partition, its psychological foundations, and its consequences. We weave an assessment of the historical event with the literature on othering. We juxtapose the history and politics of partition with the psychology of othering for a comprehensive understanding of the post-partition situation. Our goal in this chapter is not to provide detailed description of partition but to bring home the point that the partition was violent, the ideology that led to it still survives and influences the politics of South Asia, and it is necessary to explore peaceful ways to address it.

In chapter 3, we focus on post-partition politics in South Asia. The post-partition literature has focused mostly on a descriptive analysis of its consequences (for instance, the situation of refugees and displaced people). It has not focused significantly on the political dynamics of post-partition and how they could be traced to the psychology that led to partition in the first place. We examine how the partition shaped domestic as well as bilateral politics of India and Pakistan and how, operating in the same social milieu, they reinforce each other. Building on this argument, we focus on hostile India-Pakistan relations as reflected in multiple wars, limited war, border clashes, and everyday politics and actions. We use secondary literature, particularly the literature on India-Pakistan conflict through enduring rivalry and protracted conflict, and primary sources such as speeches, to argue how this rivalry is psychological and deep-rooted. In the next chapter, chapter 4, we examine peace attempts like opening roads between India and Pakistan in Kashmir and the opening of religious shrines (for example, Pakistan opening the Sikh shrine in its territory for Sikh pilgrims), from a Gandhian perspective. In the concluding chapter, we summarize the main arguments and suggest directions for the future.

1

Gandhian Conflict Resolution

In this chapter, we engage with conflict resolution literature and practice and analyze their connection to Gandhian ideas. Such an exercise provides useful insights about Gandhi's worldview, how nonviolence formed the core of Gandhian conflict resolution theory, and how transformative conflict resolution—which emphasizes transcending violence and othering and embracing nonviolence and belonging—is useful in resolving conflicts. We recast Gandhian principles and their role in contemporary conflict and peace literature. Then, we develop a Gandhian conflict resolution (GCR) framework, in which we identify three interrelated elements: first, conflict is a reality and an inevitable aspect of life; second, conflicts are not amenable to lasting solutions through violent means; and third, the goal of conflict resolution must be transcendence, embodying the idea of belonging and harmony. Gandhi accepted conflict as a normal phenomenon and offered nonviolence as an effective way of transforming it, toward enduring peace. While accepting the differences in cultures and values, Gandhi promoted the value of unity and belonging for effectively dealing with conflict. The Gandhian approach translated into politics would emphasize community unity and belonging and attempt to resolve conflicts through nonviolence. This approach, we argue, can be useful in resolving conflicts not only in South Asia but also in other parts of the world. Whereas in Gandhi's South Asia it was the clash of cultural systems, similar clashes based on race, history, or other distinct group identities are evident in many other situations.

Gandhi in Conflict Resolution Discourse

Even though 153 years have passed since Gandhi was born and 75 years have passed since he was killed, he remains an extraordinarily popular figure. Around the world, an extensive celebration took place on his 150th birth anniversary, in 2019. While paying tribute to Gandhi, US Speaker of the House of Representatives Nancy Pelosi called Gandhi an "extraordinary" man who shaped history.[1] States and international organizations held events to celebrate the occasion. The Russian Parliament displayed an exhibition on the correspondence between Gandhi and Leo Tolstoy. Poland issued a postage stamp to commemorate the birth anniversary. The tallest skyscraper located in Dubai, Burj Khalifa, was lit up with a special LED projection for one hour to pay tribute to Gandhi. A nonviolence march was organized in the Netherlands. The premier international organization, the United Nations, issued stamps to honor Gandhi. The UN secretary-general, António Guterres, in his message, noted that Gandhi's vision resonates across the world for mutual understanding, equality, and peaceful resolution of disputes. Guterres argued that Gandhi promoted nonviolence not merely "as a philosophy and a political strategy, but as a means to achieve justice and change. Indeed, many of his ideas foreshadow the holistic thinking behind the 2030 Agenda for Sustainable Development."[2]

Gandhi's life and message were not only celebrated on his 150th birth anniversary. In 2009 US president Barack Obama, responding to a question as to who the one person was, dead or alive, that he would choose to dine with, replied "Gandhi."[3] Gandhi's pictures decorate social and political leaders' offices across the globe. Leaders from all over the world visit his memorial in New Delhi. There are Gandhi statues in many countries of the world. The unveiling of a Gandhi statue in Parliament Square, London, in 2015, not far from a statue of Winston Churchill, against whom Gandhi fought during the Indian freedom struggle, demonstrates the universal appeal of Gandhi's message. At its inauguration, British prime minister David Cameron said, "This statue celebrates . . . the universal power of Gandhi's message."[4] The same year, the United Nations declared Gandhi's birth date, October 2, as the "International Day of Non-violence." Such developments indicate that Gandhi occupies a unique place in world politics. What about his place in conflict resolution discourse?

Thomas Weber argues that Gandhi was a "profound conflict theorist" and "should be viewed from within conflict resolution theory, rather than as being distinct from it."[5] A study of conflict resolution literature does not corroborate Weber's argument. There have been impressive, though only few, scholarly attempts to deal in detail with Gandhian conflict resolution theory.[6] Several scholars have used Gandhian ideas of conflict resolution in their theories, but without acknowledging the contribution of Gandhi to the development of their theories. Making a case for squarely locating Gandhian thoughts in conflict resolution discourse, Weber detects significant linkages between recent conflict resolution literature and Gandhian philosophy. Nonetheless, scholars of conflict resolution have largely shied away from engaging with Gandhi, and, as a result, Gandhian ideas have not received due credit in the literature. This apathy may be attributed to some overlapping academic concerns. For many researchers, Gandhi's "saintly image" pushes his ideas into the domain of mysticism and impracticality—making him a pariah among select academics and policy makers. Gandhi's moralistic focus has been derided by statistically oriented conflict resolution theorists who consider the scope of legitimate research limited strictly to empirical analysis. This mode of analysis is problematic, however, keeping in mind the increasing complexity of the world we live in and the increasing failures of approaches to conflict resolution that focus on its quantifiable factors without exploring its humanistic and spiritual elements. As we discuss later in detail, the Gandhian approach is practical, and he combined both prophetic and strategic considerations in his work. Thereby, "if Gandhi the saint cannot be analyzed . . . , perhaps Gandhi the tactician can."[7] Current scholarship will benefit from engaging with Gandhi the tactician, if not Gandhi the saint or the idealist. In her study on Gandhi's ascetic activism, Veena Howard describes how Gandhi, while drawing on Indian cultural traditions, combined renunciation with nonviolent social praxis.[8] Gandhi's idealism was not devoid of real-life components, and his realism was not devoid of idealistic moorings. Rather, each reinforced the other.

Contemporary conflicts are complex, and understanding them requires an examination of subtle factors and principles. Wars have defined interstate relations for most of the period since the Treaty of Westphalia and the creation of modern-day states. Hot wars and cold wars have occupied the global stage for a considerable time. Though the frequency of interstate wars has declined since the end of the Cold War, the world has witnessed a sharp ascent in conflicts within sovereign states, termed internal conflicts, civil wars, new wars, ethnic conflicts, wars of the third kind, and conflict in postcolonial states.[9] These conflicts are far more complex than traditional interstate wars.[10] To address them, states are steadily engaged in building and buying weapons. Nevertheless, peace remains elusive. International relations continue to be governed by the principle "an eye for an eye," and in our nuclearized world this may lead to, as Gandhi would argue, making "the whole world blind." The 2019 tension between India and Pakistan raised international concerns of a possible war between the two archrivals, and a study contended that even a limited nuclear war could lead to "global environmental and humanitarian catastrophe."[11]

This reliance on violence—in South Asia and elsewhere—partly originates from an instinctive aversion toward adopting alternatives like Gandhian nonviolence. Wars appear, Bose explains, to be a "spent-out device . . . (creating) more problems than they even begin to solve. Yet we continue to rely on them to solve conflicts . . . because of our preconceived notions and utter reluctance toward adopting nonviolence as the means."[12] This reluctance can be, at least partly, attributed to the fact that nonviolence is considered impractical. Studies, such as Shure, Meeker and Hansford's,[13] suggest that pacifist strategies have not been effective in attaining desired goals, and Deutsch et al. argue that "turn the other cheek" strategies may not elicit collaboration.[14] Gandhi was well aware of the link between violence and politics, but he argued that violence is not a viable means of engagement and that societies can nonviolently coexist: "I do justify entire non-violence and consider it possible . . . between . . . nations and nations."[15] For Gandhi, nonviolence is not merely a contingent plan or expediency, but imperative for peace. This conviction does not make Gandhi a dreamer but rather a leader who visualized nonviolence as a necessary guiding principle for interstate relations.[16] However, nonviolence cannot be effective unless there is a strong faith in this principle. Is this Gandhian faith lacking in the leaders and policy makers of the world today? Can violence be an effective strategy to bring sustainable peace? Though scholars assessing events with statistical tools find Gandhian methods impractical, is it not prudent to explore means other than violence and militarism to realize sustainable peace? Has too much reliance on military preparedness made this world more, rather than less, insecure, with dilemmas of (in)security being a primary factor guiding behavior of states?

Gene Sharp argues, "Nonviolent action is possible, and is capable of wielding great power even against ruthless rulers and military regimes."[17] The number of movements that have successfully used nonviolence for change has increased significantly in recent years. Global protest movements like Extinction Rebellion are ideologically Gandhian. According to Roger Hallam, one of the founders of the movement, "Extinction Rebellion is humbly following in the tradition of Gandhi and Martin Luther King."[18] Some scholars even argue that nonviolent struggles have been more successful than violent struggles: "The pragmatic use of nonviolent strategies in struggles for revolutionary goals is the dominant tendency. In the same period only a handful of armed movements have achieved successes in their fight against states."[19] The effectiveness of nonviolence in intrastate movements has also drawn scholarly attention. Empirical studies have complemented earlier theoretical scholarship on nonviolent struggle.[20] Yet in these studies, Gandhi has not been accorded due recognition. Chenoweth and Cunningham argue that in recent cases of nonviolent resistance, those involved "are doing so instrumentally, rather than because of a moral commitment to avoid arms." For them, this puts these nonviolent uprisings in contrast with Gandhian "nonviolence," which "refers to a conceptually different phenomenon—the eschewing of violent or armed action because of a moral, philosophical, or principled commitment."[21] This argument gives rise to several questions: Can an instrumental approach to nonviolence sustain itself without a moral component? Can there be practice without a theory or understanding of its ethical justification? And importantly, from the perspective of this study, did Gandhian nonviolence lack or undermine instrumentality or agency? We examine some of these questions in the following pages. For now, it would suffice to note that notwithstanding the general apathy, some scholars have credited Gandhi's example and ideas in their works on recent nonviolent movements. For instance, Jahanbegloo noted in 2013: "The past two years will remain momentous in the history of Gandhian nonviolence for people in the Middle East and around the world. Despite their geographic and cultural diversity, nonviolent movements in Egypt, Tunisia, Syria, Bahrain, and Yemen exhibited a remarkable similarity to Gandhi's . . . campaigns for checking power and opposing violence."[22]

Another factor contributing to general apathy toward Gandhi is that nonviolence as a subject of study remains underresearched. Galtung contends: "There is no systematic attempt to find the correlates of nonviolent actions in the same way as has been done for wars, external or internal."[23] Even though there are studies on nonviolence, they are meager. Jorgan Johansen reflects on this somber picture: "After some interest in the early days of modern peace research there is a renaissance in the early part of the twenty-first century. More books are published and more studies carried out today than ever before. An impressive amount of work has been done by committed individuals in academia as well as by activists. Most of it focuses on the more pragmatic understanding of nonviolent means. Evaluations and case studies of the growing number of practitioners dominate. When it comes to developing new theories, production is still relatively meagre."[24] Nonviolence has not received the kind of attention received by weapons, wars, conflicts, and violence. Though some studies indicate a relative decline in actual violence in the twenty-first century,[25] violence continues to draw significant attention. Hardiman and Nojeim in their respective works contend that, beside Gandhian ideology, nearly all other ideologies have made peace with some form of violence—making violence "normal."[26] Johansen agrees: "Almost all research on conflicts focuses on the most violent ones. . . . [C]onflicts seem only to be interesting when the groups involved are using belligerent means, and . . . are beating and/or killing each other. This focus has been so strong that some have redefined conflict and only count those cases which include violence. Other conflicts are hardly regarded as conflicts at all."[27]

Another factor contributing to this apathy perhaps arises from a lack of sophistication, or theoretical orientation, in Gandhi's writings and speeches. His ideas on nonviolence, war, and peace may appear simplistic, inadequate, unorganized, contradictory, or even "unhinged."[28] Before hazarding these judgments, we argue, a few qualifications should be borne in mind. Gandhi was not an academic scholar, nor did he claim to be one;

rather, his theories were derived from his actions. His theory was action oriented, primarily emerging from successful practice and from a desire to make the world a better place to live. Gandhi was a "practical idealist," for whom "logic comes afterwards, it does not precede the event," and "not built for academic writings."[29] He had a little concern for generating theories. He repudiated all "isms," including the one named after him "Gandhism."[30]

Gandhi often argued that his actions were experiments in the living realization of truth (*satyagraha*). His autobiography was titled *My Experiments with Truth*. His experiments did not dissuade him from changing his thoughts and actions, even at the cost of being labeled inconsistent: writing a letter to Adolf Hitler, for instance, urging him to adopt a nonviolent method against the Allied powers, and then advising the Allied powers to counter Hitler's forces through nonviolence[31]—and, similarly, contending that "self-defense is everybody's birthright," while at the same time arguing that a practitioner of nonviolence should never resort to violence in self-defense.[32] His thoughts and actions have to be viewed through the lens of experimentation and an evolving worldview, since Gandhi was a lifelong learner rather than a rigid ideologue. Jorgen Johansen explains: "Gandhi was often in doubt and experimented with different activities. He tested a number of diets, political actions and views on political and moral questions. Most of his writings are dated. In his original writings you can always see on which specific date he wrote each letter, article or comment. The reason is that he was always prepared to change his mind when he learned new things. . . . This option for changing even your core values is important to remember when reading texts by or on Gandhi."[33] In the above-mentioned example of Hitler and international conflict, Gandhi's apparent contradictions on one level do not diminish the wisdom of his evolving insight on another level. Holmes elucidates in holistic and pragmatic Gandhian fashion: "So while nonviolence obviously could not have pushed German armor back on the battlefield once the institutions of militarism had been allowed to mature and the self-propelling mechanism of a military state put into motion, it might have been effective at an earlier stage in preventing the rise to power of those responsible for all of this. If historical fact is that military means stopped

Hitler once he began to march, it is also an historical fact that reliance upon such means on the part of the world's nations did not prevent his rise to power in the first place."[34]

Though Gandhi's prescription of nonviolence methods against Hitler might appear extraneous, his nonviolent methods as an alternative to violent methods, such as wars, are worth exploring. In "the quest for an alternative to war . . . Gandhi pioneered so significantly,"[35] not only by proposing but also demonstrating the effectiveness of nonviolence in his struggles in South Africa and India. Juergensmeyer makes one case for exploring an alternative to violence by revisiting Gandhi to address the problem of global terrorism: "Immediately after the September 11, 2001, attacks . . . the idea of taking a nonviolent stance in response to terrorism would have been dismissed out of hand. But now . . . the start of a global jihadi war that seems unending, virtually any alternative seems worth considering."[36] He adds, "It is in this context that various forms of less militant response, including the methods of conflict resolution adopted by . . . Gandhi, deserve a second look."[37]

It may simply be a futile exercise to look for faults in Gandhian ideas and methods; it is more important to focus on ideas applicable to contemporary problems. For instance, Gandhi's argument that total disarmament is critical for international peace cannot just be summarily dismissed as utopian thinking. Power notes that "the arms control field is a zone . . . which . . . might benefit through a re-examination of unilateralism and the exact geometry of nuclear deterrence and peace-keeping" in light of Gandhian principles.[38] Going further, he contends, the strategy of "mutual example" in US-USSR efforts "to achieve at least surface progress towards disarmament is in the Gandhian tradition, although concepts of psychological bargaining are involved that pay scant attention to Gandhian trust in the opponent."[39] To focus on the Gandhi's relevance, Allen suggests looking at Gandhi "selectively and creatively."[40] This selective approach may be useful for multiple reasons: First, Gandhi does not have all the answers (he also never claimed to have them). Second, a selective approach provides the scope to reformulate his ideas considering modern social-political developments. Also, this approach helps rescue Gandhian ideas from any rigid encumbrance and enhances their potency for exploring the root causes of violence, and for engendering pathways for conflict transcendence.

Elements of Gandhian Conflict Resolution

Gandhi not only challenged dominant positions in the conflict resolution discipline but also offered rich resources for enhancing this discipline. Can most approaches departing from zero-sum thinking and emphasizing collaborative nonviolent problem solving be attributed to Gandhian thought? Alternatively, is it an exaggeration to think in these terms, since such ideas regarding nonviolence (which Gandhi acknowledged and called "as old as hills") have existed for millennia? That Gandhi did not develop a systematic theory of conflict resolution is a foregone conclusion. Scattered across his hundred-volume collected writings, Gandhian conflict resolution ideas and practices have been subject to varied interpretations. Johansen argues: "Probably there will never be anyone who can match Gandhi, but there are many who can follow the same path and do 'experiments with the truth.' To use creativity and empathy to develop new nonviolent tools; test them in conflict situations and build up a record of well documented experiences is the most important job for those interested in nonviolence in the years to come. In this work there are tasks for academics and activists from all parts of human activities."[41] In the following section, we propose a Gandhian conflict resolution framework by drawing on Gandhian ideas and practices. Such a framework may help explore pathways to creative engagement with contemporary conflicts. The proposed GCR framework has three overlapping A's: approach (the Gandhian worldview of conflict, or what is his conflict ontology?), action (what are the Gandhian methods or means to approach conflict?), and aim (what is the end or goal of Gandhian conflict resolution?).

Approach: Conflict Is Real

Conflicts can broadly range from competition over resources to competing needs and interests, implying pursuit of incompatible goals. Pruitt and Rubin describe conflict as a divergence of interest or a belief that the conflicting parties' aspirations cannot be achieved simultaneously.[42] For Coser, conflict is a struggle over values and claims to scarce resources.[43] Protracted conflicts that involve apparently nonnegotiable issues are what Burton refers to as "deep-rooted *conflicts*."[44] Galtung elaborates:

> "Conflict" comes from *confligere*, "shocking together"; compatible with the usual Anglo-American *Behavioural interpretation* as parties "shock-ing together," in *violence*. But it also opens for a subjective *Attitudinal interpretation* in the inner worlds of the actors, the *Lebenswelten*, as an inner shock that may cause a *hatred* that may be expressed as violence. Then the trans-subjective, relational *Contradiction interpretation*. What is "shocking together" are goals held by the parties when the realization of one excludes the realization of other(s). There is *incompatibility*, or *contradiction* of goals, like between "independence" for a province, and "unitary state" for the country. No inter-actor violence is assumed, nor that the "shocking" is known to the actors, the goal-holders. "Incompat-ible goals" does not imply "incompatible actors." That leads to A-, B- and C-oriented conflict interpretations, focused on attitude, behaviour, contradiction. In the sequence C- > A- > B, a conflict starts objectively, takes on inner, attitudinal life, and finds an outer, behavioural expres-sion, verbally and/or physically, violent, or not. But any other ABC sequence is possible empirically.[45]

Broadly there are four criteria that define a conflict situation: the participants perceive there is a conflict; perceptible difference of values, interests, goals, or relations; parties are either states or significant elements of the population within a state; and conflict outcome is important for stakeholders.[46]

Real or perceived, incompatible goals marked the twentieth-century history with wars and violence. The hopes that decolonization and the end of the Cold War would put an end to this ongoing turmoil did not materialize. Holsti argued, "Decolonization and the collapse of commu-nism," two major developments that almost coincided with the end of the cold war, "solved only two problems—foreign and/or one-party rule. But gaining freedom is not the same as building viable states based on tolerant communities."[47] Holsti was referring to internal conflicts, but his argument is applicable to interstate relations, wherein "viable states based on tolerant communities" are scarce, thus leading to conflicts. When toleration becomes equivalent to acquiescence to the dominant system, conflicts are bound to take shape. Conflicts do not have to be necessarily violent and destructive. The actions of actors with incompatible goals determine what course a conflict will take. It can become an armed conflict with violence becoming the norm, or it can be resolved amicably, peacefully, by the actors involved.

Conflicts between individuals, communities, and states have been recurring for millennia. The Hindu epics *Ramayana* and *Mahabharata* and the Greek epics *Iliad* and *Odyssey* reflect broadly how a clash of interests leads to war. Thucydides's *The History of Peloponnesian War*, considered a classic text for the realist school of international relations, is a record of the war between two alliances in ancient Greece. Gandhi understood well the reality of the conflict. However, as stated by Galtung at the beginning of this section, Gandhi would broaden the definition of conflict to include not only visible conflicts, such as interstate wars or civil wars, but also subtle ones that operate at a psychological level. Othering is an essential psychological component of such conflicts. For Gandhi, all of us confront the reality of conflict daily, on every level. In that sense, conflict, not violence, is integral to human psychology, and there is a ceaseless struggle within the individual to engage, avoid, or negotiate with this conflict. Physical manifestations of conflict were much less important to Gandhi than its subtle psychological roots. He argued that a peace activist, or what he called a "nonviolent worker," must operate at this subtle level—employing moral will or "soul force." It is important to acknowledge that conflicts are an integral part of our lives. Kurtz notes that Gandhi actually provoked conflict, rather than shunning it, since he was "neither a rigid pacifist (as he is sometimes perceived in popular culture) nor a peacemaker in the sense of wanting to prevent or avoid conflict or struggle. On the contrary, his life may be viewed, in a sense, as a series of conflicts, many of which he deliberately provoked."[48] Gandhi probed the psychosocial origins of conflict to confront its manifestations in human affairs—making them explicit so that they could be addressed peacefully. His "illegal" resistance in South Africa and India, provoking the wrath of the colonial rulers and resulting in beating and imprisonment, was not aimed at fomenting violence, but intended rather to expose and transcend systems of oppression and violence. By actively confronting injustice in the public realm, Gandhi appealed to its moral source, which he believed every individual possesses.

Gandhi was not sympathetic to violent conflict. He considered conflict valuable for mutual development and holistic transcendence, rather than violence or destruction of any kind. He did not envision conflict in terms of win-loss, victory-defeat, or zero-sum confrontations. Whereas "conflict" has a place in Gandhi's philosophy, violence has no place in it. For Gandhi, conflict is an inevitable aspect of life and society, but not violence. Conflict and violence are not synonymous, as many would claim. The two belong to different domains—conflict is a necessary element of moral evolution in people and societies that must be acknowledged, but violence is an unnecessary impediment to human progress. Galtung explains this approach, "Contradictions, conflicts, should be welcomed, not avoided. They are challenges to expand our spaces, and to furnish them creatively with new, feasible, realities. *Conflict* +crisis= opportunity."[49] Conflicts are desirable if they generate peace and address injustice nonviolently.

Action: Nonviolent Praxis

For Gandhi, certain universal principles are embedded in the human psyche. These principles, among which nonviolence figures prominently, apply to individuals, groups and organizations, and states. These principles also include truth, justice, harmony, and belonging, and they are universally valid across history and culture. Like the laws of physics governing the physical universe, moral laws govern human life and action and, by extension, societies and political systems. They form the bedrock for peace and should be adhered to by all. They are not confined to the realm of abstract speculation. They are concrete and powerful motivators for action for social change.

Ahimsa (nonviolence) and *satya* (truth) are two cardinal universal principles. They together form *satyagraha*, composed of the Sanskrit words *satya* (truth) and *agraha* (love for or abiding by), and necessitate searching for truth through nonviolent means. A practitioner of *satya-graha* is, paradoxically, both a fighter and a pacifist since he fights injustice like a warrior, but he fights without weapons. Gandhi calls such fighters "nonviolent workers" and "soldiers of peace." He illustrated the challenges that nonviolent workers faced in the context of nonviolent struggle against British colonialism, and suggested strategies for implementing satyagraha successfully despite these challenges:

> Ordered violence hides itself often behind camouflage and hypocrisy as we see them working through the declarations of good intentions, commissions, conferences and the like, or even through measures conceived as tending to the public benefit but in reality to the benefit of the wrongdoer. Greed and deceit are often the offspring as they are equally often the parents of violence. Naked violence repels like the naked skeleton shorn of flesh, blood and the velvety skin. It cannot last long. But it persists fairly long when it wears the mask of peace and progress so-called. . . .
>
> Non-violence has to work in the midst of this double violence. But if it is the supreme law governing mankind, it must be able to make its way in the face of the heaviest odds. Violence such as we have to face may well make us cowards utterly unable to discover the method of working non-violence. If therefore the forces of violence arrayed against us cannot be checkmated during our time, it would be no proof of the futility of non-violence, it would certainly be proof of the pervading cowardice . . .
>
> But non-violence has to be patient. . . . The aim of the non-violent worker must ever be to convert. He may not however wait endlessly. When therefore the limit is reached, he takes risks and conceives plans of active satyagraha which may mean civil disobedience and the like. His patience is never exhausted to the point of giving up his creed. But working in a hostile atmosphere, he runs the risk of forces of violence, which till then were held under check from mutual fear, being let loose through the restraint of such fear being removed. The Government will spread out its red paws in what it will call self-defence. The party of violence may commit the mistake of seeing its chance of coming out in the open. The non-violent party must then prove its creed by being ground to powder between the two millstones. If there is such a party,

all is well for India and the world. My hope and plans are built upon an
ever-increasing faith in the existence of that party of true non-violence.[50]

The only path to truth is via nonviolence, and there is no compromise. Nonviolence is an absolute principle; there is no partial or conditional nonviolence, and conditional conceptions of nonviolence ideas
reek of hypocrisy and lack of absolute conviction. Following the monistic
implications of his *Advaita Vedanta*–inspired ontology, all levels of ethical
qualification ultimately collapse into a single ontological reference point
that he called "Truth," which is universal and context free, and which
can be realized only through the psychic realization of nonviolence. The
means used to address conflict are also important. He once said, "One
must understand that means and ends are not separate: the means is a
seed out of which grows, like a tree, a characteristic version of the end."[51]
Nonviolence requires firm commitment and preparation. As the nonviolent worker "engages his opponent in constructive conflict . . . every
response from the opponent be accepted as genuine and that all undertak-
ings of the opponent be considered to have given in good faith."[52] Nonviolence involves active struggle, not submission or passive resistance: "Many
people mistake non-violence as compromise or avoidance of conflict. It
is not. On the other hand, it is standing up for what is right (truth) and
justice." Gandhi preferred nonviolent conflict resolution and argued that
nonviolent action is not "a resignation from all real fighting against wickedness. On the contrary, the non-violence of my conception is a more
active and more real fighting against wickedness than retaliation."[53] The
wickedness to which Gandhi referred is essentially a product of othering, which creates a perception of interpersonal separation so acute that it
evokes violent conflict. Othering and violence are inextricably linked in
this way. The counterpoint to othering and violence is nonviolence and
belonging, which are also inextricably linked.

John Sifton argues that Gandhi holds a special place in contemporary
discourse on nonviolence: "Discussions of nonviolence today, however
noble or ignoble they may be, almost always begin with an invocation
of Mahatma Gandhi. And rightly so. Political nonviolence has a limited history, but Gandhi is a central figure in it. His achievements are

legendary."[54] British journalist H. N. Brailsford, who interviewed Gandhi in 1946, argued, "Amid our preoccupations over military perils, he stands aloof and repeats with unshaken faith his creed that safety is attainable, only when men learn to treat each other as brothers and equals. No lesser means will avail."[55] Indeed, when the leaders in the different parts of the world such as Lenin, Stalin, and Mao were leading violent resistance movements, Gandhi was the lone exemplar of nonviolent struggle. Only in later eras did Gandhi-inspired movements spread across the globe.[56] Even within his political party, the Indian National Congress, which spearheaded the freedom struggle, some of his colleagues were skeptical of his nonviolent methods and theory. To Subhas Chandra Bose, a noted freedom fighter and his onetime colleague in the Congress, who argued that in the history of the past two hundred years no freedom struggle was won without violence, Gandhi replied that India could set a historic counterexample.[57] Amid a political culture hostile to this view, Gandhi not only articulated the usefulness of nonviolence for promoting desired sociopolitical change, but also demonstrated its effectiveness in action. Kripalani, another colleague in the Congress, affirmed: "Gandhi was the first in human history to extend the principle of nonviolence from the individual to social and political plane."[58] In the following pages, we demystify some of the misconceptions surrounding nonviolence. This is essential for understanding the effectiveness of nonviolence in transcending othering and promoting belonging.

Nonviolence Is the Absence of Physical Violence. Gandhi disagreed with this formulation because nonviolence involves much more than the absence of physical violence. He reconsidered the paradigm of violence and nonviolence, predominant in his time—and perhaps all times—in which violence equals physical compulsion and nonviolence equals physical submission or acquiescence. Gandhian nonviolence is not simply the lack of overt violence. It includes the absence of active as well as passive, implicit as well as explicit, violence. Violence manifests in multiple forms, including the forms of wars, religious conflicts, racism, colonialism, economic exploitation, and imperialism. War as acute large-scale violence is certainly a degrading thing, and it only proves one's "power of destruction is stronger." There are two kinds of power, "one is obtained by fear of punishment and the other by arts of love," and Gandhi preferred to obtain power by arts of love as "power based on love is thousand times more effective and permanent than power derived from fear of punishment." In this conception of power, which is required for GCR, one "must not be violent in thought, word or deed," and be "incapable of feeling or harboring anger."[59] This is what belonging entails. The question here is as follows: In a world in which violence is often used to resolve conflicts, what was Gandhi's objection to using it—even in cases, the protagonists of violence would argue, where violence could be justified as a just means? Below we discuss major reasons that Gandhi rejected violence as a means of conflict resolution.

First, Gandhi abhorred violence as immoral. Unlike thinkers in the "just war" tradition, for whom war is unavoidable, Gandhi neither supported "just" war nor defended negative peace, based on fear of violence. For him: "War, with all its glorification of brute force, is essentially a degrading thing. It demoralizes those who are trained for it. It brutalizes men of naturally gentle character. It outrages every beautiful canon of morality. Its path of glory is foul with passion and lust, and red with blood of murder. This is not the pathway to our goal."[60] While understanding that war and violence have been a predominant method of conflict resolution in international affairs since the creation of modern-day states, Gandhi considered these methods immoral as they are not natural human qualities. Gandhi's conception of the human condition in this sense was closer to that of John Locke, for whom human nature is characterized by "good will, mutual assistance and preservation," than to Thomas Hobbes, for whom human nature is "solitary, poor, nasty, brutish and short." Gandhi, like Locke, believed that there is an inherent urge in human beings toward peace, which can be further cultivated through proper education and training. Of course, the reverse can also be true—human beings can also cultivate violence. In Gandhian view, "violence 'oozed from every pore' of modern society and had so much become a way of life that modern man could not cope with his relations with himself or other men without translating them into the military language of conflict, struggle, mastery, subjugation, domination, victory, and defeat."[61]

This condition is not inherent to human nature or society. Human nature inevitably seeks its ontological-moral ground in belonging and nonviolence. Gandhi argued war is not a morally legitimate means of achieving anything permanent, including peace.

Second, Gandhi's objection to war and violence did not stem from abstract idealism. He rejected war and violence as an ineffective means to realizing sustainable peace and security. We need to mention that we have used the term sustainable peace in a general way, implying peace which is enduring or long lasting. In that sense sustainable peace is not different from positive peace, a term introduced into academic literature by Johan Galtung. According to Galtung, "With the distinction between personal and structural violence as basic, violence becomes two-sided, and so does peace conceived of as the absence of violence. *An extended concept of violence leads to an extended concept of peace.* Just as a coin has two sides, one side alone being only one aspect of the coin, not the complete coin, peace also has two sides: *absence of personal violence, and absence of structural violence.* We shall refer to them as negative peace and positive peace respectively."[62] Further, he argued that "'absence of violence' and 'social justice' may perhaps be preferred terms, using one negative and one positive formulation. The reason for the use of the terms 'negative' and 'positive' is apparent: the absence of personal violence does not lead to a positively defined condition, whereas the absence of structural violence is what we have referred to as social justice, which is a positively defined condition."[63]

Understood simply, for Gandhi, the military-industrial war machine is not sustainable—even for those who initiate war, condemn it, and support it as a "necessary evil" to establish peace. War "is almost universally condemned as something to be avoided," but it "prospers under the constant injunction that it be avoided. There is a logic of its necessity."[64] The use of force for peace is justified by theories like game theory. Claims such as "when we talk about war, we're really talking about peace" strengthen this perception. Such claims are essentially based on faulty assumptions, as peace earned through war and violence is, at the most, a "hyphen" in between the two wars.[65] Gandhi argued, "I object to violence when it appears to do good, the good is only temporary; the evil it does is permanent."[66] When defined in terms of war, the principle of peace becomes akin to war; peace is then "based on power."[67] Even in our nuclear era, where one bomb can be catastrophic, international relations remain stuck in an unshifting narrative of war as a method of restoring peace. Gandhi's rejection of war and violence thus makes sense. He argued, "It cannot be said that violence never achieves anything," but it is "absurd to say that violence has ever brought peace to mankind."[68] Boulding makes a similar argument: "Violence . . . leads to the suppression rather than the resolution of conflict; it drives conflict underground but does little to eliminate it."[69]

Third, violence does not address conflict. It can generate, at best, a negative peace—a superficial peace without positive and sustainable foundations—but it fails to address the root causes of conflict, and, since the root causes remain intact, there is a strong probability of violence reoccurring. Gandhi, writing in *Young India*, a weekly paper that he edited, termed war "a complex problem" and argued, "All activity for stopping war must prove fruitless so long as the causes of war are not understood and radically dealt with."[70] This conception of peace has helped influence a dimension of conflict resolution studies. For instance, some analysts consider conflict resolution a problem-solving exercise aimed at tackling the root causes of conflict.[71] For Gandhi, the pursuit of interests, individual or national, is not evil per se, and it is only rigid othering, narrowness, selfishness, exclusiveness, exploitation, greed, and prejudices that make it problematic. Conflicts arise out of "inequality, injustice, exploitation, greed and unbridled materialism."[72] Beliefs and perceptions play a major role in shaping conflicts. Judy Eidelson found that five belief domains play a critical role in triggering or constraining a conflict: superiority, injustice, vulnerability, distrust, and helplessness.[73] The human needs–motivation theory developed by Maslow,[74] and applied by several scholars to intrastate conflicts, demonstrates that greed, biases, prejudices, and related exclusion prompt deprivation of needs, which leads to conflicts.[75] Gandhi believed that it is possible to identify the root causes of conflicts, but it then necessitates sincere efforts to address them.

Fourth, Gandhi rejected violence because the costs are high and the consequences devastating. Violence proves that one's "power of destruction is stronger."[76] The work of Deutsch on constructive and destructive processes in the resolution of conflict is in line with this aspect of Gandhian thought.[77] States apparently continue to promote peace, through violence and war. There is no shortage of literature highlighting the negative consequences, direct and indirect, intended and unintended, of wars, conflicts, and violence.[78] Violence begets violence, and there emerges a "conflict trap."[79] All the aspects of life, sociocultural, economic, and political, become conflict accustomed. Gandhi objected to violence "because he considered violence a clumsy weapon which created more problems than it solved, and left a trail of hatred and bitterness in which genuine reconciliation was almost impossible."[80] Along these lines, Gandhi suggested that while an othering-prompted conflict leads to violence, this violence furthers othering and leads to more violence in return, thus creating a vicious cycle. There is scant literature suggesting sustainable benefits of war and violence for humankind. In any event, in this era of global connectedness, where media brings to our living rooms pictures of drowning children in the Mediterranean, child soldiers fighting and dying in Africa, the bombing of schools and hospitals in Yemen and Ukraine, beheading of journalists, and other incidents of gory violence all over the world, does one need specialized knowledge to fathom costs and consequences of violent conflicts? Gandhi renounced violence as a means of conflict resolution since this means, combined with the othering dynamics that it engenders, produces deadly results and exacts enormous costs, while peace remains elusive.

Nonviolence Is Passive Resistance. Another misconception surrounding nonviolence is that it is passive resistance. From this point of view, terms like *weak* and *pacifist* are considered synonymous with nonviolence. But for Gandhi, nonviolence is an active struggle, not passive resistance. Gandhian nonviolence does not deny the significance of conflicts, and in the same vein, for Gandhi, renouncing violent methods of conflict resolution does not imply turning a blind eye to the reality of conflict. In fact, it implies resisting evil with all the power one has in their command. The misconception may be partly attributed to Gandhi's early writings, such as *Hind Swaraj*, where he called his idea of nonusage of violence "passive resistance." He eventually changed the term to *satyagraha*, realizing that passive resistance may be associated with weakness and nonaction and implying that practitioners were victims. In contrast to this notion, he considered practitioners of nonviolence to be proactive agents with the ability to bring desired change. Nonviolence does not mean submission to violence or fatalism, in which the discontented individual leaves everything to fate. Rather, nonviolent methods encourage the nonviolent worker to engage in "active resistance" against injustice. The only Gandhian moral imperative is that the injustice must be resisted in a nonviolent manner. Often criticized for promoting passivity, Gandhi, in fact, argued that passivity is equivalent to violence, one who does not resist a wrong is a violent individual, and one should resist the wrong, but nonviolently. Nonviolence implies not only renouncing violence but also resisting violence. This method calls for social praxis, and "it is not enough that an activity is carried out without the use of violence. To fulfill the criteria of being labelled nonviolence, it must in addition be done to reduce or eliminate violence or oppression."[81] This wider meaning of nonviolence as active resistance rather than submission to exploitation remains a hallmark of Gandhian thought.

Nonviolence Is a Weapon of Cowards. Gandhian nonviolence is often conflated not only with passivity but also with cowardice. It is commonly counterpoised against the virtue of courage, in a militaristic sense. Nonviolence is the weapon of the courageous, not that of a coward. Gandhi would not prefer to be a mute spectator of wrongdoing or submitting to oppression; rather, he would prefer resorting to violent action if the situation demanded. He was indeed a radical revolutionary in that sense. We argue that this approach to nonviolence was rooted in his conviction that nonviolence all time is better than violence anytime. The original advocates of nonviolence, he claimed, were not only geniuses because they fully realized the futility of violence, but were also courageous, because nonviolent action requires more courage than violent action. In an interview with Drew Pearson, an American journalist, in 1924, Gandhi argued, "By non-violence I do not mean cowardice. I do believe that, where there is only a choice between cowardice and violence, I would advise violence. . . . I am not pleading for India to practice non-violence because she is weak, but because she is conscious of her power and strength . . . who discovered the law of nonviolence were greater geniuses. . . . Having themselves known the use of arms, they realized their uselessness and taught a weary world that its salvation lay not through violence, but through non-violence. Therefore, I respectfully invite Americans to study carefully the Indian National Movement and they will therein find an effective substitute for war."[82]

The Noncooperation Movement and Salt March are living examples of the Gandhian conviction that nonviolence necessitates courage. Webb Miller, who witnessed the Salt March, described how the followers of Gandhi practiced nonviolence despite police brutality: "In eighteen years of reporting in twenty-two countries, during which I have witnessed innumerable civil disturbances, riots, and rebellions, I have never witnessed such harrowing scenes as at Dharasana [a site of the march]. It was astonishing and baffling to the western mind accustomed to see violence met with violence, to expect a blow to be returned. My reaction was of revulsion akin to the emotion one feels when seen a dumb animal beaten: partly anger partly humiliation. Sometimes the scenes were so painful, I had to turn away momentarily. One surprising feature was the discipline of the volunteers. It seemed they were thoroughly imbued with Gandhi's nonviolence creed, and the leaders constantly stood in front of the ranks imploring them to remember that Gandhi's soul was with them."[83]

A mind "accustomed to see violence met with violence" would find it difficult to empathize with the Gandhian conviction that nonviolence is linked with courage. Gandhi argued, "Violence does not mean emancipation from fear, but discovering the means of combating the cause of fear. Non-violence, on the other hand, has no cause for fear. The votary of non-violence has to cultivate the capacity for sacrifice of the highest type in order to be free from fear."[84] Practicing nonviolence requires strength; it takes great moral, spiritual, and even physical fortitude to relinquish violence. In his work Terry Beitzel commented that, to American pragmatist William James's search for moral equivalent of war, Gandhi provided an apt alternative: that of nonviolence.[85] In 1906, James delivered a speech at Stanford University titled "The Moral Equivalent of War." He argued that war in many respects promotes laudable virtues, while pacifism is too often "passivism," bereft of any appreciable moral benefit. He noted that war builds character, including "order and discipline . . . service and devotion . . . ," and teaches "fidelity, cohesiveness, tenacity, heroism . . . and vigor." He added, "If war had ever stopped, we should have to re-invent it, on this view, to redeem life from flat denigration."[86] Gandhi offered an alternative that promotes not only the virtues of courage, discipline and service, but also "greater virtue than war because nonviolent action actually requires more courage than violence."[87]

Gandhi detested "mute submissiveness" and believed that nonviolence and cowardice cannot go hand in hand. In his words: "My nonviolence does not admit of running away from danger and leaving dear ones unprotected. Between violence and cowardly flight, I can only prefer violence to cowardice. I can no more preach nonviolence to a coward than I can tempt a blind man to enjoy healthy scenes. Nonviolence is the summit of bravery. And in my own experience, I have had no difficulty in demonstrating to men trained in the school of violence the superiority of nonviolence. As a coward, which I was for years, I harbored violence. I began to prize nonviolence only when I began to shed cowardice. . . . A rabbit that runs away from the bull-terrier is not particularly non-violent." On another occasion, he reconfirmed his belief in nonviolence as a method of courage: "For I cannot in any case stand cowardice. Let no one say when I am gone that I taught the people to be cowards. If you think my *ahimsa* amounts to that, or leads you to that, you should reject it without hesitation. . . . A nonviolent warrior knows no leaving the battle. He rushes into the mouth of *himsa*. . . . If this *ahimsa* seems to you to be impossible, let us be honest with ourselves and say so, and give it up. . . . Cowardice is worse than violence because cowards can never be nonviolent. . . . A person who has full faith in nonviolence should be a thousand times more fearless than an armed man. . . . It is the duty of every believer in *ahimsa* to see that cowardice is not propagated in the name of nonviolence." Additionally, he believed: "Nonviolence cannot be taught to a person who fears to die and has no power of resistance. . . . Not knowing the stuff of which nonviolence is made many have honestly believed that running away from danger every time was a virtue compared to offering resistance, especially when it is fraught with danger to one's life. As a teacher of nonviolence I must, so far as it is possible for me, guard against such an unmanly belief."[88]

From the above quotes, it becomes clear that Gandhi preferred non-violence as a weapon of courageousness, not as a weapon of cowardice. Gandhi's preference of violence to cowardice demands attention, as it might seem to suggest that he supported violence. For Gandhi, until one is firmly ensconced in his belief in nonviolent methods, they are unfit to be a nonviolent worker. As he advised a vacillating worker: "If like many others, nonviolence does not appeal to your heart, you should discard it. I shall not find fault with you for that, and, if others do, you should not care. The principle is this: 'That which has been propounded by the *rishis* (sages), practiced by the sages and appeals to one's heart should be followed and put into practice.'" Narrating a dialogue between his eldest son and himself, he wrote: "Thus when my eldest son asked me what he should have done, had he been present when I was almost fatally assaulted in 1908, whether he should have run away and seen me killed or whether he should have used his physical force which he could and wanted to use, and defended me, I told him that it was his duty to defend me even by using violence." Nonetheless, for him, "non-violence is a force infinitely superior to violence."[89]

Nonviolence Is a Contingent Tool. As discussed earlier, for Gandhi, non-violence is not a contingent tool, or an instrument only to be used conditionally. For him, nonviolence is an absolute universal principle that transcends contexts, divides, and binaries. He saw the nonviolent method and the goal of peace in nondualistic terms, arguing that means are equivalent to the desired goal. For him, national and international politics and goals operate in the same social environment. Booth explains: "in the traditional realist/Machiavellian formulation they (ends and means) remain essentially separate, but in the traditional non-dualistic/Gandhian formulation the idealism/realism ideal-types can be conceived as collapsing into each other."[90] The levels of analysis collapse into a single ontological reference point that Gandhi would call Truth. This Gandhian Truth is universal, realizable through nonviolent means. Nonviolence requires one to resist actively wrong as a matter of principle.[91]

There have been attempts to make a distinction between the adherents of principled nonviolence and advocates of strategic, or technical, or conditional violence. In this context, it is essential to analyze Gandhi's conception of nonviolence and its linkage to belonging. Judith Stiehm points out that there are two strands of nonviolence. First, conscientious nonviolence based on the idea of human harmony and a moral rejection of violence and coercion. Second, that Stiehm termed *pragmatic nonviolence* sees conflict as normal and nonviolence as the effective way to challenge power.[92] Explaining this duality of nonviolence, Robert Burrowes focuses on two sets of the continuum: the principled-pragmatic continuum and the reformist-revolutionary continuum.[93] The distinction between principled nonviolence and pragmatic nonviolence may be useful, for while the former takes an essentialist approach to nonviolence, the latter takes an instrumental, conditional, or contingent approach to nonviolence. The latter assumes a situational ethic: if nonviolent protest suits a situation, then it should be used in those circumstances, but not necessarily in others. This ethic fails to meet the Gandhian litmus test: nonviolence is an ethical absolute for Gandhi. If nonviolence can be practiced in one situation, it can and should be practiced in all situations. Otherwise, it will remain an instrument of expediency, to be discarded when conditions are not beneficial.

The dualism of principled nonviolence and pragmatic nonviolence is philosophically incoherent in a larger sense. Nonviolence is not just an external practice; it is a firm conviction embedded in the individual's thinking and psychology. Even further, nonviolence is an ontological choice; an expression of the natural order, or ontological structure of existence itself, it is "the supreme law governing mankind." The essence of Gandhi's nonviolence is not merely no violence but a dynamic principle of "unadulterated love—fellow-feeling," originating from "faith in the inherent goodness of human nature." This "law of love," which "rules mankind" has and continues to be fundamental to our survival as a species: "The fact that mankind persists shows that the cohesive force is greater than the disruptive force, centripetal force greater than centrifugal"; "Had violence, i.e., hate, ruled us, we should have become extinct long ago"; "If the sum-total of the world's activities was destructive, it would have come to an end long ago."[94] Gandhi reposed absolute faith in the nonviolence principle and argued that it "is a power which can be wielded equally by all—children, young men and women or grown-up people, provided they have a living faith in the God of Love and have therefore love for all mankind. When nonviolence is accepted as the law of life it must pervade the whole being and not be applied to isolated acts."[95] Here Gandhi, even without using the term *belonging,* was talking about belonging, connection, and commonalities.

Aim: Embedded Peace

Though there is significant literature on conflict management, conflict resolution, and conflict transformation,[96] our goal in this study is to examine cultural othering and belonging in South Asia and how to foster a framework that focuses on belonging and peace in the region. We agree with scholars like John Lederach that the term *conflict resolution* does not capture fully the nature and scope of the discipline, nor does it do adequate justice to related concepts. Drawing on his research experience in Latin America, Lederach explains the dilemma, "When I arrived there my vocabulary was filled with the usual terminology of conflict resolution and management. I soon found, though, that my Latin colleagues had questions, even suspicions, about what was meant by such concepts. For them, *resolution* carried with it a danger of co-optation, an attempt to get rid of conflict when people were raising important and legitimate issues. It was not clear that *resolution* left room for advocacy. In their experience, quick questions to deep social-political problems usually meant lots of words but no real change. 'Conflicts happen for a reason,' they would say. 'Is this *resolution* idea just another way to cover up the changes that are really needed?'"[97] Johan Galtung, one of the pioneers in this field, focused on this method: emphasizing how conflicts are embedded in cultures and social structures—requiring deep understanding to address them.[98] Lederach elaborates: "Conflict transformation must actively envision, include, respect, and promote the human and cultural resources from within a given setting. This involves a new set of lenses through which we do not primarily 'see' the setting and the people in it as the 'problem' and the outsider as the 'answer.' Rather, we understand the long-term goal of trans-formation as validating and building on people and resources within the setting."[99] Though Gandhi did not develop a formal theory of conflict and peace, his perspective would be closer to the conflict transformation than to the conflict resolution approach. He would probably prefer the term *conflict transcendence*, involving a more nuanced view of conflict, that considers factors beyond outward and visible aspects of culture, peace, and reconciliation. Gandhi would rather address the essentialist spirit of culture and aim at transforming not only its formal structure and institu-tions, but also the psychology of its individual members, through radical, but nonviolent, social praxis. GCR, therefore, aims at an embedded peace with two interrelated aspects: transcending the psychology of winning and losing and a spirit of conflict transcendence.

Beyond Win and Loss. GCR is not based on a zero-sum framework. Gandhi believed that conflict resolution "should be carried out in such a way that the outcome is creative and not viewed as a zero-sum process in which one of the adversaries loses, while the other wins."[100] With an objective "not to assert propositions, but to create possibilities," in her clas-sic work Bondurant points out how Gandhian conflict resolution involves synthesis rather than compromise. It entails "a restructuring of the oppos-ing elements to achieve a situation which is satisfactory to both the origi-nal opposing antagonists but in such a way as to present an entirely new total circumstance. . . . in the form of a mutually satisfactory and agreed-upon solution."[101] Interestingly, several contemporary conflict resolution theories have adopted this Gandhian framework. The "alternative dis-pute resolution" ideal is a case in point.[102] Structural prevention approach involves the creation of laws and rules that establish and strengthen non-violent channels to address conflict, accommodate competing interests, and transform conflicts, by finding common ground. Integrative nego-tiation or integrative bargaining emphasizes exploring ways to accom-modate the interests of all parties in any dispute. Such approaches are more sustainable than compromises, and they effectively consolidate positive relationships.[103] Rubin and Brown note that operative bargaining is accomplished through cooperatively formulating outcomes.[104] Weber cites examples where of "you can get to yes," "you can negotiate any-thing," "you can negotiate with difficult people," and "I can win and you can win" to argue that these negotiation guidelines have a Gandhian "fla-vor."[105] Kurtz aptly summarizes Gandhi's contribution: "Various forms of alternative dispute resolution, conflict resolution, and mediation have their roots in Gandhian nonviolence and have taken root and flourished in various spheres in recent decades. . . . Whether the management or transformation of a conflict is carried out solely by the parties themselves or with the aid of a third party (as in mediation), Gandhi's conflict para-digm is foundational, even if . . . scholars have not made the direct causal link between Gandhi and contemporary conflict resolution literature. Nonetheless, Gandhi at least sets the tone for its development. The point is not to have one party win and the other lose, but to identify the most beneficial outcome for both parties and to struggle creatively and posi-tively toward a just solution."[106]

Since the goal is to transform destructive conflict into a constructive opportunity, it is necessary not to polarize already adversarial situations, as happened between Hindus and Muslims during the partition movement in the early decades of the twentieth century. Gandhi opposed actions leading to this kind of polarization, since he could visualize their destruc-tive potentials. Considering it necessary to explore all possible options to prevent conflict escalation, Gandhi even offered Jinnah the position of the first prime minister of India. The theory of escalation explains how con-flicts that may start from trivial issues become protracted, if not handled properly. Pruitt and Rubin identify five changes that take place in the process of escalation: parties move from light to heavy tactics, conflict grows in size, adversarial issues move from specific to general, the number of hostile parties grows, and goals change from "winning" to hurting the other.[107] The concept of negative reciprocity is a crucial element of this theory and is visible in the case of India-Pakistan rivalry. In the process of escalation, a stage occurs in which parties become so negativity adver-sarial that they identify each other not as concrete individuals or groups, but as actual symbols of evil. Parties develop stereotypes of each other via selective perception and attributional distortion. They believe that they are on the winning side and continue to sacrifice resources for the conflict—falling into a "sacrifice trap" as conflict becomes ritualized. The escalation of conflict also enhances in-group/out-group bias and increases in-group solidarity and cohesion. The past seven decades in the South Asian theater witnessed acute escalation of the conflict and of in-group and out-group hostilities.

Complicated conflicts can be resolved through GCR when "a common solution of the problem begins to be the objective of both rather than the destruction of each other."[108] Doing so requires patience and persistence. Kurtz explains: "Conflicts, including violent ones, take on a life of their own, and escalate beyond the control of the participants. As conflicts are abstracted, the stakes are raised, so that each party considers itself to be fighting for a righteous cause, rather than for their own personal gain. Gandhian efforts to break the spiral of escalation involve an identification of the needs and aspirations of all involved." He then goes on to add: "If adversaries treat each other with respect and try to avoid harming one another, the likelihood of conflict resolution may be greater, Gandhi claims, because both participants gain. Otherwise, adversaries are caught up in the escalation spiral; the longer it persists, the more each party has to lose, so the less willing they are to capitulate, leading to seemingly intractable conflicts."[109] To ensure that both sides gain, it is important that conflict is not allowed to escalate.

To ensure sustainable resolution, Gandhi would not only renounce coercion but also not permit pressure tactics such as sanctions and threats. For Gandhi, coercion and sanctions are two sides of the same coin, and both are different forms of violence. Conflict parties need to ensure that the opponent is neither provoked nor humiliated.[110] Nagler explains this Gandhian approach through an example: "From the moment Saddam Hussein invaded Kuwait public debate centered on the respective merits of a military attack or economic sanctions. From the Gandhian point of view, however, such sanctions are a form of attack; a milder form, quite possibly in some situations a correct form, but one that is not different in kind from the force that sends planes over the air space of another state. In fact, we now know how many innocent children suffered and died, and continue suffering and dying, as a result of this 'alternative' to violence."[111] Pressure tactics thereby invariably undermine conflict resolution.[112] The research suggests that threats are not useful for cooperative outcomes: "An overwhelming amount of experimental research shows that threats tend to elicit counter threats, which then draw in competitive pressure, concern over restoring face, and hostility."[113] A study by Wilson and Bixenstine point out that unjustified insults or tactics posing a threat or promise of damage daunt conflict resolution.[114] Likewise, Siegel and Fouraker contend, "Some negotiations collapse when one party becomes incensed at the other, and henceforth strives to maximize his opponent's displeasure rather than his own satisfaction."[115] Bartos recommends that negotiators should be fair and avoid the enticement to coerce or exploit opponents. Such tactics often lead to stalemates or negotiation cessations.[116]

The GCR necessitates that adversarial parties continuously aspire to have a harmonious relationship and "avoid violence and militarism, and passivity and appeasement."[117] Toward this end, no chasm between preaching and practice, thought and action, is permitted. A study of current international developments, the role of states in international politics, diplomatic maneuvers, and international treaties, indicates that the chasm is indeed wide in practice. In the case of Syria, for example, all the state actors acknowledged that the problem needed to be resolved. Leaders repeatedly stressed there should be a peaceful solution to it. Little progress was made. Former UN secretary-general Ban Ki-moon expressed disappointment at the failure of state actors to contain its tragic human costs and argued, "It is time to find an exit from this madness."[118] The cease-fire agreements between parties failed, as stakeholders used the prospect of peace as leverage to realize policy objectives. One could witness a similar development in the case of the ongoing conflict in Ukraine. This was the very kind of visible chasm between intentions, words, and actions that Gandhi would abhor. It was probably for this reason he adopted a cautionary approach to even widely acceptable tools of conflict resolution: negotiation, arbitration, mediation, dialogue, and peace treaties. Peace treaties emerging from bargains may be punitive and vindictive. They can be compared to a superstructure standing on a weak foundation. Such imposed peace generates further hostility and leads to even worse violence.

Gandhi favored a creative approach to resolving conflicts that promotes belonging and "heart-to-heart" engagement. Empathy is integral to

Gandhian conflict resolution. In Gandhian psychology, nonviolence and love for truth are identical. For Jahanbegloo, Gandhi "was actually underlining the concept of empathy as a dialogical response to the presence of the other. Empathy, contrary to sympathy or compassion, demands that an individual vicariously share in the thoughts and feelings of the other and temporarily become the other. Therefore, the first step of Gandhian empathy is to assume that not only are there differences among people, cultures, and political or social conditions, but also that people may have different value systems that need to be understood and respected critically."[119] Arne Naess in his book *Gandhi and Group Conflict* puts forward the propositions that undergird an empathetic approach: personal contact with the opponent should be explored, opponents should not be judged, opponents should be trusted, and the weakness of an opponent should not be exploited.[120] It would also include, among other things, attempting to understand the opponent's goals, sacrificing nonessential goals for the sake of achieving essential goals; seeing oneself as fallible; being generous with opponents; promoting openness; and avoiding secrecy. Gandhi summarizes this policy: "It is often forgotten that it is never the intention of a Satyagrahi to embarrass the wrong doer," and "the Satyagrahi's object is to convert, not to coerce, the wrong doer."[121]

In GCR, after abandoning all forms of coercion, the stakeholders need to act creatively in a goal-consistent manner by, among other things, including cooperative and constructive elements. Diverse and innovative techniques need to be explored to build flexible relationships of trust and mutual responsiveness, emphasizing common and compatible goals. For Diesing, good relationships make genuine agreements possible. If the relationship is bad, "chances of agreement are missed through misunderstanding, energies are absorbed in useless belligerency, and dealings are distorted by attempts to retaliate for imagined past injustices and insults."[122] In his work on the constructive and destructive processes of conflict resolution, Deutsch argues against these kinds of destructive processes: "One would introduce into the conflict the typical characteristics and effects of a competitive process: poor communication; coercive tactics; suspicion; the perception of basic differences in values; an orientation to increasing the power differences; challenges to the legitimacy of the parties and so forth." And, for a constructive conflict resolution, he further argues, "One would introduce into the conflict the typical effects of a cooperative process: good communication; the perception of similarity in beliefs and values; full acceptance of another's legitimacy; problem-centered negotiations; mutual trust and confidence; information sharing and so forth."[123] As we elaborate in succeeding pages, these dynamics, including that of good communication and perception of commonalities, are missing in India-Pakistan relations.

Toward Transcendence. GCR is transformative, employing nonviolent means to achieve not only a cooperative situation in the short term, but also a nonviolent, all-embracing, psychosocial sense of belonging in a sociopolitical order with no place for othering. For Gandhi, the goal is to ensure that the psychological aspects of conflict are conducive to nonviolent solutions. The Transcendent Approach developed by Johan Galtung, who was influenced by Gandhi, employs this ideal: "The opposite of peace, violence, is seen as the outcome of untransformed conflict. . . . [F]or conflict transformation we need transcendence, going beyond the goals of the parties, creating a new reality . . . so that the parties can live and develop together."[124] Johansen argues that a cultural psychosocial belonging ethos is the antithesis of violence. He explains: "In a protracted conflict situation, violence become endemic, not only physical but also structural and cultural hence for a transformative conflict resolution nonviolent antithesis have to be adopted."[125] This conflict resolution process has three components: direct nonviolence, structural nonviolence, and cultural nonviolence. Direct nonviolence would involve "the use of nonviolent techniques to influence conflicts without the use of violence. . . . Direct nonviolence is used to directly confront those decisions, laws and systems that do not treat all humans equally." Structural nonviolence involves building societal structures "that promote cooperation, reconciliation, openness, equality and peaceful actions in conflict situations." Cultural nonviolence includes "those parts of our culture that transmit traditions of nonviolent behavior and which commemorate and honor nonviolent values and qualities."[126] These three components are integral to building peace in South Asia. In GCR, nonviolence is an effective means of transforming the conflict, not only without coercion, but also with a change in attitudes, perceptions, and behaviors. Conflict resolution pursued without a change in attitudes—with suspicions, fears, perceptional stereotypes remaining intact—holds little chance of success. Even if a resolution is reached—by any means, including fraud, compromise, or even mediation and negotiation—the possibility of violent conflict reerupting remains high. GCR, therefore, requires engaging with and transforming not only behaviors, but also attitudes and perceptions, as the very constitution of sociocultural and political structures sustains and nurtures violent conflict.

GCR positions "the Truth" at the center of interactive dynamics shared by all parties to any conflict. From the Gandhian moral vantage point, transformative conflict resolution is essentially a search for truth. This suggests that each party agrees that they possess part of the truth.[127] This understanding is important since, "if you are convinced that you alone have the truth, there is little recourse but to threaten, intimidate, bribe, or coerce those who disagree with you if they do not come around to your view—or, ultimately, if these methods are unavailing, to use force. That, more or less, is what we see on the international scene today. These methods themselves make resolution of the issues more difficult. . . . The risks of a conflict that both may want to avoid are thereby increased." Only after surrendering the claim to be sole possessor of the truth is it possible to understand disagreements "with an openness to the possibility that each of you may have hold of a part of the truth, and that only by taking seriously that possibility are either of you likely to make progress toward a completer truth." Holmes argues, "Gandhi demonstrated, rather than approaching conflict with a view to trying to prevail at any cost, it is possible to approach it with a view to trying to see that the truth prevail—trying to see that the best solution emerge, whether or not it be one to which you were predisposed at the outset."[128]

In the process of transcendence, it is crucial to replace traditional power structures based on violence, domination, and coercive or exploitive hierarchies with structures based on nonviolence, belonging, and harmony. In a sense, Gandhi intended to replace the Hobbesian security paradigm—founded on the bases of fear, mistrust and violence, and society as a "contract" made by selfish people seeking temporary respite in the inevitable "war of all against all"—with a post-Lockean kind of social contract predicated on transcendental unity rather than individual self-interest. As discussed earlier, Gandhi's approach, in terms of classical political liberalism and realism, is certainly more Lockean or Kantian than Hobbesian, since he believed that there is an inherent urge in human beings toward peace, and this urge can be transmitted to larger groups and states. His nonviolence is not a mere alternative method to organized or sublimated violence, "designed to achieve power by different means."[129] Talking about Gandhian concept of power, Galtung notes, it is not "power-over-others, by military power (sticks), economic power (carrots), cultural power (imposed identity) or political power (because it is so decided), pitting one arsenal of power against the other for balance, competition, or best of all: victory."[130] Gandhi's power, in contrast, involves power over self or governing oneself. Gandhi would therefore expect states to avoid violent conflict by cultivating a spirit of belonging. Power argues that in such a world, states would not commit aggression, not amass the military capability more than required for its own territorial integrity, profess peaceful coexistence, and foster relationships based on nonviolence so as not to alienate or exploit others.[131] State expansionism for power and resources at the expense of others would not be permitted. This would remove the kind of fear and mistrust among states that push states into (in)security dilemmas and incites them to accumulate military power. A Gandhian world would require the transformation of "politics among nations" into "peace among nations." For GCR, it is essential to distinguish between the deed and the doer: "A Satyagrahi must never forget the distinction between evil and the evil-doer."[132] For Gandhi these are two different things, and the goal is not eliminating opponents, but rather eliminating the incompatibility between them. Such an approach involves the admonition of "actions and patterns of action" and not that of the actors. Claiming that such a distinction is both principled as well as pragmatic, Kurz contends, "It goes to the heart of the processes of reciprocity that fuel upward spirals in conflicts at all levels from the interpersonal to the international and has become the bedrock of contemporary techniques of conflict resolution."[133] Following the abandonment of rigid posturing, the acknowledgment of the other's dignified existence, and accepting the need to realize transcendence, adversarial parties can move toward genuine peace. Gandhian *sarvodaya* (the well-being of all) is relevant here, as it is based on the premise that peace is incompatible with exploitation and othering. Gandhi universalized the concept of peace by arguing that only the well-being of all can engender enduring peace. This approach informs our subsequent chapters. In the next chapter, we focus on partition and the visions that shaped it, while factoring Gandhi into our analysis.

2

Othering, Clash of Visions, and Partition

In this chapter, we discuss the ideology that led to partition, its psychological foundation, and the catalysts for its consolidation. We weave an analysis of the historical event of partition with the concept of othering. We also assess the psychology involved in the analysis of two major nationalist visions, religious nationalism and secular nationalism. Gyanendra Pandey suggests that there are "different perspectives" on partition, and, hence, the history of partition appears different from diverse perspectives.[1] While acknowledging there is no one perspective on partition that provides a comprehensive ethical view, our focus is on the Gandhian perspective. We juxtapose this perspective with the perspectives of Iqbal and Jinnah to analyze how the contrasting visions shaped partition narratives, pre-partition politics, and partition itself. We discuss the contrasting visions on nationalism and the incongruities they encountered while operating in the political arena. In the first section, we elaborate on the concepts of othering and belonging. The second section focuses on nationalism and its two variants and how they interact with the psychology of othering as well as its opposite: the psychology of belonging. In the following section, we draw relationships between this debate with the respective social-political visions of Gandhi and Jinnah. In the final section, we discuss the heightened psychology of othering owing to factors such as the British divide-and-rule policy. We also offer, in this section, a glimpse of the partition violence, not only to offer a glimpse of the humanitarian cost of partition but to put in perspective the destructive and pervasive nature of this othering.

The Othering

The binary of othering and belonging is a recurring theme in social science and the study of human interactions and cultures, as it permeates all aspects of the human condition. It is part of daily life, being reflected in terms of race, color, gender, language, geographic locations, and even indiscernible markers of distinction. Edward Said applies this logic in his famous work *Orientalism*: "The Orient is not only adjacent to Europe; it is also the place of Europe's greatest and richest and oldest colonies, the source of its civilizations and languages, its cultural contestant, and one of its deepest and most recurring images of the other. In addition, the Orient has helped to define Europe (or the West)."[2] The Orient is not only the image of the prized colony but represents "recurring images of the other." Said's Orientalism focuses on the othering of Orient and Occident. In this study, our focus is on psychological othering, originating from cultural identity, within the Indian subcontinent, which led to partition and continues to persist.

In multicommunal societies, groups have multiple ethnic, religious, linguistic, and other identities. In this setting, nonmaterial needs such as security and identity are mediated through group membership. Mack, in his study of socially constructed groups and their psychological dynamics, notes that social groups have unique characteristics that separate them from other groups.[3] One of the key characteristics is an intense psychological bonding among the members of the group. For these groups, nonmaterial identity needs, such as culture, are more significant than the material needs. The material needs still play a role in shaping group identity and behavior, but in order of significance, they are secondary to nonmaterial needs. For instance, the deprivation of cultural identity may be felt more acutely than economic deprivation.[4] The deprivation of cultural needs is difficult to quantify, but is felt acutely among members of the group, and this deprivation may prompt the group to organize and strategize to accomplish its goal of satisfying nonmaterial needs, thus paving the way for conflict. What forms an identity and what may eventually prompt a community to perceive an identity crisis may be subject to varying interpretations. Still, denial of distinct identity or even a perception of this denial is sufficient for conflict generation. Othering plays a key role here. The real or perceived discrimination adversely affects interaction patterns between communities through psychological othering. The group differences in the shape of the struggle between included-excluded, majority-minority, dominant-subordinate for power and resources became quite apparent in the early decades of twentieth-century British India. The leaders of the Indian Muslim League feared that, in a Hindu-majority India, the interests of Muslims would be marginalized, as their minority group interests would not be served through the political institutions of a united India. This perceptional deprivation shaped debates between leaders of Hindus and Muslims and contributed to the bloody partition.

When deprivation is felt, real or perceived, psychological othering permeates group identity and generates sharp differences—fostering an "us-versus-them" dichotomy. This psychology becomes deeply entrenched when the group identity is religion. Avruch defines religion as a culture,[5] and we use the two interchangeably in this study. For the practitioners, the religious values are ontological, part of their core identity, and any challenge to those values is akin to challenging their very existence. According to G. Hofstede, G. J. Hofstede, and M. Minkov, "Values (in which we can include religious values) are implicit: they belong to the invisible software of our mind. Talking about our own values is difficult, because it implies questioning our motives, emotions, and taboos. Our own culture is to us like the air we breathe."[6] Culture, or religion, is not only rigidly embedded in a group's individuals, but also reflected in their practices and behaviors. It shapes their life practices and worldviews and plays a major role in communication with members of the same culture and in communication with the members of other cultures. Probably for this reason, in his work on the psychic relationship between culture and the subconscious, Devereux posed, "To psycho-analyse a Plains Indian, should you be a psychoanalyst or an ethnologist?"[7]

Culture, in its general dimensions, is related to universal attributes of human behavior; in its local dimension, it is related to systems of meanings "created, shared, and transmitted (socially inherited) by individuals in particular social groups."[8] It plays a crucial role in shaping conflict as it is rooted "in the shared knowledge and schemes created and used

by a set of people for perceiving, interpreting, expressing and responding to social realities around them."[9] When this "bank of knowledge"
is not shared and appreciated, there is a potential for conflict. Leaders
such as Jinnah and Iqbal believed that the Muslim culture was distinct
from the Hindu culture. The two communities, they believed, could not
coexist peacefully; they needed to be confined to separate territories.
Religion provides its practitioners with a deep-rooted self-concept, considered not only essential but also paramount. Deprivation of this identity
is perceived as a challenge to the very existence of the religious group.
While the embedded connection with one's culture promotes belonging within the group, it may promote othering for the members of other
groups who do not share the same values, especially when identity-based
discrimination, real or perceived, takes root. In pre-partitioned South
Asia, such othering became embedded in their cultural group identities.
The narrative of likely Muslim identity deprivation in an independent
undivided India played a critical role in generating communal conflict.
In the movement for partition of British India, economic and political
considerations played a role, as we elaborate in the succeeding pages.
However, the conflict was generated by the emerging threat of othering,
the perception of discrimination against a distinct cultural group in an
independent united India.

The scholarly attention paid to culture in exploring various dimensions
of political conflict is a relatively recent development. Lederach points
out, "It is with the growth of alternative dispute resolution and mediation
applications in North America that the relationship of culture and conflict
has become an increasingly debated topic."[10] Recent studies in the areas
of negotiation and international relations also focus on culture, particularly its macro aspects, broad values, and general orientations.[11] Critical to
our understanding here are two aspects of culture: essentialist and nonessentialist. The essentialist aspect perceives culture in terms of rigid categories, in which people are containers of culture, standing in separation
from other cultures. The nonessentialist view focuses on the constructive
nature of the culture. While for the former each culture has specific characteristics that need attention, the latter view focuses on the contextual-
ized nature of culture and its permeable and negotiable aspects. Keeping

these differences in mind, we argue that the former, in its rigid form, promotes othering and the latter promotes belonging.

Well-established cultures possess both essentialist and nonessentialist elements. The potential for conflict depends on which aspect of a culture is emphasized and which one is overlooked. Bauman, in his study of culture, argues that discourses on culture and community are neither unitary nor comprehensive.[12] For him, binaries like essentialist versus nonessentialist, or primordial versus constructivist, views of culture are not helpful since culture entails both. In his study of community relations in Southall, London, he argues that cultures have essentialist characteristics, and people tend to reify specific aspects of their culture not only to assert their identity, but also to explore agency in the political arena. Such a fixed approach to culture creates boundaries and incompatible identities among communities. Kew, in his study of conflict in Nigeria, describes how cultural systems of Muslims and Christians clashed when the two perceived each other in a rigid and hostile essentialist way.[13] Avruch takes a constructivist approach to culture and argues such an approach is necessary for understanding the complex nature of both culture and conflict resolution, since conflicts often emerge from rigid essentialism. It is necessary to make cultures inclusive and retain their flexible, nonessentialist aspects—repudiating the rigidity that leads to conflicts—in order to facilitate conflict resolution. Avruch argues:

> Our idea of culture focuses less on patterning and more on social and cognitive processing than older ideas of culture do. For another, by linking culture to individuals and emphasizing the number and diversity of social and experiential settings that individuals encounter, we expand the scope of reference to culture to encompass not just quasi- or pseudo-kinship groupings (tribe, ethnic group, and nation are the usual ones) but also groupings that derive from profession, occupation, class, religion, or region. This reorientation supports the idea that individuals reflect or embody multiple cultures and that "culture" is always psychologically and socially distributed in a group. Compared with the older approach, which connected a singular, coherent, and integrated culture to unproblematically defined social groups, this approach makes the idea of culture more complicated. Such complication is necessary,

because the world of social action, including conflict and its resolution, is a complex one, and we need a different concept to capture it.[14]

In the context of the Indian subcontinent, protagonists of partition like Jinnah were essentialist; they argued that cultural systems of Hinduism and Islam are antagonistic and irreconcilable. The advocates of national unity and cultural integration such as Gandhi and Nehru were nonessentialist; Gandhi and Nehru did not deny the distinctness of Hindu and Muslim cultures but emphasized the constructive nature of the two cultural systems. Interestingly, both Jinnah and Gandhi were aware of these two aspects of their culture. Both were products of a modern, secular English education, and both were known for their secular outlooks. Jinnah belonged to an elite social class and even had plans to retire from active politics. Iqbal persuaded him to lead the Muslim League and steer the movement for a separate Muslim state. Their essentialist view of culture turned the freedom movement, originally a movement to end British rule, toward a movement for the division of British India. This illustrates how relations between separate communities depend largely on how a focus on either othering or belonging guides the extent to which these communities perceive themselves in essentialist or constructivist terms. In her study of intercultural education, Abdallah-Pretceille, drawing on the works of Bourdieu and Lyotard, argues, "If . . . to name is to classify, then to name is also to adopt a perspective . . . for which 'the nominal definition is a designation, yet the designation, far from being a correspondence of the sign to the thing, is, like the perspective . . . . a "decision" which at once gives existence to the sign and its reference.'"[15] We argue that this kind of cultural naming, particularly in antagonistic terms, witnessed a culmination in the early decades of the twentieth-century pre-partition Indian subcontinent and consequently engendered a divisive othering in the region.

According to G. Hofstede, G. J. Hofstede, and M. Minkov, "In our societies, an analogous phenomenon (like genes in our bodies) occurs. Our societies have remarkable capacity for conserving their distinctive culture through generations of successive members and despite varied and numerous forces of change. While change sweeps the surface, the deeper layers remain stable, and the culture rises from its ashes like a phoenix."[16] From the essentialist perspective on culture espoused by Jinnah and Iqbal, Hindu-Muslim coexistence was a "surface" phenomenon. Administrative unity imposed by the British gave British India the semblance of uniformity and unity, but it could not be sustainable. Instead, it heightened the differences and prospects of marginalization in a free India, through the continuum of majority-versus-minority politics. Connor subscribes to this view. In his analysis of the struggle for freedom against British India and the united fight by the Congress and the league, he characterized this union as a tentative, contingent arrangement, a "war time alliance." His argument rests on the assumption that the communal divisions were so deep-rooted that the temporary alliance would fall apart after realization of independence from colonial rule. For him, the temporary alliance could not be considered an "all-embracing nationalism":

> A number of ethnic groups can, and often do, march under the same banner and shout the same slogans. All too often, however, such a composite movement has been misidentified as a manifestation of a single, all-embracing nationalism. In the waning days of colonialism, for example, diverse segments of the population of British India were agreed upon the desirability of ridding the subcontinent of alien rule, and this movement for the eradication of British control was generally described as Indian nationalism (further subdivided into Indian and Moslem nationalism after 1930). It would have been more accurate to characterize the movement as a wartime alliance, similar in many respects to those entered into by states. Just as alliances among states tend to weaken as the threat recedes or the goal nears attainment, so too the period dating from the British announcement of intention to withdraw has been one of rather steady deterioration of the interethnic bonds within the successor states.[17]

Was Hindu-Muslim unity against British rule a "war time alliance"? How does such a formulation account for the sizable number of Muslims who joined the freedom struggle led by the Congress Party and who decided not to migrate to Pakistan after independence? How does it explain the stand of the Muslim leaders like Maulana Azad or Abdul Ghaffar

Khan who were part of Congress and opposed partition? A broader question arises: Can a rigid view of culture be moderated by its nonessentialist or constructivist interpretation? This question is also relevant in a twenty-first-century globalized world that emphasizes cross-fertilization of ideas and values, encouraged by expansive communication, travel, and technology. One finds a countertrend equally in play. In the context of contemporary Europe, some studies have examined Muslim identity within constructed imaginings of national identity and have explored prospects for the compatibility of Muslim culture with Europe's proclaimed secularism.[18] Alami suggests, "Such critical engagements will likely persist well into the current century in dialogues that both repress and encourage constructions of new modernities in increasingly transnational and globalized world culture."[19] Though his analysis focuses on Europe, it is relevant for states in other regions contemplating the complex question of coexistence between minority and majority communities—whether Hindus and Muslims in India, Muslims and Hindus in Pakistan, Muslims and Christians in Nigeria, or Buddhists and Muslims in Myanmar. Boyce and Chunnu also apply this framework to race relations in the United States. Drawing on the works of French philosopher Emmanuel Levinas, particularly his work on othering,[20] they argue how "fear of the Other" has been used historically as a tool against African-Americans.[21] Protests in the United States and other parts of the globe in mid-2020 brought othering and belonging into sharp focus.[22]

Nationalisms: Religious and Secular

There is no single, unified, or commonly accepted definition of nationalism. A nation, for E. J. Hobsbawm, "is a historically evolved, stable community of language, territory, economic life, and psychological make-up manifested in a community of culture."[23] Prominent interpreter of nationalism Benedict Anderson emphasizes the psychological aspect: "It [nation] is an imagined political community- and imagined as both inherently limited and sovereign."[24] The concept of nationalism came to prominence after the French Revolution. Its foundation could be traced to the Treaty of Westphalia in 1648, which separated church from state and laid the groundwork of modern secular states in Europe. There is a clash of visions between the kind of secular nationalism articulated in the Treaty of Westphalia and religious nationalism as envisaged by Iqbal and undertaken as a political project by Jinnah. The concept of "one religion, one nation" stands in stark contrast to secular nationalism and to grand transnational projects like universal socialism. Austro-Marxists like Karl Renner and Otto Bauer made a theoretical argument in the early decades of the twentieth century, contending that ideas like nation, state, and society are not coterminous and that nationalist conflicts are inimical to the universal socialist project.[25] For orthodox Marxists, nationalism is a form of false consciousness and threatens socialism. Hans Kohn in *The Idea of Nationalism* focused on nationalism as an idea or doctrine rather than on its specific historical connections. The rise of fascism and the Second World War led thinkers like E. H. Carr to question ethnic nationalism.[26]

Our goal here is not to undertake a detailed exploration of nationalism and its various aspects, but to demonstrate that modern secular nationalism—emphasizing separation of religion and state—stands in contrast to the idea of religious nationalism—emphasizing exclusive intersection of religion and nationalism. This is not to argue that secular nationalism is without conflict potential. Modern secular states emphasized ethnic-cultural homogeneity to promote state consolidation, which laid the foundation for many secular conflicts in postcolonial states where borders were drawn with little consideration for demands from social groups. The policy of national consolidation prompted aggrieved and alienated ethnic minorities to mobilize. According to Smith, "State homogenization always appears to the non-dominant ethnie (ethnic group, in which we can include religion) like ethnic discrimination and exploitation. In an age of nationalism that perception is likely to prove explosive."[27] He further contends, "Today, the popular type of conflicts is the most protracted and bitter; for not only does it involve more fundamental passions than inter-state wars, it is also much more frequently entwined with the rivalries between states, so that the two kinds of conflict now flow together to produce increasingly dangerous conflagrations."[28] Connor laments, "Scholars associated with theories of 'nation-building' have tended either to ignore the question of ethnic diversity or to treat the matter of ethnic identity superficially as merely one of a number of minor impediments to effective state-integration." He further argues, "The validity of this position apparently also rests upon one of two propositions. Either loyalty to the ethnic group is self-evidently compatible with loyalty to the state, or . . . ethnic identification will prove to be of short duration, withering away as modernization progresses . . . but clearly the two are not naturally harmonious."[29] This incompatibility between the process of state consolidation and identity-based exclusivity of groups fuels conflicts. Ayoob argues that the process of state consolidation in Europe was not bereft of violence and that the developing world is undergoing a similar consolidation process, wherein groups having distinct identities oppose the process of state consolidation and resort to armed resistance for recognition and even secession.[30]

The idea of a territorial nation-state, implying all inhabitants within a territorial state constitute one nation, is in contrast with the idea of a nation-state that primarily relies on diversity. While the first idea emphasizes geographical compactness, the second idea is associated with innate qualities of life. Within the first, social identities emerge as major catalysts for conflicts as territory becomes a mechanism for power and domination, as happened in British India. Can we then view contesting nationalism, and the consequent partition of British India, through this lens of state consolidation? There was no process of state consolidation. A united independent India was never a reality, and there was no visible marginalization of one cultural group by the other—making the argument that minorities would be exploited in a united and secular independent India tenuous. True, the formation of provincial governments and familiarity with local power under British rule contributed to such a perception, but it would be an exaggeration to argue that it was the primary factor behind partition. This perception of marginalization had deeper roots, understood in terms of the incompatibility of Hindu and Muslim cultural systems.

In his study of 132 states, during the early 1970s, Connor found that only 12 could be described as substantially homogeneous from an ethnic point of view; 25 contained an ethnic group accounting for more than 90 percent of the state's total population, and in 25 states the largest element accounted for between 75 and 89 percent of the population. In 31 states, the largest ethnic element represented only 50 to 74 percent of the population, and in 39 the largest group failed to account for even half of the state's population. He observed that "this portrait of ethnic diversity becomes more vivid when the number of distinct ethnic groups within states is considered. In some instances, the number of groups within a state runs into the hundreds, and in 53 states (40.2 per cent of the total), the population is divided into more than five significant groups."[31] He contended that the conception of modern states as single homogenous states having a single ethnic identity is a misnomer. In most modern states it is difficult to find a single identity, including religious identity, as a unifying identity. Multiethnic states have promoted national symbols such as a national flag or national anthem as markers of national identity. As noted in the introduction, French sociologist Emile Durkheim was one of the first thinkers to notice this trend.[32] Robert Bellah, in his study of American nationalism, points out that a universal American identity was much pronounced than other ethnic identities within America.[33] The emergence of secular nationalism is not an easy process, and modern states struggle to reconcile aspirations of various groups within its broadly conceived national fold.

There are two major views, which are not necessarily compatible with each other, in the context of national consolidation and modernization. One argument, as forcefully made by Karl Deutsch and others, is that modernization, increasing communication, urbanization, and the fruits of economic development moderate exclusive group identities and facilitate the process of state consolidation. While arguing that modernization leads to national assimilation, Deutsch did not exclude the possibility of "more conspicuous differentiation and conflict" if the core issue of identity differences remains unaddressed. According to him, "Linguistically and culturally, then, members of each group are outsiders for the other. Yet technological and economic processes are forcing them together, into acute recognition of their differences and their common, mutual experience of strangeness, and more conspicuous differentiation and conflict may result."[34] He notes further, "Other things assumed equal, the stage of rapid social mobilization may be expected, therefore, to promote the consolidation of states whose peoples already share the same language, culture, and major social institutions; while the same process may tend to strain or destroy the unity of states whose population is already divided into several groups with different languages or cultures or basic ways of life."[35] Gellner takes a similar position. For him, nationalism is a product of modernity and essentially requires some form of homogeneity: "We do not properly understand the range of options available to industrial society, and perhaps we never shall; but we understand some of its essential concomitants. The kind of cultural homogeneity demanded by nationalism is one of them and we had better make our peace with it. It is not the case . . . that nationalism imposes homogeneity; it is rather that a homogeneity imposed by objective, inescapable imperative eventually appears on the surface in the form of nationalism."[36] Gellner rejects the argument of Elie Kedourie, for whom nationalism is imposed homogeneity.[37] Kedourie even goes to the extent of calling it an "inexplicable disease" or a "millennial religion," creating discord for rational political arrangements at their very inception.[38] While some form of national identity may be essential for a modern state to survive and thrive, the large question pertains to reconciling national identity, which demands some kind of homogeneity, and social identities, which abhor homogeneity. The situation gets more complicated when a group challenges this secular national identity and explores solutions that address its own identity needs.

For Muhammad Iqbal, secular nationalism is a misnomer. In his criticism of modern secular nationalism in Europe, he argued, "The idealism of Europe never became a living factor in her life, and the result is a perverted ego seeking itself through mutually intolerant democracies whose sole function is to exploit the poor in the interest of the rich." Rather, he argued, religion, and particularly Islam, could provide a true basis of democracy and equality: "The Muslim, on the other hand, is in possession of these ultimate ideas of the basis of a revelation, which, speaking from the inmost depths of life, internalizes its own apparent externality. With him the spiritual basis of life is a matter of conviction for which even the least enlightened man among us can easily lay down his life; and in view of the basic idea of Islam that there can be no further revelation binding on man, we ought to be spiritually one of the most emancipated peoples on earth." This conception of a spirituality-based community does not explicate in detail how it can be operationalized in a multireligious society. Iqbal's Islamic nationalism displays a bias, that only under Islam can democracy and justice flourish—not under other religions like Christianity, Buddhism, or Hinduism. This assumption is not merely problematic from the vantage point of other religious interests, but also a dangerous one, impelling adherents toward a conviction that, as Iqbal states, "even the least enlightened man among us can easily lay down his life."[39]

The rise of Islamic movements in other parts of the world shaped subcontinental communal politics. Annemarie Schimmel points out that Iqbal dreamed of a global Islamic movement and conceived the foundation of an independent Islamic state in the Indian subcontinent as a part of this movement. Iqbal wrote, "I had seen in a dream that a black dressed army was riding on Arab horses; I felt that they were angels. As to me the explanation of this dream is that in the near future a new movement will appear in Islamic countries. The meaning of Arab horses is the spirit of Islam."[40] This vision colored his view to the extent that he repudiated the separation of religion and state as an impossible aspiration. Secular states as envisaged in the Treaty of Westphalia, he believed, cannot provide real equality and justice for their constituencies. He stated, "The biggest blunder made by Europe was the separation of Church and State. This deprived their culture of moral soul and diverted it to the atheistic materialism . . . The European war of 1914 was an outcome of the aforesaid mistakes made by the European nations in the separation of the Church and the State."[41] If Iqbal rejected European secular nationalism, based on separation of church and state, then what are the practical modes of consolidating nation-states? Is religion the only way to retain a "moral soul" and deter "atheistic materialism" in order to prevent "war"? Is this practiced in any religious state? For Iqbal, the scope of this vision does not end with the formation of a separate territory for Indian Muslims. It is a step toward the establishment of an international brotherhood of followers of Islam, *ummah*.

Ummah or *umma* broadly means "community" or "community of believers." Fred Halliday explains, "The Arabic term, umma, is cognate with Hebrew, am, people, both derivative of Aramaic and Akkadian. It occurs frequently in the holy texts that constitute the Islamic tradition or Sunna: at least 62 times in the Qur'an and frequently in the hadith or sayings of the Prophet Muhammad. . . . A closer examination of these elements of tradition reveals a diverse set of meanings and options. . . . The most important, but by no means exclusive, usage relates to the community of believers who were ruled by Muhammad during his period in Medina (AD 622–632)."[42] He examines its flexible and rigid interpretations and its relationship with the idea of nationalism. In his study of the politics of *ummah* or *umma*,[43] Ahsan refers to German historian Reinhard Schulze, who adopted a flexible approach to the concept. Schulze, in *A Modern History of the Islamic World* argues, "This concept [umma] too was flexible, and indeed served to reinforce, rather than challenge, the hold of the territorial and national state. Not only secular nationalism of the mid-twentieth century, up to around 1970, but even later Islamist movements espoused a concept of politics, and legitimacy, focused on the state."[44] This flexible notion of *ummah* as elaborated by Schulze is possible in a modern globalized world. Elisabeth Özdalga also adopts a flexible interpretation. She argues that Islamism or an Islamic view of the state is compatible with modern nationalism, originating from Europe, and calls them "sister ideologies." In her study of Middle East state formation, she argues that Islam is compatible with the secular state idea and consolidation of state power in a defined territory. She explains, "Statements concerning the lack of separation between political and religious institutions in Islam have most often been taken as indications that Islam is not 'secularizable,' implying that it is not compatible with modern political institutions like democracy."[45] James Mellon takes a cautionary approach and argues that Pan-Islamism and Pan-Arabism as a "supranational ideal transcending individual states" may influence state policies as a cultural force, but independent states continue to dominate the politics of the Middle East and, by extension, international politics.[46] It can be argued that such an assertion may conform to a middle or intermediary stratum of Islamic *ummah*, with a global ambition.

A rigid *ummah*, arguing for an Islamic state all over the world, as reflected in the ideologies of radical organizations such as al-Qaeda, or Islamic State in Iraq and Syria, warrants attention, as this notion challenges the modern secular democratic system, in which multiethnic states, not religious-driven ideologies or movements, are primary actors in domestic and international politics. Mehdi Mozaffari makes a distinction between Islam and Islamism and, while arguing that Islamism has multiple dimensions and various ramifications, says that "despite sectarian and other differences between various Islamist groups, their final objective remains the same. They all aim at the re-instauration of the Islamic might in the world: to achieve this goal, the use of violence is not rejected."[47] Mozaffari quotes Sayyid Qutb, the Egyptian Islamic thinker: "Those who say that Islamic Jihad was merely for the defence of the 'homeland of Islam' diminish the greatness of the Islamic way of life and consider it less important than their 'homeland.' This is not the Islamic point of view, and their view is a creation of the modern age and is completely alien to Islamic consciousness. . . . Of course, in that case the defence of the 'homeland of Islam' is the defence of the Islamic beliefs, the Islamic way of life, and the Islamic community. However, its defence is not the ultimate objective of the Islamic movement of Jihad, but is a means of establishing the Divine authority within it so that it becomes the headquarters for the movement of Islam, which is then to be carried throughout the earth to the whole of mankind, as the object of this religion is all humanity and its sphere of action is the whole earth."[48] Is this vision of Qutb different from the vision of religious nationalism of Iqbal? Is it not based on othering—excluding other visions and asserting its own as the only viable one for the universal brotherhood it conceives?

The Islamic *ummah* is a teleological concept—supporting whatever serves the purpose of realizing the universal brotherhood of Islam. It would support a territorial nation on contingent grounds but not as a final destination since, as Iqbal points out, Islam does not recognize "artificial boundaries and racial distinctions." A territorial Islamic nation would consolidate Islam as a life force in that particular territory, but, by the very logic of *ummah*, it would not stop there. Once it fully consolidates the Islamic life force in that territory, it would gear its state power toward supporting this movement in other places, until universal Islamic brotherhood is realized. Iqbal would affirm that in Islamic brotherhood there is no concept of a fixed state, although they may exist for "facility of reference only."[49] The rights of non-Muslims in this framework have not been made clear by Iqbal, that is, whether as nonadherents of Islam they will have equal rights or be disenfranchised because of their religious status.

Pakistan's origin could be traced to religious othering, but the country continued to grapple with the issue of othering. It witnessed a conflict of ideas between its European-educated intelligentsia, who had faith in democratic secular ideals, and those pushing for a religious-based political system.[50] This conflict almost ended with Zia-ul-Haq assuming power in the late 1970s. Zia promoted a rigid interpretation of *ummah* and stated, "The basis of Pakistan was Islam. The basis of Pakistan was that the Muslims of the sub-continent are a separate culture. It was on the two-nation theory that this part was carved out of the sub-continent as Pakistan. And in the last 30 years in general . . . there has been a complete erosion of the moral values of this society. . . . These are the Islamic values and we are trying to bring these values back." He then advocated for a universal brotherhood of Muslims: "Islam does not recognize any geographical limits dividing its followers. Muslims are Muslims, regardless of whether they are also Ajami [foreigner] Arab, Pakistani or Russian. Nationality is irrelevant within the Ummah, with the universal brotherhood of Islam."[51] Pursing this vision, Zia used state machinery to promote radical Islamization of state as well as society. The consequences of this impetus have been enormous and have promoted the cancerous growth of religious extremism and violence. Zia's democratic successor, Benazir Bhutto, remained a critic of this vision. She wrote, "The stakes could not have been higher. Pakistan under military dictatorship had become the epicenter of an international terrorist movement that had two primary aims. First, the extremists' aim to reconstitute the concept of the caliphate, a political state encompassing the great Ummah (Muslim community) populations of the world, uniting the Middle East, the Persian Gulf states, South Asia, Central Asia, East Asia, and parts of Africa. And second, the militants' aim to provoke clash of civilizations between the West and an interpretation of Islam that rejects pluralism and modernity. The goal—the great hope of the militants—is a collision, an explosion between the values of the West and what the extremists claims to be the values of Islam."[52] The military-led Islamic drive by Zia offered an answer to the question unaddressed by Iqbal: What will be the fate of religious nonadherents in an Islamic state? The non-Muslim population has dwindled significantly in Pakistan. Farahnaz Ispahani, a former member of Pakistan parliament, wrote in 2013, "At the time of partition in 1947, almost 23 percent of Pakistan's population was comprised of non-Muslim citizens. Today, the proportion of non-Muslims has declined to approximately 3 percent."[53]

The larger question is, if nationality is unnecessary for the universal brotherhood of Islam or ummah, as Iqbal and Zia would argue, then how can one justify the need for an Islamic state or a territorial limit of a state encompassing Islamic ideas? If Islamic brotherhood cannot be confined to territorial limits, then is the two-nation theory, which contended that Hindus and Muslims are two nations and need different territories, dubious? Was it simply the rhetoric of some Muslim elites to fulfill their ambition for power, which was deemed impossible in a Hindu-majority yet secular India? What about the Muslims who did not leave India after the creation of Pakistan—did they emerge as a counterforce to Iqbal's two-nation vision by not migrating to Pakistan? Iqbal never addressed these issues, as he was preoccupied with the idea of Pakistan and universal Islamic brotherhood.

Gandhi stood for secular nationalism. He would probably have accepted a flexible concept of *ummah* or brotherhood, but his brotherhood would not be religious. It would be multireligious and pluralistic within a liberal democratic social-political order. Any orthodox religious *ummah* or brotherhood of the kind championed by Iqbal was anathema to Gandhi. Gandhi was firmly opposed to any religious state—whether Islamic, Hindu, or any other religious identity. Referring to Gandhi's conception of God, Gregg argues, "People who do not believe in God or who dislike references to what they call supernatural should know that Gandhi said that God is another name for Truth. Truth and God, he said, are the same. Instead of Truth, some people would prefer the term Ultimate Reality or Unity or Spirit. Moslems would prefer the name Allah; Hindus might use the name Brahma or Shiva or Rama; Buddhists of different schools might use still other names or no name at all. We need not quarrel over the name. We know that Gandhi was referring to a supreme intangible Power, and that success in nonviolent resistance requires a firm belief in such a Power."[54] Gandhi's interest in religion was not sectarian. He was interested in exploring the peaceful potentials of all religions. Bertrand Russell wrote about Gandhi in 1952, "He had a wide and unsectarian interest in religion, and listened to Christian teaching without hostility, though without acceptance."[55] The nonsectarian in Gandhi would not hesitate to listen to other religious texts and be equally comfortable reading the Gita or the Quran. According to Russell, "However that may be, it is impossible to understand him psychologically so long as we think of him in purely modern terms. To build him up psychologically from European ingredients we must make a combination of early Christian saint with medieval ecclesiastics, adding to both, however, something of the sweetness of St. Francis."[56] Hence, for Gandhi, as for the compassionate Saint Francis, the idea of othering—or more so the idea of violent othering—would be positively deplorable, something contradictory to the spiritual core of his philosophy and his being.

Ambedkar in his *Pakistan or Partition of India*, published in 1946, a year before the partition became a reality, examined both Jinnah's argument that Muslims are a separate nation and Gandhi's argument that Hindus and Muslims can have a single Indian national identity and found support for both. Ambedkar adopted a dispassionate perspective on partition politics. He was neither pessimistic like Iqbal and Jinnah (concluding that there is no scope for a harmonious relationship between Hindus and Muslims) nor optimistic like Gandhi (concluding that Hindu-Muslim unity is a permanent feature of Indian character, wedded to the destiny of India) or the idea that India would be incomplete without this harmonious relationship. He argued:

> Reliance is placed not only upon racial unity but also upon certain common features in the social and cultural life of the two communities. It is pointed out that the social life of many Muslim groups is honeycombed with Hindu customs. . . . Hindu surnames are found among Muslims. For instance, the surname Chaudhari is a Hindu surname but is common among the Musalmans of U.P. and Northern India. . . . In the religious sphere, it is pointed out that many Muslim *pirs* had Hindu disciples; and similarly some Hindu *yogis* have had Muslim *chelas*. Reliance is placed on instances of friendship between saints of the rival creeds. . . . That a large majority of the Muslims belong to the same race as the Hindus is beyond question. . . . But the question is: can all

this support the conclusion that the Hindus and the Mahomedans on account of them constitute one nation or these things have fostered in them *a feeling that they long to belong to each other?*[57]

An important point that Ambedkar emphasized for building a nation-state, and which we emphasize throughout this study, is a "feeling that they (people of different religions and cultures, in the context of India—Hindus and Muslims) long to belong to each other." His point about the importance of belonging in this context is an important one. Iqbal and Jinnah considered national unity artificial, since Hindu and Muslim cultural systems, they believed, were inimical to one another. The partition-related violent sectarian upsurge seemed to corroborate their perception and undermine Gandhi's vision of a united India. The larger question, keeping in view post-partition politics, is whether the vision of belonging or the vision of othering has more salience for peace in South Asia. We have addressed this question in the next chapter. In the next section, we examine the clash of these visions.

The Clash of Visions

Gandhi remained an ardent advocate of Hindu-Muslim unity, and the optimist in him never allowed him to discard his view despite setbacks and criticisms from within his party or from opponents. For instance, many Congress leaders were critical of Gandhi supporting the Khilafat Movement of 1919–24, which aimed at restoring the caliph, and his stance on the Mopla Riots in 1921, which initially erupted as an uprising against oppression but later turned into sectarian violence targeting Hindus.[58] In his call for an all-India movement to support the Khilafat movement, Gandhi, in his "tenacious quest for Hindu-Muslim unity," as Ambedkar described it, called upon all Indians to take a vow: "With God as witness, we Hindus, and Mahomedans declare that we shall behave towards one another as children of the same parents, that we shall have no differences, that the sorrows of each shall be the sorrows of the other and that each shall help the other in removing them. We shall respect each other's religion and religious feelings and shall not stand in the way of our respective religious practices. We shall always refrain from violence to each other in the name of religion."⁵⁹ Ambedkar saw Gandhi's stand on these developments as "too heavy a price for Hindu-Moslem unity." While Ambedkar clearly understood both points of view, on the issue of othering and belonging he was closer to Gandhi than to Iqbal.

To critics who objected that he was too conciliatory in attempting to placate Muslim aspirations and anxieties, Gandhi responded with a spiritual appeal for interfaith belonging: "It has been whispered that by going so much with Mussalman friends, I make myself unfit to know the Hindu mind. The Hindu mind is myself. Surely I do not live amidst Hindus to know the Hindu mind when every fibre of my being is Hindu. . . . But I must labour to discover the Mussalman mind. The closer I come to the best of Mussalmans, the juster I am likely to be in my estimate of the Mussalmans and their doings. I am striving to become the best cement between the two communities. My longing is to be able to cement the two with my blood, if necessary. But, before I can do so, I must prove to the Mussalmans that I love them as well as I love the Hindus. My religion teaches me to love all equally."⁶⁰ Gandhi presented a counterpoint to calls for brotherhood by Muslim League leaders rallying for a separate state. He broadened the definition of brotherhood itself and argued that both Hindus and Muslims are brothers, engaged in a family quarrel. He even called mobilization for a separate state "un-Islamic" and "sinful." For his contemporaries, the difference persisted—both in conceptual and political terms. For Iqbal, brotherhood or *ummah* was specifically confined to the Muslims, and this brotherhood is guided exclusively by the principles of Islam. This led inevitably to the political project of Pakistani nationhood to promote universal Islamic brotherhood.

Gandhi's conception of brotherhood could never be a religious one, as it undermined the multicultural and multireligious fabric of India. The only legitimate Gandhian brotherhood would be one of humanity encompassing all religions within a radically pluralistic political community. A free India, in his view, had to be a "shining" example of this multireligious and multicultural brotherhood. Gandhi spared no effort to prevent a religious division of British India. He replied to a question about religious partition in 1946 that he would prefer to be "cut to pieces" rather than accept Iqbal's notion of religious brotherhood. He challenged the claim that Muslims would be persecuted in an independent India: "It is nonsense to say that any people can permanently crush or swamp out of existence one fourth of its population, which the Mussalmans are in India. But I would have no hesitation in conceding the demand of Pakistan if I could be convinced of its righteousness or that it is good for Islam. But I am firmly convinced that the Pakistan demand as put forth by the Muslim League is un-Islamic and I have not hesitated to call it sinful. Islam stands for the unity and brotherhood of mankind, not for disrupting the oneness of the human family. Therefore, those who want to divide India into possibly warring groups are enemies alike of India and Islam. They may cut me to pieces but they cannot make me subscribe to something which I consider to be wrong."[61]

At a glance, Gandhi might appear a devotee of the status quo and Iqbal an advocate of change. This perception is somewhat unfounded, though. Gandhi was interested in preserving a long-standing tradition of peaceful community relations, and, in the event of any social injustice, he preferred gradual, nonviolent, change. Iqbal was averse to maintaining community relations in a multireligious framework, as he perceived that religion-based injustice and repression might result from this arrangement. He preferred swift social-political change, even with violence if necessary. The view of Gandhi as an agent of change and Iqbal as an advocate of the status quo would seem to be more accurate. Gandhi would continuously champion the transformation of both society and human nature through nonviolent praxis—a progression from the Hobbesian solitary, brutish, and nasty life of othering to a Lockean cooperative and inclusive life of belonging. He advocated genuine work to effectuate this change, not only at the individual but also at the state and cultural levels—and this was evident in his movements for religious harmony, addressing untouchability, gender equality, and the freedom struggle for India. In contrast, Iqbal adopted a status quo interpretation of religion, and promoted his political projects without ever considering crucial questions—such as how minorities would be treated in his ideal state or, more important, how his conceptualization of cultural homogeneity would develop if all Indian Muslims did not cross the border to become citizens of a newly formed Islamic state.

Gandhi's conviction persisted until the end of his life. Repeated failures and frustrations did not attenuate his philosophy of belonging, even at a time when partition was about to become a reality. Talbot noted in the early 1940s, "On many sides in India today one hears that Gandhi is through, finished. That his era is past, the world has gone beyond him, his old magic won't work anymore, the hour of youth is at hand. This old cry was sounded after the civil disobedience movement, again when he resigned from the Congress in 1934, again when the Congress Working Committee temporarily divided from him (soon to scurry back rapidly under his leadership) after this war broke out, and again and again and again."[62] India being a multireligious and pluralist nation, losing this multicultural identity would be to lose India: "[If] India is divided she will be lost forever. Therefore . . . if India is to remain undivided, Hindus and Moslems must live together in brotherly love, not in hostile camps organized either for defensive action or retaliation."[63] Gandhi the optimist argued that all Indians, irrespective of their religions, shared a common ancestry, lifestyle, and language: "In actual life, it is impossible to separate us into two nations. We are not two nations. Every Moslem will have a Hindu name if he goes back far enough in his family history. Every Moslem is merely a Hindu who has accepted Islam. That does not create nationality. . . . We in India have a common culture. In the North, Hindi and Urdu are understood by both Hindus and Moslems. In Madras, Hindus and Moslems speak Tamil, and in Bengal, they both speak Bengali and neither Hindi nor Urdu. . . . [I]t is our superstitions that create the trouble. . . ."[64] Hence, Iqbal and Jinnah on one side and Gandhi on the other side had opposing visions: for Iqbal, Islam via the *ummah* as the basis for a state; for Gandhi, secular and multireligious national unity.

The meetings and letter exchanges between Gandhi and Jinnah—particularly between 1940, when the Lahore Resolution was passed, and 1947, when the partition occurred—provide useful insights into their opposing worldviews and incompatible visions. The resolution used the term *Muslim India* while talking about discontent among Muslims of British India and the need for a separate homeland. The resolution read, "This Session of the All-India Muslim League emphatically reiterates that the Scheme of Federation embodied in the Government of India Act, 1935, is totally unsuited to, and unworkable in the peculiar conditions of this country and is altogether unacceptable to Muslim India."[65] It further argued, "Muslim India will not be satisfied unless the whole constitutional plan is reconsidered."[66] In contrast, Gandhi viewed all constituencies— whether Hindu India, Muslim India, Buddhist India, Jain India, Christian India, Jew India, or Parsi—as coalescing within a single India. While Iqbal conceived of Islam as a life force that can flourish only in an independent geographical territory of its own, Gandhi affirmed that Islam as a life force can flourish within a pluralistic and multiethnic India. For Gandhi, partition, as envisaged in the Lahore Resolution, would bring "nothing but ruin for the whole of India." Iqbal considered partition to be the only viable solution to India's problems. And in a letter to Gandhi, on September 17, 1944, Jinnah wrote, "Muslims and Hindus are two major nations by any definition or test of a nation." Though criticized by some of his Hindu colleagues for favoring Muslims, Gandhi also faced criticism from Jinnah as loyal only to his Hindu constituency. Responding to Gandhi's unyielding commitment to inclusive nationalism, Jinnah retorted, "When you proceed to say that you aspire to represent all the inhabitants of India, I regret I cannot accept that statement of yours. It is quite clear that you represent nobody else but the Hindus, and as long as you do not realize your true position and the realities, it is very difficult for me to argue with you."[67] Contra Gandhi, Jinnah considered competent political leadership to be exclusive to religious identity. This argument can also be extended to caste, language, race, color, ad infinitum, and even an imagined identity.[68] On another occasion, Jinnah wrote to Gandhi, "An ocean separated you and me in outlook." In a letter from September 23, 1944, Jinnah criticized the August 1942 resolution of the Congress to launch the Quit India (leave India) movement. He considered the resolution a move toward establishing a "Hindu Raj," "inimical to the ideals and demands of Muslim India," and even a "death-blow to Muslim India."[69]

As othering became more firmly established in Indian affairs and communal divisions intensified, the popularity of the Muslim League increased. Guha estimates that in 1927, the league had only thirteen hundred members, but by 1944 it had more than a half-million members in

Bengal alone, as "Muslims of all classes flocked to the League. Artisans, workers, professionals, and businessmen all rallied to the clarion call of 'Islam in Danger,' fearing the prospect, in a united India, of a 'Brahmin Bania Raj.'"[70] One major victim of this sustained othering was the freedom struggle. Jinnah eventually identified himself as a Muslim leader, with seemingly no active interest in furthering any freedom struggle against the British. Talbot writes, "Mr. Jinnah stands as the mouthpiece, protector and defender of the Muslim peoples of India. . . . When, soon after war broke out, it looked as if a common front of Indian leaders might advance the independence issue and Mr. Jinnah refused to associate himself with any parleys except as the recognized sole representative of the Muslims in India." Attempts by the Congress to work with the league were shrugged off: "Each new effort (to bring the two parties together) gives Mr. Jinnah another opportunity to slap on the wrists of the Hindu leaders (and the 'renegade Muslim,' Maulana Abul Kalam Azad, the imprisoned president of the Congress) for being audacious enough to assume an all-India representative character."[71] Jalal presents Jinnah as a leader committed to the idea of Pakistan throughout the partition negotiations. This commitment originated not primarily from a longing for a Muslim state, but from a craving to gain recognition as "sole spokesman" for India's Muslims.[72] The primary motivation behind Jinnah's activism for Pakistan was the fact that he was not the sole political voice of Muslims in the 1940s. The idea of Pakistan and commitment to it catapulted Jinnah's popularity as the champion of Muslim unity. The real struggle was not so much to create a separate territorial homeland as it was to create a launchpad for establishing a united "Muslim community" in India.[73]

Interestingly, even while contending that an "ocean" stood between him and Gandhi, Jinnah at one point in time seemed to have agreed with Gandhi that Hindus and Muslims can coexist in a united community. This "ocean" did not exist during the initial Indian freedom struggle when a secular Jinnah was an important leader of the Congress. Here we are talking about the stage in the freedom struggle's history when partition was about to become a reality and a large section of the Indian Muslim population had been convinced that they could not coexist with Hindus in the same civil society. Jinnah, by then resolutely devoted to the two-nation theory, argued in a speech to the Constituent Assembly of Pakistan, on August 11, 1947—just a few days before partition—that in an independent Pakistan, all people, including Muslims, Hindus, and other minorities, could coexist as "equal" citizens of Pakistan: "I cannot emphasize it too much. We should begin to work in that spirit and in course of time all these angularities of the majority and minority communities, the Hindu community and the Muslim community . . . will vanish. . . . You are free; you are free to go to your temples, you are free to go to your mosques or to any other place or worship in this State of Pakistan. You may belong to any religion or caste or creed—that has nothing to do with the business of the State. . . . We are starting in the days where there is no discrimination, no distinction between one community and another, no discrimination between one caste or creed and another. We are starting with this fundamental principle that we are all citizens and equal citizens of one State."[74]

Was this argument in contradiction to Jinnah's contention that Hindu-Muslim coexistence was impossible? How could Jinnah conclude that such coexistence is possible in Pakistan but not in a united India? Stephen Cohen notes this contradiction: "A few speeches could not erase four decades of emphasis on *differences* between Hindus and Muslims, and the threat to Muslims from the larger community. As Shahid Burki questioned, 'How could Muslims cease to be Muslims and Hindus cease to be Hindus in the political sense when the religions to which they belonged were, in Jinnah's passionately held belief, so utterly different from one another? Was Jinnah giving up the two-nation theory, the ideological foundation of the state of Pakistan?' The fact is, he was a pragmatic leader trained in the British constitutional framework, scornful of the religious leaders who had opposed the idea of Pakistan—and who in turn castigated him for being irreligious."[75]

Jinnah projected himself as a champion of secular nationalism, which he diligently clung to until the idea of Pakistan became widely accepted. Is this not what Gandhi stood for throughout his life? For Gandhi, Bhikhu Parekh argues, "the very idea that each nation should have its own state was preposterous and impractical. In any case, the new state of Pakistan would include a large number of Hindus, even as India would include millions of Muslims. Since both states were bound to be multi-religious and had to find ways of accommodating minorities, there was no reason why the united India could not do the same. . . . What in Gandhi's view Jinnah was not entitled to do was to arouse religious passions and threaten mass violence if he did not get his way."[76] Were there parallels between the ideas of Gandhi and Jinnah on this score? Probably not. Throughout his life, the former was firmly ensconced in his belief that a multireligious state is possible, while the latter oscillated between secular nationalism and religious nationalism. Initially a secular nationalist, even called "ambassador of Hindu-Muslim unity," Jinnah later subscribed to the separatist religious vision of Iqbal and led the movement for a religious state—even though he later advocated for multireligious coexistence within his religious state. For Gandhi, in a united secular India, all religious communities could coexist harmoniously. For Jinnah, a Hindu-majority yet secular India could not provide equal rights to religious minorities, but an Islamic Pakistan could.

Jinnah's ideological vacillations notwithstanding, partition happened. Richard Gregg in his book *The Power of Nonviolence* argues that partition occurred because Gandhi's agenda was undermined by his rivals. He contends that the partition of India, and the violence before and after it, could have been avoided had the British, the Congress, and the Muslim League heeded Gandhi's advice. Gandhi's methods and thoughts themselves did not contribute to the partition or the violent outcome, but it was "insufficient following of Gandhi's constructive program," among other factors, which led to both. The British failed to listen to him regarding partition (the religious rather than the geographical division hurt Gandhi more). Nor did Congress heed his advice to keep India united and accommodate Jinnah's political ambitions (Gandhi had proposed making Jinnah prime minister of an independent united India).[77] Gregg notes:

> In granting independence (to India), Great Britain insisted, contrary to Gandhi's advice, on splitting the country into Pakistan (predominately Moslem) and India (predominately Hindu). On this point, Congress leaders rejected Gandhi's advice. Immediately, on Moslem initiative, dreadful riots, murders and arson broke out between Moslems and Hindus. Gandhi finally quelled them. None of the violence was directed against the British. I regard the debacle as a combination of the

breaking-forth of the energy of century-old frustration in subjection to foreign rule, moral fatigue of the nation at the end of the 28-year struggle for freedom, and insufficient following of Gandhi's "constructive program" which, had it been adhered to, would have cured that moral fatigue. The failure was due to not enough nonviolence.[78]

Gandhi was not as much opposed to the territorial partition of British India as he was to its psychological partition. He argued that such a partition would lay the foundation for perpetual conflict in the Indian subcontinent. Even though he grudgingly accepted political partition, Gandhi firmly believed India and Pakistan could reconcile their differences and coexist peacefully. His exasperation to avoid partition was visible. Seeing its inevitability, he said in one place, "I have, therefore, suggested a way out. Let it be a partition as between two brothers, if a division there must be."[79] Even if partition was inevitable, he insisted, the physical division should not color relations between the two states. Detailing how Gandhi's opposition to partition emerged from his opposition to othering based on religious nationalism, Parekh argues that once partition became inevitable, Gandhi channeled his energy into minimizing partition-related violence and promoting a sense of belonging between the newly formed states. He contends that Gandhi opposed partition "not because he was worried about India's territorial shrinkage but because he considered it a 'falsehood.' It denied a thousand years of Indian history and the basic spirit of Indian civilization, and rested on the inherently 'evil' principle of religious nationalism. He was also afraid that it would lead to much bloodshed and permanently sour the relations between the two countries. When he realized that the fast that he had long threatened was likely to make matters worse, he gracefully accepted the partition and strove to create a climate that would both minimize violence and maximize future reconciliation."[80]

Sharpening of Othering and Partition

These cultural differences became more prominent in the early decades of the twentieth century. Several factors contributed to the rise of psychological othering leading to partition. Below we have elaborated those factors.

Divide and Rule. Though it has been argued that before Iqbal and Jinnah there were thinkers who viewed Hindus and Muslims as different socio-cultural units, destined to have different homelands, it should be emphasized that this notion arose primarily during the colonial period and led to partition at the end of the colonial rule. For administrative expedience, the British Empire found it convenient to fuel social and ideological divisions between the two communities. The classic "divide-and-rule" policy, a bureaucratic vehicle for othering, was employed by the British to weaken any united freedom struggle. In 1946, to a question by Louis Fischer, "Is there less social contact between the Hindus and Muslims?" Gandhi replied, "No, rather the contrary. But politically there is a bar, thanks to Lord Minto."[81] It was under the colonial administration of Lord Minto, viceroy of British India, that the communal electorate was introduced to this political system. The establishment of communal electorates in 1909 was not simply a practical administrative decision, but rather an intentional policy designed to distance the two communities. Before Gandhi, Aurobindo Ghose, who was a stalwart of Indian freedom struggle in the first decade of the twentieth century, flagged the policy of othering being promoted by colonial administrators, which was undermining what he termed "unity of heart" in India. Referring to the partition of Bengal in a speech delivered in 1908, Ghose made a fervent appeal for belonging and unity, to attain Swaraj:

> Swaraj (self-rule or independence), finally, is impossible without unity. But the unity we need for Swaraj is not a unity of opinion, a unity of speech, a unity of intellectual conviction. Unity is of the heart and springs from love. The foreign organism (a reference to British rule) which has been living on us, lives by the absence of this love, by division, and it perpetuates the condition of its existence by making us look to it as the centre of our lives and away from our Mother and her children. It has set Hindu and Mahomedan at variance by means of this outward outlook; for by regarding it as the fountain of life, however, we are led to look away from our brothers and yearn for what the alien strength can give us. . . . [I]n the old days we did not hear of this distress of the scarcity of water from which the country is suffering now so acutely. It

did not exist and could not exist because there was love and the habit of mutual assistance which springs from love.[82]

The Muslim League was formed in 1906 with patronage from the British rulers. Nawab Salimullah of Dacca, who was a major force behind the foundation of the Muslim League, enjoyed the support of British authorities. Aurobindo Ghose wrote in *Bande Mataram*, a weekly newspaper advocating freedom of India, on March 15, 1907, "His (Salimullah's) whole history since he was shoved into prominence by his Anglo-Indian patrons, has been one long campaign against the Hindus with attempts to excite the passions and class selfishness of the Mahomedans and inflame them into permanent hostility to their Hindu fellow-countrymen."[83] Detailing how colonial rule promoted othering, Gilmartin argues, "It was the state itself, in the end, which provided the political structures necessary for the League's efforts. Critical to the League's political imagining of an encompassing Muslim community was the gradual introduction into twentieth-century India of elected legislatures, of arenas of electoral contestation that were, like other public arenas. . . . Elections played an increasingly important role in the 1920s, 1930s, and 1940s as a new kind of public realm linking society and state. Separate electorates thus embodied, simultaneously, the image of a common Muslim community, fixed by state definition, and the reality of deep provincial and local divisions."[84] And, elaborating on the British role in accentuating the communal polarization between Hindus and Muslims, Guha writes:

It is also true that the British did welcome and further the animosities between Hindus and Muslims. In March 1925, by which time the anticolonial struggle had assumed a genuinely popular dimension, the secretary of state for India wrote to the viceroy: "I have always placed my highest and most permanent hopes upon the eternity of the Communal Situation." Within England the growth of liberal values placed a premium on the sovereignty of the individual; but in the colonies the individual was always seen as subordinate to the community. This was evident in government employment, where care was taken to balance numbers of Muslim and Hindu staff, and in politics, where the British introduced communal electorates, such that Muslims voted exclusively for other Muslims. Most British officials were predisposed to prefer Muslims, for, compared with Hindus, their forms of worship and ways of life were less alien. Overall, colonial policy deepened religious divisions, which helped consolidate the white man's rule.[85]

Though the British promoted othering and eventually supported the idea of partition, this was probably not the case initially. In fact, there seems to be no clear indication that the original motivation for British-supported othering policies was to divide British India before granting independence. The divide-and-rule policy was aggressively promoted to sustain the empire, but not necessarily to ensure that Muslims received equal rights within British India or to grant them a separate homeland. It was not until the 1940s that the British accepted the possibility of an independent Pakistan, though this idea had been around at least since Iqbal's presidential address to the Muslim League calling for a separate Muslim state in the 1930s. Though British policy enthusiastically endorsed othering to maintain control of subcontinental politics, it was, arguably, not inclined to support separate statehood for Muslims. The idea of independent Pakistan circulated at the Round Table Conference in the early 1930s was known to the British, but it was not explicitly acknowledged or promoted. Ambedkar noted, "The proposal (for partition) was circulated to the members of the Round Table Conference but never officially put forth. It seems an attempt was made privately to obtain the assent of the British Government, who declined to consider it because they thought that this was a 'revival of the old Muslim Empire.'"[86] Notwithstanding these prevarications with respect to Pakistani separatism, the role of colonial rulers in promoting othering was significant.

Power Politics. Othering was exacerbated by internal power politics. The desire for political power and its unequal distribution in the provincial and interim governments exacerbated tensions between Congress and the Muslim League. The formation of ministries by the Hindu-led Indian National Congress accentuated the alienation of the league from substantial power, and this led Muslims to seek a political alternative via Muslim majority political agency. Their alienation was further accentuated when the political parties realized that the British had decided to leave the subcontinent and hand the reins of power to Congress. This power tussle was visible already in the 1930s, but subsequent political developments accentuated antagonism and belied hopes for a solution. Two factors could be identified in this regard: "the refusal by the Congress to recognize the Muslim League as the only representative body of the Muslims" and "the refusal by the Congress to form Coalition Ministries in the Congress Provinces."[87] Parekh blames Congress for the missed opportunities to avoid a confrontation: "The Congress in particular missed the opportunity to win over Jinnah and the Muslim League during its period of office between 1937 and 1939, and to prevent an opportunistic alliance between the middle-class Muslims of which he was a spokesman and the feudal classes whom he had long loathed. It was this alliance that made Pakistan possible and explains its subsequent history. Given more time, a more relaxed political environment, a less manipulative colonial government, and greater sensitivity and understanding on the part of both the Congress and the Muslim leadership, ways could perhaps have been found to allay these fears. Whatever the explanation, the Hindu-Muslim estrangement was so deep that many well-meaning constitutional schemes collapsed without a fair trial, and the much-dreaded partition of the country with all the attendant violence seemed inevitable."[88]

Divisiveness between the Congress and the league became more pronounced, with the two taking different stands on the Second World War. The league supported Britain in the war, and Congress opposed the British decision to declare war on India's behalf. As a result, "During the war years, Jinnah secured a much stronger position than before and could begin bargaining for a separate homeland."[89] Further, the socialist rhetoric of congressional leaders, particularly that of Nehru, was not favored by league supporters: "The increasing use by Congress of socialist rhetoric frightened away Muslim landlords and upper classes, from whom many of the ardent advocates of Pakistan were drawn."[90] Nehru had visited the Soviet Union in 1927 and was enamored by its socialist policies. He became interested in adapting those policies to the Indian system. In his book *Soviet Russia*, he had elaborated his impressions of the Soviet system.[91] In a letter to Jinnah on May 28, 1937, Iqbal, while deliberating on the issue of poverty and inequality among Indian Muslims and possible solutions to them, wrote, "The atheistic socialism of Jawahar Lal (Nehru) is not likely to receive much response from the Muslims" and argued that the solution lies in "the enforcement of the Law of Islam."[92]

The psychological influence of this political power struggle was more entrenched than the visible struggle for power; whatever its outward manifestations, psychologically it was viewed as a power struggle between Hindus, who were once subjects, and Muslims, who once ruled. The power parity imposed by the colonial administrations through a series of steps—including, among other things, dismantling the Muslim criminal law and justice system, introducing British law, abolishing the system of Qazi, introducing English in place of Persian as the court language, and introducing a democracy-based interim government in a Hindu-dominated British India—was received adversely by Muslims, Ambedkar claimed. He believed that these arbitrary measures to establish power parity played a critical role in determining and producing an "us-versus-them" psychology: "Exclusion from political power is the essence of the distinction between a ruling race and a subject race. . . . The British conquest of India brought about a complete political revolution in the relative position of the two communities (Hindus and Muslims). For six hundred years, the Musalmans had been the masters of the Hindus. The British occupation brought them down to the level of the Hindus. From masters to fellow subjects was degradation enough, but a change from the status of fellow subjects to that of subjects of the Hindus is really humiliation." The majority of Muslims and their leaders in British India had not witnessed Mughal rule. The psychology of this unconsciously held privilege, combined with the felt loss of that position when the interim government was enacted, increased their sense of alienation. It persisted in the generation advocating partition via their, as Comte famously put it, "living dead men's lives"—exulting in past glory and fearing that it would be permanently lost with the new political dispensation to be formed after the British departure. This fear and anxiety sharpened communal differences.[93]

While Muslim consolidation formed around the narrative of lost glory and the potential of possible oppression in a united India, a fringe section of Hindus clung to the narrative of exploitation and humiliation by Islamic invaders and rulers. Ambedkar provides a graphic description of Islamic invasion from the eighth century and its psychological, cultural impact: "The methods adopted by the invaders have left behind them their aftermath. One aftermath is the bitterness between the Hindus and the Muslims which they have caused. This bitterness between the two is so deep-seated that a century of political life (by the British rule) has neither succeeded in assuaging it, nor in making people forget it. . . . [W]hat wonder if the memory of these invasions has ever remained green, as a source of pride to the Muslims and as a source of shame to the Hindus?"[94] Larry Collins and Dominique Lapierre, detailing the psychological rupture between the Hindus and Muslims, write, "The root of the problem was the age-old antagonism between India's 300 million Hindus and 100 million Moslems. Sustained by tradition, by antipathetic religions, by economic differences, subtly exacerbated through the years of Britain's own policy of Divide and Rule, their conflict had reached a boiling point. The Moslem leaders now demanded that Britain rip apart the unity she had so painstakingly erected to give an Islamic state of their own. The cost of denying them their state, they warned, would be the bloodiest civil war in Asian history. Just as determined to resist their demands were the leaders of the Congress Party representing most of India's 300 million Hindus. To them, the division of the subcontinent would be a mutilation of their historic homeland almost sacrilegious in its nature."[95]

As these exclusivist and othering narratives were increasingly emphasized, the amalgamation of cultures and values of Hinduism and Islam were conveniently forgotten. Through selective amnesia, cultural differences and age-old political animosities were highlighted, while memories of harmony and coexistence were increasingly forgotten, in the public consciousness. Gandhi was a firm believer in India's tradition of sociocultural harmony and hoped this unity could guide communal relations. Prithwindra Mukherjee argues that during the partition of Bengal, India's legacy of united struggle was exemplified in the life of Jatindranath Mukherjee, also known as Bagha Jatin. He explains how, "In 1905, during the agitations against the Partition of Bengal, Jatin was to seat side by side militants—Muslims and Hindus of all classes—around communal meals, to affirm the fraternity between Indians. He welcomed all his brothers—disciples and political associates—from all social levels and to put them up as his household members."[96] It is probably humanly impossible to document all the instances in which Hindus and Muslims worked together during, before, and even after the freedom struggle. It is also worth mentioning that many Muslims who opposed the narrative of othering and creation of Pakistan were publicly shamed as "renegades." Jinnah certainly never hid his contempt for Muslim leaders like Maulana Azad.

The formation of the Muslim League inspired some Hindu impetus for religious mobilization in response. The Hindu Mahasabha was established in 1915 and the Rashtriya Swayamsevak Sangh in 1925 to promote Hindu interests. Talbot writes, "The strongly communal Muslim League has naturally inspired the rise of a virulent Hindu community body. It is the Hindu Mahasabha. The Mahasabha ('great association') takes for its creed 'India for the Indians; let the foreigners go back where they came from.'"[97] The formation of Hindu organizations in response to Muslim identity movements provoked heightened Muslim fears about Hindu identity movements. Kulke and Rothermund describe the deep influence of this psychology in shaping the conflict between Hindus and Muslims that became particularly acute in the early decades of the twentieth century:

> More popular movements of Hindu solidarity—such as the cow-protection movement in northern India—were positively resented by them (Muslims) as a direct attack on their own religious practices, which included cow-slaughter at certain religious festivals. The Hindi–Urdu controversy in northern India added more fuel to the fire of communal conflict. The Hindus asked only for equal recognition of their language—Hindi, written in Devanagari script—as a language permitted in the courts of law, where so far Urdu written in Nastaliq script had prevailed; the Muslims, however, resented this as a challenge to Urdu and identified this linguistic advantage more and more with their existence as a religious community. Even illiterate Muslims whose language hardly differed from that of their Hindu neighbours could be called upon to defend Urdu for the sake of their Islamic identity.[98]

Mobilization movements by Hindus prompted Muslims to consolidate their religious identity for political bargaining power, by rallying behind Jinnah. Hindu organizations, however, largely failed to mobilize the majority of Hindus. Since none of the major Hindu leaders in the freedom struggle—most notably Gandhi—subscribed to the idea of othering, when they eventually agreed to partition it was for practical political reasons, rather than for ideological cultural reasons.

Partition and Violence

After the British announced in February 1947 that they would leave India by June 1948, political activities ratcheted up. They were accelerated after Mountbatten assumed the viceroyship in March and announced the partition and exit plan. The partition took place in August 1947 and was recorded as one of the bloodiest divisions in human history. Khushwant Singh presents the somber mood accompanying the gory partition:

> The summer of 1947 was not like other Indian summers. . . . The summer before, communal riots, precipitated by reports of the proposed division of the country into a Hindu India and a Muslim Pakistan, had broken out in Calcutta, and within a few months the death roll had mounted to several thousand. . . . [B]oth sides killed. Both shot and stabbed and speared and clubbed. Both tortured. Both raped. From Calcutta, the riots spread north and east and west: to Noakhali in East Bengal, where Muslims massacred Hindus; to Bihar, where Hindus massacred Muslims. Mullahs roamed the Punjab and the Frontier Province with boxes of human skulls said to be those of Muslims killed in Bihar. Hundreds of thousands of Hindus and Sikhs who had lived for centuries on the Northwest Frontier abandoned their homes and fled toward the protection of the predominantly Sikh and Hindu communities in the east. They traveled on foot, in bullock carts, crammed into lorries, clinging to the sides and roofs of trains. Along the way—at fords, at crossroads, at railroad stations—they collided with panicky swarms of Muslims fleeing to safety in the west. The riots had become a rout. By the summer of 1947, when the creation of the new state of Pakistan was formally announced, ten million people—Muslims and Hindus and Sikhs—were

in flight. By the time monsoon broke, almost a million of them were dead, and all of northern India was in arms, in terror, or in hiding.[99]

Gandhi made several efforts to stop the partition. Toward this end, he engaged Jinnah, the Congress, and the British government. As mentioned earlier, he even offered Jinnah the leadership of the first government of free India, which neither many of the congressional leaders approved nor Jinnah accepted. Gandhi was unhappy with the partition already, but the intense violence that started with the call for Direct Action in August 1946 saddened Gandhi even more than the geographical partition. Communal violence exploded after the Direct Action Day was initiated by the Muslim League to pressure the British administration to acknowledge an independent Pakistan. The message was clear: if the demand for a separate homeland was not met, the league would force its implementation by using all available means, including violence. Thousands of people died in the communal riots that followed, and no part of British India remained untouched. Guha explains the logic of this event: "By starting a riot in Calcutta in August 1946, Jinnah and the League hoped to polarize the two communities further, and thus force the British to divide India when they finally quit. . . . The bloodshed of 1946–7 seemed to suggest that the Muslims were just such an element, who would not live easily or readily under a Congress government dominated by Hindus. Now 'each communal outbreak was cited as a further endorsement of the two-nation theory, and of the inevitability of the partition of the country.'"[100]

With partition, the Gandhian project of a multireligious united India was shattered. The principles for which he stood played a significant role in the independence of India, but they could not prevent the partition of British India. While much of India was celebrating independence, Gandhi sat in a twenty-four-hour fast. When the *Hindustan Times* approached him for a message on independence, his reply was that "he had run dry," and when the BBC wanted him to convey a public message, he referred the reporter to Nehru. Far from celebrating, Gandhi was visiting areas affected by communal violence areas and pleading for harmony. When Nehru was delivering his famous "tryst with destiny" speech in the Indian parliament, Gandhi was in Kolkata—fasting, praying, and attempting to douse the sectarian fire.

Psychosocial belonging failed to take root despite Gandhi's best efforts, while othering persisted and pervaded the policy making of independent India and Pakistan. The othering-inspired partition did not end the Hindu-Muslim conflict or effect enduring peace in the post-partition subcontinent. There is significant literature on how the creation of borders in the two modern states has addressed the aspirations of groups, including minority groups, despite failing to establish enduring peace.[101] Zamindar makes a useful argument in the context of post-partition politics that the border between India and Pakistan is not only an international border but also a psychological, internal border (a manifestation of othering), questioning, shaping, and interrogating the people's, particularly the refugees', identity and loyalty as well as legitimacy in the aftermath of the creation of the two states in the subcontinent.[102] In the next chapter, we elaborate how this othering has persisted and engulfed the post-partition South Asia.

3

Post-partition South Asia

Our focus in this chapter is on the post-partition politics of South Asia, particularly how the psychology of othering shaped India-Pakistan relations. There are several studies on post-partition South Asia and India-Pakistan relations, but seldom has any study examined how the psychology of othering shapes these relations. After presenting a broad picture of South Asia and various challenges it confronts, we examine relevant aspects of India-Pakistan relations and demonstrate how intensely the legacy of the past informs them. Developments of the past seven decades have rigidified the hostility there. As reflected in its wars, limited wars, border clashes, cyber warfare, propaganda, and other forms of explicit and implicit violence, othering-generated violence has become a mainstay in India-Pakistani bilateral relations. We also examine the literature on enduring rivalry and protracted social conflict, useful in explaining its legacy of violence. In the final section, we focus on the economic, sociocultural, and psychological costs of the conflict.

South Asia

Most postcolonial state borders were drawn without considering the fact that ethnic identities may not end at their unequivocal perimeters. The border drawn between India and Pakistan was no different. The Radcliffe Commission, which was assigned this task, drew the border in a few weeks in a region spreading over thousands of miles and inhabited by diverse demographics and cultures. In an interview with Kuldip Nayar in 1971, Cyril Radcliffe said, "I was so rushed that I had no time to go into details. . . . Even accurate district maps were not there and whatever material there was, was also inadequate. What could I have done in one and a half months? . . . It was impossible to undertake a field survey because of the heat."[1] The haphazardly drawn border, passing through villages, houses, and backyards, divided thousands of families.[2] The hope that the end of colonialism, partition, and creation of the two states would ensure peace remained unrealized. The border separating respective nations of Hindus and Muslims was intended to ensure peace, as envisaged by the two-nation theory. However, as a marker of territorial integrity and sovereignty, it marked regions "of contested power, in which local, national, and international groups negotiate relations of subordination and control."[3]

Beyond South Asia, most developing postcolonial societies have had similar experiences; most postcolonial state borders were drawn haphazardly and without considering the concerns of the communities living in the divided areas. Being multiethnic societies, the attempts to create homogeneity and unity by creating borders produced complex results—including postcolonial ethnic conflicts. Burton writes: "Most modern societies are multi-cultural or multi-ethnic. Most have problems of poverty and plenty. Most have problems of inequality and opportunity. Most have problems of frustration and lack of participation and identity. Most, as a consequence, have high levels of alienation, leading to conflict situations of many kinds that affect the whole of a society and, indirectly, the world society."[4] The aggressive postcolonial pursuit of nation-state consolidation and obsession with security produced a psychology of discrimination among minorities and compelled them to challenge the identity narrative provided by the colonially generated nation-state. Smith notes: "State homogenization always appears to the non-dominant *ethnie* like ethnic discrimination and exploitation. In an age of nationalism that perception is likely to prove explosive."[5] Lack of internal cohesion, a weak nation-building process that failed to address fear of discrimination, and a crisis of legitimacy caused by minorities' mistrust for majority leadership contributed to, and continue to perpetuate, the quagmire of majority-minority conflicts in South Asia.

South Asia suffers from multiple challenges, including, but not limited to, compounded nation-building travails, poor human development, economic underdevelopment, a "governability crisis," incongruity between ethnic aspirations and national sovereignty, religious fundamentalism and terrorism, and natural disasters. Almost all states in the region experience separatism and internal conflicts to varying degrees. A study covering the period from the summer of 2000 to the summer of 2001 found fifty-nine violent political conflicts in the Asian region, out of which thirty-eight were in Central and South Asia.[6] Sri Lanka had to contend with the Liberation Tigers of Tamil Eelam, and even after the war of 2009 that led to the demise of Eelam and ended the conflict, it is difficult to conclude that ethnic conflict in Sri Lanka has ended and interethnic harmony has been realized. In Nepal, though a violent Maoist movement has diminished as leaders of the movement opted to join mainstream politics, ideological elements of the movement have not withered away. The vision of a classless society that inspired the movement has not died, and, to make things more complicated, democracy remains fragile in this landlocked state. Bangladesh suffers from multiple challenges, among which the dominance of military and religious extremism is prominent. Religious extremism in recent decades has become pervasive, threatening its ethnic minorities. Afghanistan also presents a perpetually dismal chronicle of cultural-political anarchy. Its challenges have always been compounded by its geopolitical location and position in the "grand chessboard" of Eurasia.[7]

Though the conflict between India and Pakistan occupies the center stage in South Asian politics, the rivals confront similar challenges. As the philosophy behind their creation indicates, Pakistan under Jinnah was conceived as a religious state, whereas India under Gandhi and Nehru emerged as a multiethnic and pluralistic state. It would be an exaggeration to argue that this contrast accounts for all the historical challenges for these states. Weiner, in his study of India in the 1960s, argues that its underlying political problems revolve around "how to modernize a State within a democratic framework, in spite of pressing political demands that appear to impede economic planning, national unity, and political order."[8] This argument is relevant and also applies to Pakistan, which swings between two types of political governance and has witnessed vacillating episodes of military dictatorship, Islamic radicalization, and repression—dwindling its minority populations. India in comparison, despite its challenges, has maintained a democratic system of governance. Notwithstanding the complex matrix of conflict in the South Asian region, the India-Pakistan conflict is a particularly salient problem in regional and international politics.

Manifestation of Othering

As we elaborated in chapter 2, India-Pakistan hostility has deep roots, and to understand the present it is important to look at the past. Taya Zinkin writes: "Unlike Athena, countries do not spring fully armed from Zeus's head; like hulls encumbered with barnacles they are weighted by their past. This is true even of the ex-colonial newly independent countries," including India and Pakistan. Further: "To appreciate the tensions which exist—always ready to flare up—between India and Pakistan one has to go back into history." India and Pakistan are shouldering the weight of their past. A "poisoned atmosphere" surrounds them "like a rotting albatross" resulting in "wars and endemic distrust."[9] However, the rivalry cannot simply be traced to 1947. Ayesha Jalal notes: "A defining moment that is neither beginning nor end, partition continues to influence how the peoples and states of postcolonial South Asia envisage their past, present and future."[10] Reporting for the BBC in 2017, Andrew Whitehead contends that wounds of partition are festering: "Partition triggered one of the great calamities of the modern era, perhaps the biggest movement of people—outside war and famine—that the world has ever seen. Those wounds have been left to fester. No one has been held to account—there's been no reconciliation process—and for a long time, the full story of what happened has been smothered in silence. Literature and cinema found ways of representing the horror of what happened. Historians initially focused on the politics of Partition. It took them much longer to turn their attention to the lived experience of this profound rupture. Big oral history projects have got under way only in the last few years, as the number of survivors dwindles."[11]

Assessing the lived experience of partition in post-partition South Asia is essential to understanding the present in light of the past. Such an understanding will help to open peaceful pathways to address current hostility there. Partition-related violence is not what ultimately caused hostile

India-Pakistan relations; instead, these hostile relations are the consequence of othering psychology that took root much earlier than 1947, as
we demonstrated in the last chapter. India and Pakistan remain burdened
by the narratives built not only around memories of violence during partition but around the very psychology of othering that led to it. Partition
was the first significant outcome of this othering, and post-partition India-
Pakistan hostility is a manifestation of the same psychology. More than
one and a half billion people in the region live under the shadow of the
past and shoulder the legacy of othering.

To better understand India-Pakistan relations, it is helpful to consider
general theories of protracted conflict and enduring rivalry, as they provide insights into the othering-oriented hostility particular to this region.
Protracted social conflicts are "hostile interactions extending over long
periods of time with sporadic outbreaks of open warfare which fluctuate
in frequency and intensity. These situations can involve either group in
one nation-state or in different nation-states of the same region, where
deep-seated racial, ethnic and religious hatreds may generate or intensify
domestic and international hostilities. Because protracted social conflicts
are rooted in ethnic hostilities and the ingroup/outgroup effects which
accompany them, the actual distribution of power and resources or the
perception of these distributions play a critical role. . . . Protracted social
conflicts, especially in the Third World, are insidious and pervasive. They
tend to pose several interlocking crises at once (a sort of crisis-nest), affect-
ing present leadership and past and present injustices."[12] The characteristics of a protracted social conflict include duration (protractedness),
fluctuation in the intensity and frequency of interaction, conflict spillover
into all domains, strong calibrating forces that keep interactions within
the existing Normal Relations Range, and the absence of any distinct termination.[13] Threats emerging from protracted conflicts tend to be "more
mercurial since they are behavioural and structural in cause; overt and
covert in behaviour; and internal, external or both in their source."[14] The
literature on enduring rivalries[15] indicates that deep-seated conflicts are a
reality in interstate relations. As Maoz and Mor explain, enduring rivalry
is characterized by a "persistent, fundamental, and long-term incompatibility of goals between two states," which "manifests itself in the basic

attitudes of the parties toward each other as well as in recurring violent or potentially violent clashes over a long period of time." They enumerate four major characteristics of such rivalries: "outstanding set of unresolved issues," "strategic interdependence," "psychological manifestations of enmity," and "repeated militarized conflict."[16] The India-Pakistan conflict displays many characteristics of protracted conflict and enduring rivalry, which we have elaborated below.

High-Intensity Violence. The first war between India and Pakistan was fought in 1947 over Kashmir,[17] which was one of five hundred–odd princely states at the time of partition. The partition plan left the decision about joining either nation to their rulers. Both India and Pakistan sought Kashmir, the only princely state that abutted both. As the two states were pursuing strategies to shape Kashmir's politics, the situation was further complicated by the infiltration of armed groups, including Hazara and Afridi tribesmen, paramilitary forces like the Muslim League National Guard, and even regular Pakistani army personnel.[18] These armed infiltrators took control of Muzaffarabad in the western Jammu region on October 22, 1947, and advanced toward Srinagar, Kashmir's capital and center of power. Neither the king's forces nor forces from the neighboring state, Patiala, were able to contain the infiltrators' advance and, as a result, King Hari Singh sought India's help, which India promised on the condition that Kashmir acceded to it. The king signed an Instrument of Accession in October 1947. The timing of this accession subsequently became a major source of contention: India claimed that it intervened militarily after the king signed the accession agreement. Pakistan claimed that Indian forces arrived in the disputed region before the accession was formalized, and hence the accession has no established standing in international law.

War between the two neonatal states continued for more than a year. In 1948 India filed a complaint at the United Nations Security Council under Article 35 of the UN Charter, which galvanized the international body to broker a cease-fire.[19] The hostility did not end. Rather, the cease-fire served to escalate the conflict via numerous debates at the United Nations instigated from both sides, the involvement of big powers in the conflict, its propagandized coloring through the Cold War prism, and, ultimately, laying the ground for future wars. The United Nations created a commission to investigate the dispute and noted that the warring parties had agreed to determine the question of Kashmir's accession through a plebiscite, which also required Pakistan withdrawing its troops from the region. Neither of the two happened: Pakistan did not withdraw its troops, and no plebiscite was held. The cease-fire line divided Kashmir between India and Pakistan, and China also took control of parts of the region.

Studies suggest that the India-Pakistan conflict persists owing to a range of factors, including territorial disputes, national identity, strategic importance, irredentism, differing internal power structures, realpolitik, and Great Power involvement.[20] The territorial dispute over Kashmir, however, is considered the core source of hostile relations between them. It is often argued that if the Kashmir issue were resolved, India and Pakistan could enjoy at least a civil, if not amicable, relationship. Tir and Diehl estimate that as many as 81 percent of enduring national and international rivalries have been partly or predominantly caused by territorial disputes.[21] In the case of the India-Pakistan conflict, it is certainly important to acknowledge the role that territorial disputes play, but it would be an exaggeration to consider such disputes to be the sole, or even primary, impetus behind the conflict. India has territorial disputes with other neighbors, but the level, nature, and scope of its rivalry with Pakistan are significantly more intense and impassioned. This indicates that the India-Pakistan dispute has much deeper causes. Suggesting that resolution of Kashmir issue would end the India-Pakistan conflict assumes that territoriality is its primary point of contention. There are many other, even more compelling, underlying issues of contention.

Simply reducing the Kashmir conflict to a territorial dispute, a resource-led dispute, or a geopolitical dispute becomes problematic. Understanding the conflict based on these determinants alone would, at best, explain the formal nature of the problem—enduring and multilayered as it may be—but any comprehensive account of the India-Pakistan conflict would be incomplete without acknowledging how the psychology of othering has shaped it. Brines concurs: "Kashmir crystallizes the fear, the mistrust and the bigotry that darken the subcontinent and provides a vehicle for enlarging them with modern political complications."[22] Famously touted as "an unfinished agenda of partition," the Kashmir dispute is an acute manifestation of psychological othering. The two-nation theory that created Pakistan is predicated on the argument that for the subcontinental Muslims, the home state is Pakistan. Such an argument also holds that since Kashmir is an adjacent Muslim majority state, it should merge with Pakistan. India, disapproving of the two-nation theory, argues that India's secular framework can accommodate the aspirations of Kashmiri Muslims.

Acknowledging the legacy of research contending that the Kashmir dispute is a major element in this historically political rivalry, we argue that the Kashmir conflict is also an acute manifestation of the region's history of psychological othering. The seeds of the Kashmir dispute were sown long before 1947 and long before the actual war broke out. Zinkin notes: "Pakistan is the first-born of Muslim Fundamentalism. Islam, nothing else, was the reason for its birth. From this follows its incapacity to accept that Kashmir with its overwhelming Muslim majority remains with India of its own free will. To accept that would be to cut at the foundation of the Pakistani State."[23] We argue that the psychology of othering, which was so fervently held by philosopher Iqbal and politician Jinnah, spawned not only the partition but also the Kashmir dispute and many other problems that now characterize India-Pakistan relations. Kashmir is just one manifestation of this othering. Hagerty characterizes the Kashmir dispute as a "zero-sum test for each state's legitimizing ideology."[24] While the resolution of the dispute would go a long way toward improving the political relationship between them, it would be extraneous to argue that resolution would transform the India-Pakistan relations in a comprehensive way—a Gandhian way—toward authentic belonging.

Returning to the historic narrative, after a brief period of contingent peace following the first war, the two neighbors fought their second war in 1965, which ended after UN intervention. This resulted in the Tashkent Agreement of 1966, in which both states agreed to maintain the status quo. Less than a decade later, in 1971, the third war started. In July 1972, both signed the Shimla Agreement and agreed to resolve contentious issues through dialogue. Enduring-rivalry theory entails a repetition of the actions, including violent actions, producing the same outcomes. In such rivalries, there is no decisive outcome of any of the disputed issues even following repeated open conflicts. This point is important, since maintaining this kind of rivalry necessitates that the disputed issues remain unresolved, and this inability to challenge the status quo is what perpetuates the probability for further confrontation. India and Pakistan have fought three wars with no resolution of contentious issues, accomplishing nothing but augmenting distrust and rigidifying othering between the adversaries. While zero-sum perspectives still characterize the rivalry, the geographical neighbors are becoming increasingly conscious that another full-scale war is impracticable, particularly after their acquisition of nuclear weapons in the late 1990s. This awareness notwithstanding, the persistence of rigid othering makes the prospects of another war palpable. The othering phenomenon, in its earlier incarnations, led to the loss of millions of lives through the history of partition. In its new incarnation, it may wreak nuclear destruction of catastrophic proportions.

Nuclearization and Its Impact on the Conflict. The nuclearization of the subcontinent in the 1990s ensured that formally regional rivalry reached a new apex, generating fears across the globe of possible nuclear conflagration with worldwide ramifications. Wolpert explains: "With their capitals and major cities less than ten ballistic missile-minutes from each other the two countries have become the world's most dangerous match for the potential ignition of a nuclear war that could decimate South Asia and poison every region on earth."[25] The politics of nuclear armament and the history of this rivalry cannot be delinked.[26] It is important to note that the two rivals have refrained from using nuclear weapons so far. When, after a year of nuclearization, India and Pakistan clashed in the Ladakh region, in 1999, it was only a limited war. These two simultaneous developments in succession—the nuclearization in 1998 and the 1999 limited war—led to a debate about whether nuclearization somehow moderated the intensity of hostilities permanently, or if it was merely a temporary measure guided by strategic calculations. The debate on the role of nuclear weapons in contributing to stability or instability is not new generally, but in the case of South Asia it is relatively recent. Some scholars argue that the principle of nuclear deterrence is operative in India-Pakistan relations.[27] Ganguly and Hagerty argue, "The nuclear-deterrence proposition provides the strongest explanation for the absence of major war in the region over the last two decades."[28] It is contended that the India-Pakistan war in Kargil remained limited because of the nuclear angle. Adopting a similar stand, Basrur argues that the possession of nuclear weapons has had a moderating impact on their rivalry.[29] A counterargument, particularly given the persistent rigid othering and hostility, appears equally forceful: "It is risky to think that classical nuclear deterrence will continue to prevent nuclear war ad infinitum."[30] Khan reasons: "Although deterrence is achieved in terms of preventing full-scale wars in the presence of nuclear capabilities due to their devastating effects, the actors are unlikely to perceive an urgency to negotiate because a degree of parity is achieved between them."[31]

Has nuclear deterrence, or a fear of a nuclear war, helped promote peace in the subcontinent? The answer would be no if we think in terms of Gandhian peace, which is not possible in an atmosphere of fear or intimidation. If we think in terms of negative (Hobbesian) peace, a peace grounded in fear of war or further devastation, the answer would probably be yes, but in that case peace would not be enduring. Regardless of whether or to what extent nuclear armament has aggravated or deterred hostilities, it is critical to note that hostilities have not ceased. A year into the Kargil war, Leng noted: "Far from showing signs of improved crisis management, each successive Indo-Pakistani crisis escalated to a more violent conclusion than its predecessor."[32] The nuclearization may have shaped the bilateral relations in recent decades, but it does not herald an end of the conflict or the end of violent engagements through alternate means.

Protracted-conflict theory suggests that keeping conflict sustenance to acceptable levels is possible, since actors in conflicts cannot remain engaged in explicit violence indefinitely. At the same time, they cannot refrain from engaging and reengaging in clashes to keep the rivalry alive; hence, "when animosities (or frustrations or simple calculations) result in the outbreak of hostilities at the level of war, outside powers or the costs of sustaining high-intensity military operations may push interactions back from war to lower-level conflict." To keep conflict at acceptable levels, even cooperation cannot be permitted to exceed an established threshold. When the cooperation level seems to be defying this threshold, interaction levels must be decreased to facilitate lesser cooperative levels.[33] The

India-Pakistan conflict did exhibit some breakpoints. Cease-fire agreements reached after each war aimed at cooling the conflict. Peace negotiations raised hopes, but they seldom brought desired peace. The Agra Summit of 2001 was an attempt to address the conflict, but the conflict equilibrium became active to lower the cooperation levels. The summit meeting between Indian prime minister Atal Bihari Vajpayee and Pakistan president Pervez Musharraf became part of a long list of failed attempts at genuine peace in the history of the rivalry.

Low-Intensity Violence. Besides resulting in the outbreak of both full-scale and limited wars, othering was evident in other more low-intensity violent events like border tensions, skirmishes, and standoffs. These events perpetuated the psychology of othering and maintained rivalry at accepted levels. While it is not possible to document all the incidents of low-intensity violence, we list some of them below.

After the first war, there were two consecutive war scares in 1950 and 1951. Both countries reached the brink of war again in 1955. With the rise of a separatist movement in Jammu and Kashmir, there was a war scare in 1986–87 and again in 1990. Troop mobilization on the border occurred in 2001–2 following a terrorist attack on the Indian Parliament carried out by Pakistan-based terrorist organizations. The terror attack in Mumbai in 2008 again led to troop mobilization on the border. At that point, "military tensions and clashes appear to be just another terrorist attack away."[34] Surgical strikes by India on the Pakistan side of Kashmir in 2016, following a militant strike that killed more than a dozen Indian security personnel, prompted an intense border standoff and fire exchanges for months, resulting in dozens of military and civilian casualties on both sides. In 2019 there was a military standoff following a terrorist suicide attack on a convoy of India's security personnel that resulted in forty deaths and retaliatory air strikes by India to demolish terrorist camps in Balakot, Pakistan. The two states also engaged in a minor aerial fight following the Indian air strikes.

The India-Pakistan border is an active site of violent engagement, war or no war. The border is a crisis point of psychological othering. Of the 3,323 kilometers of the land border that India and Pakistan share, about one-third (1,225 kilometers) passes through the conflict-ridden region of Kashmir. There is significant literature in border studies making a case that many borders between states have generated conflicts instead of resolving them, creating a sense of fear and "cartographic anxiety" and contributing to already deep-seated othering. Martinez's alienated borderlands characterization as having "extremely unfavourable conditions," including "warfare, political disputes, intense nationalism, ideological animosity, religious enmity, cultural dissimilarity and ethnic rivalry," as well as "militarization and establishment of rigid controls," aptly describes the border between India and Pakistan.[35] Aggarwal defines the India-Pakistan accepted border in Kashmir: "Drawn and redrawn by battles and treaties, the line is identifiable by traces of blood, bullets, watchtowers, and ghost settlements left from recurring wars between India and Pakistan."[36] The border in Kashmir is militarized with heavy deployment of military personnel, land mines, electrified fencing, and observation towers.[37] The heavily armed security personnel are on near-permanent high alert. Border clashes are common and transpire even without any apparent reason. In 2003 there was a cease-fire agreement to halt the exchange of low-grade combat along the border, but that agreement has remained ineffective, as violations are frequent. The situation is equally tense at the Siachen Glacier, with no clear demarcation. The glacier has become the highest, coldest, and probably costliest battleground for India and Pakistan since the mid-1980s.

Proxy Wars. The India-Pakistan conflict is also characterized by proxy war. John Mitton explains: "Rivals may exploit new opportunities for confrontation . . . by injecting themselves into ongoing civil conflicts, supporting opposing sides, and seeking to gain even limited strategic, economic, and/ or tactical advantage over their enemy."[38] One strategy of proxy war in recent decades is employing nonstate armed groups to counter a rival. States may also use religious extremists to perpetuate rivalries by using these groups "to exact real costs on rivals—the targeted state must spend resources on counterterrorism and often sustains casual ties—while preventing higher stakes and more costly military conflict."[39] Proxy wars not only are cost-effective in comparison to direct military confrontations, but can, in the long run, help overcome power asymmetries in conventional capabilities.[40] There is a power asymmetry between India and Pakistan, with India having superiority in terms of conventional weapons and economic power. The establishment of a "Kashmir Desk" in Pakistan's Inter-Services Intelligence department, Prime Minister Benazir Bhutto's public call to Muslims in Kashmir to revolt against India's rule, Pakistan's oft-repeated affirmation that it supports the Kashmiri separatist movement, and its cavalier approach to religious extremist groups that openly target India are some of the indications of Pakistan's proxy role in the separatist movement on the Indian side of Kashmir.[41] An International Crisis Group report of 2002 terms Pakistan's intervention in the movement as a proxy war: "Notwithstanding its denials, however, the . . . [Pakistan] government has continued its proxy war in Kashmir as part of a broader long-term strategy to make the costs of controlling the territory untenable for India."[42]

A separatist movement in Kashmir emerged during the late 1980s. The alienation of a significant section of Kashmiris from India was a factor that contributed to the rise of the separatist movement.[43] Pakistan claims it supports the movement only morally, diplomatically, and politically. In contrast, the International Crisis Group report of 2003 notes that sections of the Pakistani establishment supported the militancy in Kashmir not only morally but also financially and logistically as "an obligation towards their co-religionists."[44] There is extensive literature that charts Pakistan's explicit and implicit role in the movement.[45] Cohen argues, "Pakistan's role was not the decisive factor in starting the uprising, although a critical one in sustaining it."[46] Scholars contend that, by aiding armed militancy, Pakistan aimed at weakening India.[47] Most of the active militant organizations on the Indian side of Kashmir operate from the Pakistan side of Kashmir. In his study of six militant groups operating in Kashmir, Staniland contends that they received material support from Pakistan. This external support facilitated sustenance of separatist movements in Kashmir, "making this an easy case for theories that attribute a clear effect to external resources."[48]

There are internal tensions in the parts of Kashmir that are under the control of Islamabad. Pakistan uses every available opportunity to highlight India's role in human rights violations in Kashmir, but India, until recently, remained somewhat apathetic toward developments on the Pakistan side of Kashmir. Despite a resolution in India's parliament in the 1990s stating that the whole of Kashmir, including areas with Pakistan, is an integral part of India, New Delhi seemed reluctant to talk about Pakistan-controlled Kashmir. The incumbent Bharatiya Janata Party–led government in New Delhi, particularly in its second term starting in 2019, displayed an interest in the region. Indian news channels have started showing daily weather reports on the parts of Kashmir under Pakistan's jurisdiction. Political posturing is evident. In September 2019, External Affairs Minister Subrahmanyam Jaishankar said, "Our position on PoK (Pakistan Occupied Kashmir. Pakistan terms this part of Kashmir, Azad Jammu and Kashmir and Gilgit-Baltistan) has always been and will always be very clear. PoK is part of India and we expect one day that we will have the physical jurisdiction over it."[49] Going beyond Kashmir, both states have blamed each other for various issues. India has accused Pakistan of supporting the violent Khalistan movement in Punjab during the 1980s. India also claims that Pakistan supported militant organizations that carried out terrorist attacks in many Indian cities, including in Mumbai in 2008. India has often decried Pakistan's inaction against, and patronage of, terrorist organizations in Pakistan side of Kashmir and other parts of Pakistan, which foment terrorist activities in India. Pakistan has accused India of meddling in its internal affairs, particularly supporting the separatist movement in Balochistan.

Conflict Spillover: Implicit Violence

These high- and low-intensity confrontations are not the only forms of hostility. They are overt manifestations, but there are also myriad implicit or subtle examples that emerge in almost all aspects of life. It can be reasonably argued that the entire South Asian region remains enthralled to the psychology of othering—so much so that it may not be an exaggeration to claim that the region is othering habituated. It is as if the British gave the region a single administrative identity and then handed over the reins of power, via a psychology of partition, to leaders who remain bewitched by this psychology. No aspect of life remains outside of the spell of othering, and hence "there is . . . a tendency for all issues to become linked into one grand issue—us versus them." While enduring-rivalry theory focuses more on the material and political aspects of power in shaping rivalries, we argue that, in the case of India and Pakistan, the rivalry is much deeper, emerging from psychosocial polarization. As a result, both countries perceive each action of the other through the prism of suspicion. The cost-benefit analysis of conflict here seems to be eschewed in favor of a policy of mutual destruction, as "contenders become more concerned with hurting or denying their competitor than with their own immediate satisfaction, and with this, hostility deepens and goes beyond that associated with normal conflict."[50]

Describing how such rival states behave, Thompson and Dreyer note: "The states that collide in international space tend to do so repeatedly, especially if they are unable to resolve the conflicts. To the extent that the conflicts persist, the two states in question look at, and treat, each other in ways that are different from the way in which most states interact. They regard each other's diplomatic and military maneuvers with considerable suspicion. Past defeats and victories are lamented or celebrated. Future attacks or threats are anticipated. As a consequence, the two states surround themselves in a cognitive web of intensifying antagonism, mistrust, and threat expectation that makes future conflict all the more likely."[51] The India-Pakistan conflict aptly matches this description of the "cognitive web of intensifying antagonism." The two seem to be frozen in a conflict continuum, which at times erupts overtly and otherwise simmers. Notwithstanding occasional peace gestures in terms of agreements, negotiations, and rapprochements, hostility remains the dominant reality of South Asian politics. While Gandhi would grudgingly accept fierce opposition as a flawed but possibly workable mechanism for resolving a conflict, here the opposition involves hopelessly intransigent enemies. Deep mistrust marks this rivalry, which is so deeply embedded in their respective psychology and policy apparatuses that—notwithstanding their shared culture and history—they are not simply rivals, but perpetual enemies. Their hostile relations fluctuate in frequency and intensity, with sporadic outbreaks of open warfare combined with subtle hostility aimed at hurting the other, geographically, economically, or psychologically, through all possible means. This plays out on an almost daily basis nationally, bilaterally, regionally, and internationally. While Gandhi advocated refraining from violence not only in actions but also in words and cautioned the nonviolent worker to "work in the midst of this double violence (overt and covert),"[52] India and Pakistan have apparently moved in the opposite direction and engaged in unremitting hostility without any genuine movement toward resolution. It is difficult to do justice to the extent of this daily cycle of hostility, violence, and recrimination. A brief analysis of it may suffice to understand how profoundly the psychology of othering has configured its scope.

Each episode of confrontation, high intensity or low intensity, expands it, which in turn paves the way for further rigidity that leads to a vicious cycle in which conflict leads to more conflict. By becoming a source of further hostility, the conflict's proliferation has become endemic. The two rivals constantly aspire to gain the upper hand not only in political and economic antagonism, but also in sociocultural spheres. Diplomatic relations are fragile, and diplomat harassment and expulsions are constant. The two have attempted to block each other's membership in international associations. The hostility is clearly reflected in their international relations. India and Pakistan stood in opposite camps during the Cold War. Each regards the other's relations with foreign countries suspiciously. Pakistan is wary of India's involvement in Afghanistan. Pakistan's ties with China have not been received well by India. India is engaged in a border conflict with China. China has been supporting Pakistan militarily and economically. Pakistan ceded a portion of its part of Kashmir to China in 1963, to the chagrin of India. While Pakistan has enthusiastically supported China's "One Belt, One Road" initiative and allowed the use of its territory and its part of Kashmir for infrastructure and military developments, India has decided not to join this initiative. More recently, amid an India-China brawl at the border in June 2020, Pakistan's foreign minister visited China to boost relations. In mid-2020, Pakistan offered support to Nepal in its dispute with India. A news report read, "Imran Khan to Join Xi Jinping to Shore Up Nepal's PM Oli against India."[53]

Pakistan's attempts to internationalize the Kashmir issue, and India's efforts to brand Pakistan a terrorist state, are manifestations of deep-seated hostility, indicative of an even deeper dynamic of othering. The annual meeting of the UN General Assembly provides a public forum for displaying this othering mentality internationally. In the 2019 meeting, Pakistan asserted that India indulged in "false and duplicitous claims on normalcy in Jammu and Kashmir." Pointing at India's policy of bifurcating its part of Kashmir, Pakistan argued that the measure was the "first step" toward suppressing its Muslim community. It also stated that India had issued political maps claiming not just its side of Kashmir but also the parts that are with Pakistan and that India had violated the cease-fire along the Line of Control three thousand times in 2019. India castigated Pakistan for its "misinformation" campaign, and its representative argued, "One delegation (Pakistan) that epitomises the dark arts has, yet again, displayed its wares by peddling falsehoods. . . . These we dismiss with disdain. My simple response to Pakistan is even though it is late, neighbour, heal thyself of your malaise. There are no takers here for your malware."[54] The blame game is played regularly at this international platform.

The implicit violence is not confined to international stages. Incendiary rhetoric is frequent, particularly during a crisis or election time. Pakistani leader Zulfiqar Ali Bhutto's vow to "wage war for a thousand years" is well known. In the postnuclearization era, despite being aware of the costs associated with a possible nuclear conflagration, both countries have used inflammatory rhetoric to keep the fear of a war alive. Indian prime minister A. B. Vajpayee, during the Kargil crisis, stated that India was ready for a "decisive battle," and Pakistan president Musharraf retorted, saying Pakistan would give "a fitting reply." Then Indian defense minister George Fernandes proclaimed that if the conflict turned into a nuclear war, India would survive, but Pakistan would be destroyed.[55] Both unleashed intense war rhetoric after the 2019 Pulwama terrorist attack and subsequent Indian air strikes. In January 2020, Indian Army chief M. M. Naravane told a news channel, "We have our forces deployed all along the border, including Jammu and Kashmir, and we have various plans and if required, those plans can be put into action." Pakistan called this statement irresponsible and asserted that its security forces are prepared to counter any "aggressive move" by India.[56] The war of words, at times, makes it difficult to differentiate between truth and falsehood.

India and Pakistan have different versions of who won the limited military engagement in 2019. The Indian government described the air strike as a "non-military preemptive action" that was successful in destroying terrorist camps via air strikes.[57] Pakistan claimed it gave a "befitting response to India's Balakot misadventure."[58]

Protracted conflicts "involve whole societies" and act as agents "for defining the scope of national identity and social solidarity."[59] They shape identities and worldviews of political leadership and the vast majority of citizens affected. In the case of India and Pakistan, not only political leadership but societies in general have come to view each other as enemies—to the extent that there is public aversion to any kind of concession to the "enemy." A vast majority of the people in both countries were not born when partition occurred. Still, they endure the legacy of othering. The rivalry has become integral to both nation's national prestige. On both sides, most people stick to their state's narratives. The projected hostile intentions of the other are frequently used as a unifying political force. The inflammatory effect of this hostility is apparent during elections and domestic crises like economic failures, which are invariably attributed to the enemy neighbor. Portraying the other as an archenemy facilitates both the consolidation of votes and fervid jingoism, which is a powerful unifying force on both sides of the border.

Stereotypical images of the "other" are promoted through media and popular forums such as movies and shows. The media seems to be enamored with the image of the other as enemy. A Strategic Foresight Group report explains: "Indian and Pakistani media are obsessed with each other. Even tangential news about India makes it to the front page of Pakistani newspapers and vice versa. Also, media in both the countries are more or less influenced by their respective government's policies—when governments of both the countries are engaged in talks, the media focuses on prospects of friendly relations between the two countries, and when the governments are at loggerheads, the media also adopts a hostile stance."[60] There are instances when the media engages in hostile propaganda and misinformation campaigns, offering conflicting narratives and promoting competitive jingoism by disseminating distilled, exaggerated, distorted, and even "fake news." A recent example is the India-Pakistan standoff in

2019, during which many journalists brushed aside their professionalism and became warmongers.[61] Prime-time news shows draw massive ratings and revenue for the media houses but also bring dangerously inflammatory propaganda into the living rooms of citizens of both countries. The conflict's proliferation at this level seems to keep intensifying, with hardliners becoming more vocal and moderate voices being marginalized. The entertainment industry joins media houses in promoting jingoism by producing movies and shows that depict the "other" disparagingly. Common people have joined this trend, as social media becomes widely popular. Grassroots jingoism has become entrenched this way, with citizens becoming the social media soldiers, fighting with the means available to them.[62] As social media becomes increasingly influential, common people leisurely engage in hostile exchanges from the comfort of their homes. Patriotic hacking drew media attention in 2015 when Indian hackers compromised several Pakistani websites. In 2017 the websites of some Indian universities were hacked by a group named "Pakistan Haxor Crew." The group claimed the hacking was in retaliation for the hacking of Pakistan's Railway Ministry website.[63]

The ongoing rivalry—and othering—is sustained as educational institutions promote negative and stereotypical images of the "other." This is quite apparent within Pakistan, where religious education institutions frequently engage in India- and Hindu-bashing narratives. A 2019 video called "Ab Hind Banega Pakistan" (India Will Become Part of Pakistan) featuring Pakistani children calling for India's destruction, released by Pakistan-based Islami Jamiat-e-Talaba, is an instance of how young minds are conditioned in the psychology of othering. The video shows children describing their plans after Pakistan conquers India, with one minor saying, "We will employ the Indian Army to clean the streets."[64] The adverse impact of such othering is not only confined to the "enemy." It also occurs within the respective countries, as the hostility propagated by othering turns inward. Select groups in India suspect Indian Muslims of harboring loyalty toward Pakistan, and slogans such as "Go to Pakistan" or "You Are a Traitor" are directed against the moderate voices—or even those suggesting peaceful resolutions. Non-Muslim minorities in Pakistan have dwindled, particularly after its rapid Islamization since the 1980s. Attacks on minorities and forceful conversions are frequently reported. Communal violence is a reality for both states.

There are other striking examples of how the conflict has saturated all aspects of life. Perhaps no other sociocultural activity displays the hostility as acutely as sports events, particularly cricket. While the rivalry is also visible in other sports, such as hockey and soccer, it is most apparent in cricket, both countries' favorite sport. The "politics, passion and national identity" coincide when the game is played.[65] Cricket matches between the two adversaries take on the appearance of a war with bats and balls rather than with guns and bullets. A *Guardian* report detailed a cricket match between the two in Manchester in 2019: "It is a match. . . . But when India and Pakistan face off in Manchester on Sunday the sporting contest will be magnified and warped by so much else: the 70-plus years of shared history and antipathy between the two countries, the recent political tensions in Kashmir, and the stultifying pressure that comes when several hundred million eyeballs are watching on. Few sporting contests carry as much baggage."[66] The winning side usually celebrates, while the losing side mourns the defeat, expresses anger, and experiences anguish in the extreme—losing to any other country is tolerable but not to the archrival. Zealous fans resort to hooliganism in anger. When India defeated Pakistan at the 1996 World Cup, angry fans stoned the house of Pakistan's cricket-team captain. Matches have been suspended several times following wars, terrorist attacks, and other crises. The rivals sometimes play in a third country, which may be as near as Bangladesh and Sri Lanka or as far as England or Canada. They have not played any bilateral cricket for the past several years and compete against each other only at global or continental events.

Violence is also embedded in travel, literature, and other aspects of life. Travel between them is not easy, despite kinship affiliations running across the border for centuries, or what Gandhi would term "common ancestry." Border crossings by foot are few, and air travel is restricted. Whitehead notes: "It's about 700km (430 miles) from Delhi to Islamabad—less than the distance between London and Geneva. A short hop in aviation terms. But you can't fly non-stop from the Indian capital to the Pakistani capital. There are no direct flights at all. It is only one of the legacies of seven decades of mutual suspicion and tension. . . . But both have been unable to overcome the legacy of the tragedy which accompanied what should have been their finest moment 70 years ago."[67] Getting a visa is difficult even for those having relatives on the other side of the border. Conferences and dialogues on India-Pakistan relations are organized in third countries to avoid the visa-related inconvenience. Cultural exchange is fragile and restricted, even though Bollywood movies and actors are popular in Pakistan, and Pakistan's television shows have a dedicated audience in India. At times, Indian directors and producers cast Pakistani performers in Indian movies and shows, but occasionally doing so has resulted in public outrage.[68]

The above discussion on implicit violence helps clarify the depth of a rivalry borne of othering. It offers glimpses of the sociocultural costs of the conflict. In the next section, we analyze the material costs. We provide a relatively cursory synopsis of the costs, as the main argument of the book does not necessitate a detailed analysis or quantification of material costs. The goal here is to indicate how costly the conflict has become and why it is necessary to reflect on whether it is fruitful to carry on the legacy of othering.

The Costs

Examining the costs of conflict is an important exercise, as it helps to reveal its quantifiable dynamics and may point toward pathways for peace. A Strategic Foresight Group report of 2004 elaborates: "It is often suggested that we should talk about benefits of peace rather than the cost of conflict. Such a proposition is meant to situate the debate in positive semantics. The costs of conflict and the benefits of peace are two sides of the same coin. We emphasize costs rather than benefits . . . because the former are wide ranging, while the latter are specific. It is important to make it possible for the people of India and Pakistan to benefit from peace and reconciliation through trade, cultural exchanges and cooperation in general. It is much more crucial for them to rid themselves of cost and their interdependent relations of such costs, with other evils in the society."[69]

In his 2001 book on the costs and benefits of peace, Mahmud Ali Durrani, a former Pakistani army general later turned peace activist, examines how the conflict is an ever-impeding socioeconomic development there.[70] Discussing "the futility and grave risks of militarisation, the heavy cost of the adversarial relationship and the multiple benefits of cooperation," Durrani then examines prospects for how "the existing bedrock of deep-rooted cultural and racial ties between the two nations" can "facilitate an honest effort to reduce the equally deep-rooted mistrust that has been created by certain historical experiences and misguided propaganda." Bharat Bhushan of the Indian newspaper *Hindustan Times* in the foreword to his book advocates such efforts as "holding a mirror up to the political leadership."[71] As we discussed in chapter 1, one of the reasons Gandhi abhorred violence and wars is their huge costs and disastrous material consequences. It seems nearly impossible to document all the costs the rivalry has exacted for more than seventy years at physical, economic, sociocultural, and psychological levels. This exercise is difficult because of the intensity and duration of the conflict. Nonetheless, an overview is warranted.

Burdened with a violent past and a present that perpetuates the legacy of the past, both India and Pakistan have ignored human security, or security of their citizens, as they have become obsessed with state security. Traditional conceptions of state security—based on the military defense of territory—are an important but not a sufficient condition of human welfare.[72] Recent studies have looked beyond the "one-dimensional" or "territorial" aspect of security and expanding horizon of security to include multiple aspects of human welfare.[73] The United Nations conceives of human security in the form of seven interrelated components: economic security, food security, health security, environmental security, personal security, public security, and political security. The security of people, rather than just political-strategic borders, gained some ground after the Cold War; such a realization has not yet dawned in South Asia. Violent othering along the India-Pakistan border in the form of barbed-wire fencing, war towers, electrified fences, frequent firing, shelling, and border skirmishes ensures border security in a superficial sense, but at the cost of human security. Every year, dozens of security personnel and borderlanders become victims of these tensions. Positioned at the front of a state-to-state power contest, borderlanders negotiate their lives every day amid life-threatening conditions. Our research on the impacts of tense borders, including frequent displacements, suggests the prospect of a dismal scenario unfolding along the India-Pakistan border in Kashmir.[74]

The dismal scenario is not confined to the borderlands. Both countries have lost numerous military personnel and civilians to explicit violence. The Strategic Foresight Group report offers details: "In 1947–8 war India suffered 1,104 military casualties and Pakistan 1500. The number of casualties increased in the two subsequent full wars. In 1965 India lost 3,264 military personnel and Pakistan lost 3,800. In 1971 war, 3,843 Indian soldiers and 7,900 Pakistani soldiers lost their lives. The 1999 Kargil War led to 522 casualties on the Indian side and 696 on Pakistan side. The combined death toll was 22,600 and about 50,000 were injured. At least 100,000 families suffered direct costs due to the three full and one limited wars between the rival neighbors." These estimates from 2004 do not include the numbers of those killed in other manifestations of hostility. On Siachen Glacier, soldiers from both sides remain posted at altitudes ranging between ten to twenty-two thousand feet above sea level. The Strategic Foresight Group report estimates, "Approximately Rs. 50,000 per soldier is spent on clothing to put up with temperatures as low as −50° Celsius. Helicopters ferry food and other supplies to the troops, making Siachen the most expensive air maintenance operation in the world. Human costs for troops, apart from casualties, include psychological disorders, frostbite, hypoxia, high altitude pulmonary and cerebral edema and snow blindness. Enemy firing accounts for hardly 3 per cent of the total casualties; the weather extremities of the glacier cause the rest."[75] Earlier, a 1999 report on the glacier noted, "Rs 3 crore (INR 30 million) per day, (is) the Indian Army's expenditure. . . . But the damages, monumental as they are, are not merely financial. The conflict has resulted in 2500 soldiers losing their lives, and 10,000 others being incapacitated more due to harsh terrain, adverse climatic conditions—which lead to frost bite, hypoxia, whiteouts and severe mental stress—than actual military engagement."[76] The situation has not changed much since this writing, aside from the exponential increase in material and human costs.

The economic costs are also enormous. Between December 2001 and January 2002, India spent $600 million and Pakistan $400 million on the military standoff following the Indian Parliament attack. By the end of the confrontation, the rivals ended up spending about $3 billion. During the 2002–3 confrontation, India spent Rs 14.6 billion per day and Pakistan Rs 3.7 billion per day.[77] Following the Balakot air strikes of 2019, Pakistan closed its airspace to India for months, which adversely affected hundreds of commercial and cargo flights. The closure not only led to additional flight time for passengers but also added to economic costs. Indian airlines lost nearly $80 million,[78] and Pakistan's losses were about $100 million.[79] This was neither the first nor the last time that rivalry clouded the airspace. Nearly a month after the reopening in August, Pakistan again partially shut down its airspace for India, as a countermeasure against India's revocation of Article 370 and Article 35A, which dealt with Jammu and Kashmir.

It is difficult to gauge the nature and scope of probable gains were peace and cooperation established. Some studies are worth noting. Pakistani economist Parvez Hasan estimates economic gains for Pakistan:

> One is tempted to speculate on what might have happened if defence spending, . . . resources had been allocated to social and economic development and potential economic gains from regional economic co-operation had been optimized. It is not frivolous to suggest that Pakistan's economic growth rate over the long period of 1970–2010 could have been at least 2 percentage points higher than it actually was—that is, 6–6.5 per cent per annum, rather than 4–4.45 per cent per annum. This would have meant an economic size double of what we have, higher education levels, lower poverty incidence, and less social tensions, including less extremisms. It is also interesting to note that, with an economic size twice the present level, the actual defence spending, would not be any lower, even if the percentage of GDP [gross domestic product] allocated to it was half the present level. If one adds to the mix the assumption of greater trade and economic co-operation between India and Pakistan over the past four decades, one can argue that the whole history of the subcontinent could have been a happier one.[80]

Loss of potential economic gains is not the only casualty of the conflict; limited trade relations also contribute to the conjunction of economic underdevelopment. Poor trade relations exacted a heavy cost in terms of GDP, investment, infrastructure, and employment. India enjoys relatively higher trade than Pakistan with states as close as Bangladesh and Sri Lanka and as far as Nigeria and South Africa. A 2012 Federation of Indian Chambers for Commerce and Industry report suggests that despite its potential for economic gains, the trade value between them is "small."[81] Sengupta explains: "Indeed, if there were friendly relations between the two neighbours, trade and investment partnership would have flourished and the welfare gains would have benefited the common person on both sides. In agriculture, manufactures and in services, much complementarity exists between the two countries. . . . The official trade between the two countries is small at $2.4 billion. It could have been many times more." Smuggling along the border amounts to $5 billion, and trade via third countries such as the United Arab Emirates and Singapore amount to somewhere between $5 billion and $10 billion.[82] In his foreword to a report of the Atlantic Council, George P. Shultz, former US secretary of state, writes, "The cost of the military is substantial for the two. But the cost of arms and armies is only part of the problem. Here we have two countries full of competent people and many complementary capabilities. In this setting, trade should be booming, much to the benefit of people in both countries. Instead, trade is at a mere trickle. This situation contrasts sharply with other areas in the world, such as North America, where the vibrant trade among the United States, Canada, and Mexico raises the level of living in all three countries."[83] The continuity of tensions ensures that economic relations remain perpetual hostage to the politics of violent othering. Even minimal trade is annulled when tensions are high. Regional cooperation platforms such as the South Asian Association for Regional Cooperation remain stymied by this adversarial relationship.

Despite economic challenges such as high inflation, debt, and vulnerable currencies, a substantial part of the annual budget is spent on defense. In this context, the economic situation of Pakistan is relatively dismal. Heavy investment in military supplies and sophisticated armaments is an impediment to economic growth in the region. Investments also take place despite social and economic problems including poverty, infant mortality, malnutrition, poor education, unemployment, and lack of access to basic amenities. The rivals are ranked low in the human development index, with India ranking 130 and Pakistan 161 among 191 countries in 2020.[84] And, notably, even exorbitant military expenditures have not brought foolproof security for the two. New security challenges, such as internal conflicts, have emerged partly owing to overemphasis on security challenges from outside. This analysis is not to suggest that the two states disband their militaries or annul spending on defense. What we argue instead is that moderation of this violent othering by following the Gandhian methods of peace by peaceful means would facilitate trans-formation and a diversion of the resources to the welfare of both nations' citizens. Nawaz and Guruswamy write about the choice between "butter and guns":

> Apportioning resources appropriately is important to ensure both inter-nal and external security is intact. The challenge for both is to balance state security with human security. The choices they face between defense and development are not new. It was the Nobel Prize-winning economist, Paul Samuelson, who in 1948 first labeled productive and unproductive activities "butter" and "guns" respectively. In coining the terms, Samuelson had the experience of Nazi Germany in mind, where the government was committed to increasing military expenditures (guns) at the expense of civilian production and consumption (butter). That is, the choice between butter and guns was a matter of economic policy. As guns increase, butter must decrease; there is no alternative allocation for available resources.[85]

As resources are limited, reflecting on their use and misuse is important. US president Dwight D. Eisenhower, also a general, who took part in the Second World War, offered a brilliant insight in 1953: "Every gun that is made, every warship launched, every rocket fired signifies, in the final sense, a theft from those who hunger and are not fed, those who are cold and are not clothed. The world in arms is not spending money alone. It is spending the sweat of its laborers, the genius of its scientists, and the hopes of its children. . . . This is not a way of life at all, in any true sense.

Under the cloud of threatening war, it is humanity hanging from a cross of iron."[86] The leaders of India and Pakistan can use such sober reflection and would be well advised to engage in actions that emerge from those reflections.

Indian strategist Brahma Chellaney argues that India missed an opportunity after the 2001 Indian Parliament attack. He wrote, "Had the then Prime Minister Atal Bihari Vajpayee quickly responded with punitive airstrikes to the December 2001 Jaish-e-Mohammed attack on Parliament—at a time when much of Pakistan's F-16 fleet was not airworthy due to a lack of spares—India probably would have been spared the Pakistan-scripted terrorist carnages that have followed." He further reasons, "The lost golden opportunity was compounded by nearly 18 years of political dithering on allowing limited uses of air power, such as taking out trans-border terrorist launch pads. India's belated use of air power to strike a terrorist safe haven has finally sent a clear message: it is not afraid to escalate its response to the aerial domain in order to call Pakistan's nuclear bluff."[87] While Chellaney's argument might be appealing from a strategic and realpolitik viewpoint, and even if one concedes that such actions might discourage Pakistan from engaging in proxy confrontations, the larger question is whether such air strikes ensure enduring peace. Our prognosis would be no. Wars, Gandhi famously said, put aesthetic canons of morality to shame, and a politics without moral considerations cannot be constructive. Given their violent past and uncertain present, the need is, we argue in the next chapter, to explore, in the spirit of Gandhi, possible pathways to promote belonging in India-Pakistan relations.

4

Promoting Belonging

An analysis of the conflict's history reveals that violent methods to resolve it have proved futile and that it is time to think outside the box and embrace alternative methods. In this chapter, we apply Gandhian methods for promoting peace and belonging in South Asia. Even while acknowledging that psychosocial othering is deeply embedded in the subcontinent's politics, and that it has been nurtured continuously for more than seven decades, a Gandhian optimist would persist in exploring nonviolent means to transform it. The geographical partition was engineered as a solution to communal cultural conflict, but postcolonial history shows that partition did not end the conflict. Instead, the othering that led to partition has been formalized and institutionalized. The hostile relationship exacted high costs, and present fear of a nuclear conflagration looms large. What is the way out? What are the alternatives? We draw a broad canvas of possible means to address othering-generated conflict and focus on its psychological, sociocultural, political, and economic possibilities. They need to be employed simultaneously, as they complement and reinforce each other. Our goal is not to offer a detailed or permanent set of recommendations to address this othering, but rather to illustrate how the problem of psychological othering requires deeper reflections from policy makers of both countries, and consequent plans of action based on those reflections are integral to its resolution.

Fragile Peace

Peace efforts in South Asia are inherently fragile. The first India-Pakistan war ended after the UN-mediated cease-fire in 1948. Following a brief period of uneasy peace, the two countries fought their second war in 1965. Indian prime minister Lal Bahadur Shastri and Pakistan president Ayub Khan met in Tashkent to negotiate a settlement. Both leaders negotiated the Tashkent Agreement and agreed to abjure violence. That did not happen. A third war was fought in 1971, and a new agreement was signed following the cease-fire. The Shimla Agreement aimed at solving contentious issues peacefully through dialogue. There have been other agreements since then as well, but peace remains elusive. War scares, the limited war of 1999, the intense border tensions, and the clashes of 2001, 2002, 2016, and 2019 are all instances of how the two countries keep the conflict kettle boiling. The varied peace initiatives between these events could, at best, be considered respites in an ongoing saga of hostility. Agreements like Tashkent in 1966, Shimla in 1972, Islamabad in 1988, Lahore in 1999, and many others raised hopes, which ceased shortly after being initiated. The bilateral engagement in the late 1990s and early 2000s continued for a relatively long time, but, as developments in recent years have demonstrated, the momentum could not be maintained and relations lapsed into uncertainty.

A. B. Vajpayee of India and Nawaz Sharif of Pakistan initiated a peace process at the outset of the twenty-first century. This was considered unusual, keeping in view the "hard-line image" of the Bharatiya Janata Party to which Vajpayee belonged. Vajpayee's 530-kilometer bus ride from Delhi to Lahore in February 1999 was portrayed as a major move toward peace. Vajpayee sought to address Pakistan's fear of insecurity by going to Minar-e-Pakistan, the symbol of Pakistan's independence. He stated that a stable, secure, and prosperous Pakistan is in India's self-interest. The joint statement emphasized that "an environment of peace and security is in the supreme national interest of both sides and that the resolution of all outstanding issues, including Jammu and Kashmir, is essential for this purpose."[1] Three months after Vajpayee's visit, the Kargil war took place in May 1999. An army coup ousted the elected government of Sharif in Pakistan in October 1999. Despite these developments, Vajpayee expressed readiness to build relations with Pakistan. He sent a letter of invitation to the new military ruler of Pakistan, Pervez Musharraf, for talks, in May 2001. He wrote, "For the welfare of our peoples, there is no other recourse

but a pursuit of the path of reconciliation."[2] Vajpayee's approach implied
that despite their mutual mistrust, Pakistan as a neighbor could not and
should not be ignored. He invited Musharraf to a summit-level meeting in
Agra. Though the Agra Summit in July 2001 "made a modest step in the
right direction," it failed to produce tangible results.

The India-Pakistan Composite Dialogue was initiated when, in the
early 2000s, a series of confidence-building measures were proposed to
improve relations. Vajpayee met Musharraf on the sidelines of the South
Asian Association for Regional Cooperation summit in Islamabad in
January 2004. They agreed to resume a constructive dialogue, which was
stalled after the attack on the Indian Parliament in December 2001. Before
his Islamabad visit, Vajpayee stated in an interview to a Pakistan TV channel, "We want that in improving bilateral relations, he (Musharraf) will
come forward and take part. I am hopeful that the attempt will be successful."[3] Responding to Musharraf's reference to Vajpayee as "man of peace,"
he said, "I have been working for peace all along and will continue to do so
in the future."[4] In February 2004, delegations of the two countries met in a
"cordial and constructive atmosphere" in Islamabad to discuss modalities
and a time frame for the resumption of composite dialogue. This engagement was considered historical, as "in contrast to previous talks, both sides
deviated from their obstinate positions and took up talks on a broad range
of issues such as confidence-building measures, disputed territories or
the stimulation of bilateral trade."[5] Significant progress in some areas was
achieved. This included a memorandum of understanding on confidence-
building measures in the security sector such as a permanent hotline between the foreign ministries, de-escalation of fighting in disputed regions,
a memorandum of understanding on addressing the concerns over the use
of nuclear weapons, agreement on combating terrorism, resuming bilateral trade, removing nontrade barriers, and establishing trade associations.
The measures also included increasing communication between the two
countries through the land (buses and trains) and water (ships). Earlier, in
late 2003, a cease-fire along the tense borders in Kashmir became a reality.
It was the first time that both agreed to a formal truce on the border.

Vajpayee's policy of engagement with Pakistan was carried forward by
his successor, Manmohan Singh, who led the United Progressive Alliance

(UPA) government. Singh declared that India would accept a solution and move forward, but without compromising its territorial sovereignty. This progress was slow and bumpy, but the peaceful bilateral engagement was a real achievement. Despite sporadic violence, India and Pakistan considered the engagement irreversible. In 2005 a cross-border road connecting Srinagar on the Indian side of Kashmir and Muzaffarabad on the Pakistani side of Kashmir was opened. This new road facilitated travel across the border. In 2006 another cross-border road connecting Poonch on the Indian side of Kashmir and Rawalakot on the Pakistani side of Kashmir was opened. With the opening of these roads, negotiations for cross-border trade commenced. In 2008 both roads were opened for trade.

Leaders of India and Pakistan, in a joint statement of September 2008 on cross-border trade through Kashmir, "agreed that the forces that have tried to derail the peace process must be defeated." Further, they confirmed that trade would "allow the continuation and deepening of a constructive dialogue for the peaceful resolution" of conflicts.[6] The joint statement implied that, notwithstanding these achievements, political leaders of the two states were aware that there were hard-liners on both sides interested in the continuation of the conflict. Prime Minister Manmohan Singh said in October 2008, "History will judge how big these steps (opening cross-border roads for trade and people-to-people interaction) were. The fact is that they have taken place after many lost decades of mutual recrimination, violence and war."[7] His statement reflected a twofold acknowledgment: first, decades have been lost to violence; and second, realization of the significance of peace measures. Earlier, in 2007, Manmohan Singh had observed: "There can be no question of divisions or fresh partitions, but the Line of Control (dividing Kashmir between India and Pakistan) can become a line of peace. We are committed to winning the hearts and minds of all. We will never allow anyone to stop the heartbeat of peace-loving people in whatever cause."[8] Singh spoke the language of Gandhi, which calls for "winning hearts and minds."

Bilateral engagement was not smooth and was discontinued on several occasions. After assuming office in 2008, Asif Ali Zardari appeared to follow a policy of rapprochement and preferred to emulate the policies of Prime Minister Singh. The bumpy road to dialogue abruptly ended after terrorist attacks in Mumbai in November 2008. The dialogue resumed in late 2011, without significant outcomes. In the initial days of Narendra Modi–led National Democratic Alliance government, there were signs that the India-Pakistan relations might gather speed. India's invitation to leaders from all neighboring countries, including Pakistan, to the oath ceremony of new prime minister Narendra Modi in May 2014, was a positive gesture. Modi's stopover in Islamabad in December 2015 to participate in a family event of Sharif was hailed as another positive step toward peace. Later developments did not corroborate this optimism. Amicable relations waxed and waned with the cancellation of meetings at the foreign secretary level in August 2014. The relations declined further after the attack on an Indian Air Force base in India, a few days after Modi's visit to Lahore. Then Indian foreign minister Sushma Swaraj, in a joint meeting with US secretary of state John Kerry, stated, "Talks with Pakistan will happen only when it takes steps on the Pathankot terror attack," since "terror and talks cannot go hand-in-hand."[9] Relations worsened after an attack on an Indian military base in Kashmir in 2016, killing seventeen Indian soldiers.[10] After another attack in Pulwama in February 2019, which killed forty members of India's paramilitary force, India revoked Pakistan's most-favored-nation status and significantly increased customs duties on some Pakistani trade imports. Subsequent aerial strikes by India to destroy terrorist camps in the Pakistan side of Kashmir added fuel to the fire. Trade through Kashmir, which had continued for more than a decade with occasional closures, came to a complete halt in April 2019. Relations deteriorated further when, in August 2019, New Delhi revoked Article 370 of the Indian Constitution, which accorded a special status to Jammu and Kashmir.

The literature on "spoilers" is relevant to explain this hostile situation.[11] Spoilers in conflict situations are elements attempting to perpetuate and exacerbate hostilities. Perpetual conflict for spoilers is "normal," and any peace attempt disturbs that normalcy.[12] According to Stedman: "Peacemaking is a risky business. . . . [T]he greatest source of risk comes from spoilers—leaders and parties who believe that peace emerging from negotiations threatens their power, worldview, and interests, and use violence to undermine attempts to achieve it."[13] In India-Pakistan relations, institutional structures in both countries are working as "spoilers," fueling conflict and resisting peace. Gandhi would contend that peace remains elusive, as these peace efforts were concealed by "camouflage and hypocrisy," and that "the declarations of good intentions, commissions, conferences and the like, or even through measures conceived as tending to the public benefit" were promoting othering and hostility.

The Gandhian Way

India-Pakistan hostile relations are marked by several overlapping fault lines. How would the Gandhian way address these multiple fault lines? Gandhi would not recommend another partition, war, or any other solution that emerges from violence. The prolonged conflict, as pointed out by Azar and others, "has been a process manifesting continuous overt hostilities and producing the mentality and circumstances of the participants to it; that, as such, it cannot be stopped, on short notice, by specific action either by participants or 'outsiders,' but must run a very difficult and dangerous course before it decays or transforms itself."[14] Diehl and Goertz put forward a punctuated-equilibrium model to argue that a "political shock," internal or external, is an essential precondition for change, which includes, among other things, war and domestic regime changes.[15] Others consider a major crisis or impending war as a precondition for the termination of festering, immanent hostilities.[16] Some theorists focus on the necessity of visionary leadership along with other conditions favorable to peace.[17] Gandhian conflict resolution would acknowledge the relevance of these ideas, but it would go deeper into the psychology of othering to address the conflict.

There is literature on the prospects for enduring social and political dialogue and peace between India and Pakistan.[18] Those studies have seldom considered the importance and impact of othering and belonging in their analysis. Most emphasize political dialogues and economic cooperation, but rarely focus on the kind of psychological othering that has informed bilateral relations. As we have explained, each war and crisis served a double purpose: it exacerbated the psychosocial mentality of othering that fuelled cross-cultural political hostility, which, in turn, further inflamed the othering that spawned it. To end this cycle of othering and hostility, Gandhian methods are indispensable. The cycle can be broken by the creation of fertile conditions for peace, fostered by visionary leadership and bold political will. Gandhi would call this condition a "union of hearts," a prolific psychological ground for creative peace, in which violence has no *locus standi*. At the height of violence that preceded and succeeded partition, Gandhi repeatedly called for a unity of hearts, making use of this logic: though geographical partition is a reality, psychological partitioning (othering) is not inevitable "if . . . our hearts are true we can behave as if they had not been partitioned."

The conflict emerging out of othering, as it has shaped the external and internal politics of India and Pakistan, is simply not amenable to resolution by engagement at an exclusively political, economic, or sociocultural level. As discussed in the last chapter, othering has penetrated so deeply into the national psyche that even a cricket match between the two states enlivens war. The violent partition cannot be undone, but the violent psychic othering that led to partition can, and must, be ended— and the catharsis it generated needs to be channeled toward building a peaceful South Asia. The othering is deep-rooted, and it may not end soon, but that does not mean there should be no attempts to address it. As we explained in the chapter 1, the Gandhian conflict resolution mantra is composed of three elements: approach, means, and end. The two rival states must acknowledge that the conflict is a reality and then embark on a journey to not only resolve but also to transcend it through psychological, sociocultural, political, and economic means. All these means are significant, but their psychological-spiritual foundation is an essential prerequisite to all of them; it provides the substratum for all other means or goals.

Political Engagement

There is significant literature focused on India-Pakistan dialogue.[19] Arguing that dialogue may not lead to conflict resolution until Pakistan accepts the reality of India's strategic superiority, Tellis argues: "A lasting cordiality between India and Pakistan ultimately hinges on the Pakistan Army reconciling itself to India's strategic superiority within South Asia. It cannot be induced by continual bilateral engagement, irrespective of whether it is structured or nonstructured or whether it is conducted through open diplomacy or secret parleys."[20] Gandhi would not accept Tellis's superior-inferior dichotomy, as Gandhian ethics undercuts this dichotomy. For Gandhi, "Nonviolence is infinitely superior to violence," and nonviolent political engagement requires repudiating any hierarchical dichotomies that may inspire further conflict. Peaceful parties must reject categories like superiority and inferiority—with all the class and military antagonisms that these entail—and cultivate engagement in a spirit of equality and belonging. It would be understandably difficult to operationalize such a Gandhian scheme, which appears naive or utopian in the contemporary milieu, and seems inapplicable to the realpolitik canons of politics. Given the obvious inability of realpolitik to resolve decades of violent conflict, and the obvious inability of realpolitik policy to address the deeper dimensions of psychosocial alienation (othering) underwriting this conflict, Gandhi's psychosocial-spiritual mode of conflict resolution—which is addressed directly to the psychology of othering—would appear to be a hopeful alternative to the status quo. Gandhian conflict transcendence demands ingenuity and political vision, a vision that accepts the region's realities as they are and, at the same time, prompts its rivals to play their respective parts in addressing the conflict.

Certainly, peace cannot be the result of a dialogue if the "hearts and minds" of its participants are disengaged, or if one side clings to peace and the other promotes violence. Indeed, as Gandhi would agree, dialogues are only genuine, and successful, if they come from the heart. Channels of high-level communication need to be open all the time, even during a crisis. They cannot be subject to political whims or the machinations of "spoilers." In the past, on several occasions, high-level meetings were abruptly canceled because of a violent event. There should be established procedures, institutionalized and sustained dialogues, and mutually agreed-upon methods to continue dialogue while peacefully resolving crises. India and Pakistan can no longer afford communication deficiencies or breakdowns. No opportunity to meet, or even greet, should be lost. Regular summit meetings should become common practice rather than hopeful expectations. Meetings on the sidelines of international platforms, such as the UN General Assembly, should become a norm. Such intense political engagement would provide regular opportunities to discuss points of contention and common goals. Moving beyond the symbolism and practice of stalling communication during a crisis, sustained bilateral contacts can facilitate crisis management and build trust. All types of diplomacy—"formal," "track-two," "multitrack," and "silent"—should be put into practice diligently.[21] Back-channel diplomacy can be very effective and should be encouraged, as it will help open innovative channels for negotiation. All engagements should ensure that more confidence-building measures are added to the list. A mutual assurance of "no first use of nuclear weapons" can also be an effective way to move forward. A dedicated hotline between the two prime leaders was a useful mechanism when first introduced and can be resumed. Such arrangements between the leaders of the United States and the Soviet Union during the Cold War helped avert confrontations in Cuba and elsewhere.

Economic Engagement

Economic engagement should accompany political engagement. The theory that economic engagement can play a positive role in conflict situations and help moderate rigid positions is pertinent to conflict in South Asia. Following the liberal argument that economic ties facilitate interstate peace and when economics is prioritized over politics, conflicts can be managed effectively, we explore prospects for economic cooperation here. We do not argue that economic cooperation will be enough to address the sort of deep-seated othering causing this conflict. We argue that in the quiver of the belonging project, economic cooperation can be a useful arrow. Economic engagement is one spoke in the wheel of promoting belonging. Here, we focus on select aspects of India-Pakistan trade and opening the Silk Road for facilitating the free flow of goods, ideas, and peoples.

Wars prove detrimental to economic growth, as the rival countries divert resources for arms and armaments. Dwight Eisenhower reflected on the costs of World War II: "The cost of one modern heavy bomber is this: a modern brick school in more than 30 cities. . . . We pay for a single fighter with a half million bushels of wheat. We pay for a single destroyer with new homes that could have housed more than 8,000 people."[22] According to Cordell Hull, the US secretary of state during the war, "If trade crosses borders, soldiers won't."[23] Though the liberal school of politics is associated with this conception of economic interdependence and peace,[24] it can be traced back to an earlier period. Immanuel Kant's idea of permanent peace and Norman Angell's idea of peace through commerce both emphasized economic interdependence between states.[25] Angell described war as an "orthodox statecraft," as it is beneficial to neither the victor nor the vanquished. Drawing from the developments in Europe, Angell pointed out how the population of small and peaceful but financially prosperous countries such as Belgium and Switzerland, with small armies, were better off than the population of big militarily extravagant countries such as Germany, with a powerful army, owing to the former's economic interdependence. For Angell, war is "commercially suicidal," as it destroys prospects for trade and commerce in warring states.[26] In this context, one could also consider the formation of the European Coal and Steel Community in 1951 and its later transformation into the European Union as an exemplary case of economic interdependence and its influence on peaceful relations between European nation-states.

In South Asia, the Silk Road,[27] the traditional network of routes crisscrossing the subcontinent between East and West, played a significant role for trade and for transporting cultures and religions.[28] Before 1947 the road acted as a bridge between India, China, and Central Asian countries. Merchants, explorers, soldiers, spies, and missionaries traversed the rugged and remote region because of this transportation network. The Munshi Aziz Bhat museum located in the Ladakh region testifies to the role the Silk Road played in trade and human interaction. We visited the museum in 2006 and 2007, located on a hillock on the outskirts of Kargil and found collections of headgear, caps, overcoats, shoes, utensils, and machetes traded from the medieval period to the nineteenth century. Some of the collections were from Samarkand, Bukhara, and Ashkhabad.[29] Economically, the Silk Road could open floodgates of trade between India and Pakistan, which can also be expanded toward Central Asia and China.

In recent times, a robust demand for the Silk Road's reopening has begun in Kashmir. Our interactions with the borderlanders in Kargil in 2006 and 2007 revealed their overwhelming interest in reopening of the Silk Road.[30] Many older people became emotional while recalling the times when the road was open. Most respondents expressed the view that an open Silk Road would be of tremendous benefit not only for the people of Kashmir but also for India, Pakistan, and entirety of South and Central Asia, culturally as well as economically. Even after more than a decade since our field research in the Kargil region, the situation has not changed. Hence, we argue that a revived Silk Road can provide opportunities for India, Central Asia, and China to conduct trade. An undivided Kashmir abuts Afghanistan and China, and the Karakoram Highway from China to Pakistan passes through this region. Opening this route would provide a direct link to Central Asia and promote tourism. Before the division, the whole region was a popular destination for tourists. Its older generation remembers the region as a "trekker's paradise." As argued earlier, it would be farfetched to contend that economic linkages will serve as a panacea for all issues that divide the region, but the benefits of trade will positively impact politics in the region. The resulting connections could play an effective role in the economic development of the region and facilitate the formation of regional organizations such as the Silk Road economic cooperation organization.

Other areas where both countries can cooperate economically include infrastructure development, developing hydroelectric power in the Indus River basin, managing watershed development, and cultivating fruits and vegetables. There are prospects for cooperation in building multistate pipelines for Iran-Pakistan-India and Turkmenistan-Afghanistan-Pakistan-India. Both states confront issues of food, energy, and water insecurity. Through the Indus Water Treaty, Pakistan and India have managed water resources of the Indus Basin. Many such agreements are needed. The region is prone to environmental challenges, including earthquakes, droughts, and flooding. Such disasters do not respect human-made borders, as was demonstrated by the 2005 earthquake in Kashmir, in which people from both sides of the border were adversely affected.[31] Due to interstate hostilities, these common challenges have not, thus far, been addressed properly.

A substantial increase in trade is projected if relations between the two nations are normalized.[32] A 2018 World Bank report suggests that India-Pakistan trade has the potential to increase to US$37 billion from US$2 billion.[33] As per a Brookings Institute report, India's percentage share of global trade with South Asia is less than 4 percent, thus making South Asia one of the least economically integrated regions of the world.[34] The report advises focusing on free-trade agreements, eliminating barriers and protectionist policies, and the development of cross-border infrastructure as effective measures to address lack of economic integration. Toward this end, stakeholders here need to actively promote the South Asia Free Trade Area and strengthen the South Asian Association of Regional Coopera-tion. Nawaz and Guruswamy contend: "Clearly there is much India and Pakistan can do to bring prosperity to their people faster if they worked together to build their economies. Economically intertwined and mutu-ally beneficial economic systems in both countries will create a huge peace constituency that will not only be good for the two nations but also for the region and for the entire world."[35] They make a case for a compre-hensive approach: "Both countries need to shift this trajectory of military spending and turn toward greater confidence building. They can do this by many means, including: increased people-to-people contacts and thus eliminate old stereotypes that fuel fears of each other; direct communica-tions between their militaries, through exchange visits and more transpar-ency about their military plans and movements; open borders for trade and tourism; and joint investments in energy, water, and export indus-tries."[36] Economic interdependence has played a role in building peace among many rival states, and leaders of India and Pakistan need to reflect seriously on it in their relations.

Sociocultural Engagement

Alongside political and economic engagement, sociocultural engagement is a significant force for integrating all aspects of life. Kuldip Nayar, who migrated from Sialkot of Punjab, Pakistan, and Asif Noorani, who migrated

from Bombay (now Mumbai) to Karachi, recount their memories of partition in *Tales of Two Cities*. Theirs are not merely stories of migration but
voyages—physical, emotional, and spiritual—deeply invested in belonging but shattered by othering. Nayar, recounting his days in Sialkot, narrates how Hindus and Muslims were peacefully coexisting:

> The people of Sialkot were mild, austere and tolerant. They were cast
> in a different mould. Our religions or positions in life did not distance
> us from one another. We numbered about a lakh (a hundred thousand):
> 70 per cent Muslims and 30 per cent Hindus, Sikhs and Christians. . . .
> [W]e had never experienced tension, much less communal riots. Our
> festivals, Diwali, Holi or Eid, were jointly celebrated and most of us
> walked together in mourning during Moharram. Even our businesses
> depended on cooperative effort. There was a mixture of owners and
> workers from both communities. Sports goods were the main indus-
> try and many labourers worked at home with their families to meet
> the orders, given piecemeal. Manufacturing surgical instruments was
> another business in which local people were employed. Such work had
> brought us together, Hindus and Muslims, in a common endeavour.[37]

The people of South Asia have multiple cultural similarities and
differences. Ambedkar, as we elaborated earlier, argued that to restore
peaceful coexistence between Hindus and Muslims, commonalities must
be emphasized. His argument on commonalities is relevant, and one
encounters examples of cross-cultural harmony even today. In Kashmir,
Nund Rishi for Hindus is Noor-ud-din for Muslims. The emphasis on
commonalities by Ambedkar also matches the narrative of Nayar, who
mentions how his family in Sialkot was worshipping a Muslim saint.
Nayar also talks about how "trivial" issues were exaggerated by the effects
of othering: "The few weeks of madness (during the partition) on both
sides of the border embittered relations between the two countries for
generations to come. . . . Fear and mistrust of each other made even trivial
matters major issues."[38]

Nayar narrates his encounter with Jinnah, who visited Law College at
Lahore, where Nayar was a student, three years before the partition. To his
question, "Would Hindus and Muslims be just at each other's throats once

the British left?" Jinnah replied that the "bitterness and antagonism . . . between the two communities would go after Pakistan was constituted. The two countries would be the best of friends, as were France and Britain after hundreds of years of war. This was the lesson of history."[39] As we have seen, the past seven decades of relations between India and Pakistan have not been peaceful like those between France and Britain. Othering between the South Asian neighbors has only rigidified. The period witnessed three full wars and much more in South Asia, whereas the two European countries had no similar confrontations. The border-crossing point at Wagah, Punjab, witnesses the rigid mentality on a daily basis, during daily ceremonies for lowering of the flag, so much so that Michael Palin, the British filmmaker who shot the ceremony, called it "carefully choreographed contempt."[40]

Noorani and Nayar narrated a multicultural experience much affected by the partition and othering. They experienced initial belonging, witnessed partition, and resisted the animosity and hatred that partition brought in its wake. During extensive research in the border areas of Jammu and Kashmir, we came across hundreds of borderlanders who have familial ties across these borders.[41] These people, mostly nonagenarians and octogenarians, witnessed the violent partition but cherished pre-partition memories of belonging. Even those not having cross-border family ties aspired for peace between India and Pakistan. These narratives remain unheard. They are not dominating cross-cultural or international discourse. To facilitate conflict transcendence, these narratives can play a powerful role. An emphasis on narratives of othering and exclusion might reactively raise awareness about the counterproductiveness of violent conflict, but an emphasis on those of belonging and inclusion would proactively facilitate peace. Partition happened and is a reality, but bitter memories of the past need not define the present and the future.

The problem for current generations is that they did not experience pre-partition harmony and coexistence. At the same time, they did not experience partition-related violence. They are shouldering the legacy of othering by adhering to preselected narratives. The younger generation could benefit immensely from the narratives of partition and then reflect on historical developments in light of democracy, technology, and globalization. In this context, "the 1947 Partition Archive," a nongovernmental organization, aimed at "documenting, preserving and sharing eye witness accounts from all ethnic, religious and economic communities affected by the Partition of British India in 1947," serves a useful purpose in preserving partition memories. This preservation provides insights into partition and exposure to firsthand accounts of partition, which could be used to heal the deep fissures of othering wrought over decades. The website's "About Us" page provides such a long-range perspective: "It is our view that a strong foundation in history will pave the way for a more enlightened future for the subcontinent and hence the world."[42] It is crucial to highlight commonalities and belonging, which existed for centuries. On the memories of a shared past a shared future can be built. Through narrating a history of belonging, a future of belonging may be envisioned. It is important, therefore, to document stories of hope, coexistence, and belonging.

There is a need to foster new narratives of hope and harmony. In this media-dominated age where social media tools are used universally, civil society and nongovernmental organizations can play a role in promoting belonging. Various nongovernmental organizations including the South Asian Free Media Association; Aman Ki Asha (Hope for Peace); Society for the Promotion of Indian Classical Music and Culture amongst Youth (SPIC MACAY); Women in Security, Conflict Management and Peace; and South Asia Forum for Art and Creative Heritage are active in promoting belonging throughout the subcontinent. SPIC MACAY has actively pursued the goal of promoting an interethnic subcontinental popular culture among the youth of India and Pakistan. In June 2018, it hosted seventy-two Pakistani students at its event at the Indian Institute of Technology, Kharagpur. One participant stated, "We have a shared history and culture and we have so much to learn from each other."[43] Gandhi would have approved this vision of shared history and culture, or what he called "common ancestry." There is a need to encourage such interactions between the younger generations of both countries, as such interactions help them explore and reconcile diverse narratives in the spirit of belonging. These interactions also help the generation of emerging thinkers and policy makers to experience meaningful belonging. Symbolically, the song "Pasoori," released by Coke Studio in Pakistan, in May 2022, became immensely popular and had 111 million views in the same month. Shah Meer Baloch wrote in the *Guardian* reflecting on this popularity and its prospective for building bridges between the two countries: "The song has been heralded for transcending boundaries, particularly between India and Pakistan, continuing a long tradition of culture uniting the two countries where politics always failed."[44]

Face-to-face engagement is key to creating commonalities and eliminating stereotypes that fuel rivalry. Celebrating centuries of integrated culture needs to become part of the dominant discourse. Music, drama, and food cross borders and have the capacity to transcend even rigidly defined Indo-Pak boundaries. Noted Bollywood actors like Balraj Sahni, Dilip Kumar, Raj Kapoor, Dev Ananad, Sunil Dutt, and many others were born in present-day Pakistan, while noted Pakistani singers like Munni Begum, Mehdi Hassan, Reshma, and many others were from present-day India. During an orchestral concert in Srinagar in September 2013, the famous conductor Zubin Mehta said: "I have waited and dreamt of this moment for years. . . . We only want to do good. Music must go out from here to all our friends everywhere."[45] Collaboration in popular media such as films, dance, and drama needs to be actively encouraged via joint sponsorship and production to deepen understanding on both sides of the border.

The history of cross-cultural linkages is indeed legendary, and this past needs to be revived and made explicit. There is a need to appreciate the cultural map of respective religions and ethnic traditions. Religious sites crisscross the subcontinental landscape. Many of them are currently unapproachable because of border restrictions. Kuldip Nayar notes: "It was a strange partition which left so many famous Muslim monuments on the Indian side and the sites of ancient Hindu civilizations on the Pakistan side."[46] Some examples in this context are Ajmer Sharif in the city of Ajmer in India, a famous Sufi pilgrimage site, and Katas Raj Temples in Punjab of Pakistan, a Hindu religious site. Gurudwara Darbar Sahib in Kartarpur, a Sikh religious site, which Pakistan opened on the 550th birthday of Guru Nanak in November 2019 for Sikh pilgrims, is a welcome move. While inaugurating the Kartarpur corridor, connecting the Pakistan-based Sikh shrine to the border in a visa-free regime, then Pakistani prime minister Imran Khan said, "We believe that the road to prosperity of region and bright future of our coming generation lies in peace." As pilgrims crossed the border, Indian prime minister Narendra Modi thanked his Pakistan counterpart and said: "He (Imran Khan) understood India's feelings on the Kartarpur Corridor issue, gave respect and, keeping in view those feelings, worked accordingly." One of the pilgrims from the Indian city of Amritsar observed, "We are the same people, divided by a border."[47] Gandhi would encourage the opening of more such religious and cultural sites on both sides of the border.

Psychological Engagement

To use a Platonic phrase,[48] pretenses of peace via terms like *dialogue* create a semblance of peace, but they would not address the more deep-seated othering at their root. We are not arguing that economic, political, and cultural engagements have no relation to psychological belonging, and they certainly have value as conduits for encouraging unity in current India-Pakistan relations. Unless the othering at the psychological level is addressed, resolving problems at these more superficial levels is a "Band-Aid solution." This is what has been happening over the past several decades. Political agreements remained short-lived, as genuine understanding and belonging did not guide them. At best, these agreements offered a temporary reprieve in adversity before conflict reerupted. Psychological engagement is more important than economic and political engagement for addressing psychological othering, which is the impetus behind political, economic, and cultural conflict and is amplified with each act of violence: "A culture of belonging must inhabit stories, symbols, and how we see ourselves and each other. It also must inhabit the systems, policies and practices of society that make up the substance of culture."[49]

Gandhi would be doubtful about the ultimate effectiveness of agreements and treaties, based on "camouflage and hypocrisy," in promoting peace. They are bound to fail despite their "declarations of good intentions." Peace treaties emerging from political and economic bargains are akin to superstructures built on weak foundations. Imposed peace contains seeds of hostility and even leads to worse violence. This explains the failure of agreements between India and Pakistan, in which they renounced war but resumed it after a few years or decades. For example, at Tashkent in 1966, the rivals decided to maintain the status quo and cultivate peaceful relations but engaged in another war within less than a decade. Gandhi remained unshaken in his faith that a peaceful transformation is possible but, for this, half-baked, halfhearted treaties must be renounced. Such treaties might temporarily lead to the absence of direct fight and bring about a truce or delay war. Enduring peace can be realized only when there is a sincere meeting of minds and hearts. The India-Pakistan conflict is a living testimony to this Gandhian analysis—demonstrating that unless political relations emerge from a psychospiritual vision of peace, supported by statesmanship, they will not be successful. The usual political-economic arrangements based on mutual mistrust and suspicion will not produce sustainable peace.

There is a fundamental antagonism between the kind of contingent realpolitik calculus aimed at short-term gains and a Gandhian vision of peace involving long-term possibilities for promoting belonging via nonviolence. During a discussion with Gandhi in December 1947, K. M. Kariappa, the first commander in chief of the Indian army leading India in its war against Pakistan, asked, "Pakistan has no use for non-violence. How then can we win their hearts and prove the efficacy of ahimsa (nonviolence)?" Gandhi replied, "Violence can only be overcome through non-violence. This is as clear to me as the proposition that two and two make four. . . . This applies to true non-violence. But very few people have grasped this eternal truth."[50] For Gandhi, nonviolence is an effective means to counter violence but only so long as disputants grasp "this eternal truth," as he did and have similar unwavering faith in this means. This faith is a necessary bulwark against deep-seated hostility.

For Gandhi, conflict resolution is not merely resolving a crisis or a conflict. His method involves transcendence, which can only happen when psychologically there are no traces of conflict. It must entail a spiritual transformation in the souls of the parties involved in the dispute. We argue that because the India-Pakistan rivalry is not primarily territorial but psychological, embedded in the legacy of othering, it can be resolved only on a psychological plane. Such a resolution would promote an atmosphere that does not harbor or encourage mistrust and violence. From the Gandhian perspective, politicking has no place, and any diplomatic maneuvers or policies with othering at its roots are bound to fail. It seems hopelessly idealistic or naive for those "accustomed to see violence met with violence"[51] to appreciate Gandhi's moral realism—which calls for positive engagement in a project of reconciliation, peace, and belonging. Hence, when Gandhi talks about viewing one's opponent as partner rather than enemy, he is attempting to foster a spirit of belonging. The emphasis is on not using violence in any form—in words or deeds—in the attempt to promote belonging. By not offending and humiliating an opponent, a solid foundation is developed for building trust and empathy. Gandhi would assert that it is important to transcend stereotypical narratives and understand opponents' points of view while attempting to address the insecurities that prompt them.

Actions to promote peace should be genuine, not halfhearted. A political gathering or engagement solely for media coverage or consolidation of targeted constituency would be a repudiation of Gandhian principles. As Clark argues in the context of the United States, "Engagement must *both* make space for new constituents' whole selves, *and* make them equal 'co-owners' of the agenda and struggle. The former without the latter is inclusion without belonging."[52] It is difficult to have genuine engagement unless there is understanding and harmony at the level of culture and values, which inform the psychology of the group. And unless othering at these levels is addressed, it will be difficult to consolidate political and economic cooperation. Even if political and economic engagements at the purely instrumental level are successful, they will ultimately falter or remain instruments of political expediency. Policies directed toward collective belonging, and a creative disremembering of past animosity, help foster cooperation. Toward this end, the Gandhian perspective that "even if partition has happened we should behave as if there is no partition of hearts" must permeate the psychology of policy makers. New narratives must be nurtured. The narratives of "us versus them" must be replaced by the narrative of "we." Emphasizing this kind of narrative, leaders must reject the stereotypical "us-versus-them" discourse of nationalist or ethnocentric rhetoric of superiority. Akhtar reflects Gandhian principles in arguing, "It may be a long haul, but there is hope yet that 'India vs. Pakistan' eventually gives way to a shared future beyond militarism, establishments and hate."[53]

Gandhian conflict resolution assumes that, in conflict situations, all the stakeholders represent elements of truth; hence, there is no absolutely right side or absolutely wrong side in any conflict. A cooperative journey to transcend the conflict, by transgressing the binary of right and wrong, lies at the heart of this perspective. For Holmes, the Gandhian approach "assumes that in any conflict there may be truth on both sides. It strives to see that the best solution emerge whether or not it is the one to which you were initially predisposed, and even if it should require abandoning views to which you might originally have been committed. According to this approach, there is no interest in seeing either side prevail; only in seeing that the truth, in a sense that includes acknowledgment of the legitimate interests of both sides, be the final outcome of the process."[54] Indian and Pakistani narratives generally stand in sharp contrast, portraying "self" as the victim of injustice requiring defense and "the other" as the unjust aggressor deserving to be defeated and punished. Working past these narratives, they must consider each other as partners in a common cooperative effort, rather than as enemies.

Gandhian principles imply that in promoting belonging-based policies, both states must understand the congruence between rights and duties. He wrote: "I venture to suggest that rights that do not flow directly from duty well performed are not worth having. . . . If you apply this simple and universal rule to employers and laborers, landlords and tenants, the princes and their subjects, or the Hindus and the Muslims, you will find that the happiest relations can be established in all walks of life without creating disturbance in and dislocation of life and business, which you see in India and in other parts of the world."[55] This is an important statement for conflict transcendence in South Asia. The two rivals have thus far viewed conflict through the prism of their respective rights. Above and beyond this, they need to consider their duties—bilateral, national, and international—as significant as their rights. Moral duties transcend and subsume the human rights that they engender, so that recognizing rights without acknowledging and respecting moral duties is akin to treating an illness's symptoms while ignoring its causes. The rivals must decide how they want to perceive themselves and each other. If they decide to order their relations in terms of rigid othering, then the status quo of hostile relations or an all-annihilating war will remain a perpetual threat.[56]

Gandhian conflict resolution would necessitate a change in the established understanding of the means to be used and ends to be accomplished along these lines. The spirit of mutual hostility, in all forms and at all levels, needs to be eliminated. An empathetic attitude toward each other's interests and constraints is essential. Leng's contention about the need for trust and empathy to resolve the rivalry seems to emanate from Gandhian ideals: "The termination of the rivalry itself would require learning at a higher level, that is, a shift in goals as well as means. A significant reduction in the mutual distrust that infects Indo-Pakistani relations requires that both sides publicly disavow hostile goals. . . . It is not enough to change goals; the changes must be communicated to the other side in a manner that leads to trust in the other's intentions. Ultimately, diagnostic learning would have to extend to empathy, that is, an understanding of the interests of the other party, and the constraints under which it operates. Without mutual trust and empathy, there is little likelihood of . . . terminating the rivalry."[57]

Promoting belonging is indeed an arduous task. Hofstede, Hofstede, and Minkov argue that—particularly in situations like this one—a substantive change in values, or transformation in core values, is not easy. Such a transformation process necessitates sustained efforts and involves risks of failure. They conceive an onion-shaped model of culture and argue that transforming the outer layer or the outward laws, customs, and traditions of a culture are relatively easy. Learning and changing the core part of the culture is a painstaking and time-consuming process. For them, "Culture change can be fast for the outer layers of the onion diagram, labeled *practices*. Practices are the visible part of cultures. New practices can be learned throughout one's lifetime. . . . Culture change is slow for the onion's core, labeled *values*."[58] Applying this framework to South Asia, we argue it is not possible to foster belonging and dispel othering psychology overnight. New ideas, practices, and, indeed, a sea change at the psychological level must occur to promote belonging.

Ashutosh Varshney's work suggests that with continuous interactions, through social and educational institutions and intercommunal associations, communal conflicts can be minimized.[59] Applying this argument, India and Pakistan must divert their energy and resources to promote belonging.

This kind of psychological transformation necessitates a process that challenges the deep-seated othering hardened over the decades. For this, visionary leadership is essential. Nawaz and Guruswamy, while elaborating possible pathways to promote development in South Asia, argue: "Although there have been occasional moves toward confidence-building measures and most recently toward more open borders for trade, deep mistrust and suspicion mark this sibling rivalry."[60] This "sibling rivalry" is indeed deep, and unless it is addressed at the deeper psychological level, with bold decisions and visionary leadership, ad hoc political measures will not help much. Taking into account this tussle and slow curve of the learning process among the South Asian leaders, Leng suggests, there is a need for the leadership to learn the right lessons, going beyond the lessons of realpolitik and coercion, as they only fuel the conflict. He contends: "To choose to accept the risks of peace in a rivalry saturated with distrust and hostility requires extraordinary leadership skills and great personal courage. The requisite leadership skills include not only the vision to see beyond the realpolitik boundaries of the rivalry, but also the ability to impart that vision to the rest of the nation."[61]

Bissel offers four cultural strategies to promote belonging: "cultivate vibrant and diverse forms of cultural practice that support the growth of leadership and practice of those directly and deeply impacted by systems of oppression"; "amplify the knowledge, insight and vision that comes through culture and cultural production and create containers and experiences where this knowledge, insight and vision can be expressed and understood on its own terms"; "align with efforts for material, political, and social change"; and "make social and cultural change into a new 'common sense.'"[62] These strategies are important in the context of India and Pakistan relations. As both these traditional societies are guided by the top-bottom approach, in which top leadership and power holders make policies and decisions and high politics guides lower politics, it is crucial that the political leaders of both countries actively promote engagement. Leadership on both sides must develop and dynamically participate in a joint project of belonging. This cooperative spirit would undermine the current conflict emerging from lack of trust. Gandhian conflict resolution also necessitates an understanding and cocultivation of values that can address structural elements that fuel conflict. The growing trust would foster new narratives and build peaceful relationships and nonviolent institutions. For such a project of collaboration and cocultivation, a meeting of minds and hearts is more important than signing treaties and agreements.

Media can play a constructive role by bringing about the desired shift from hostility to empathy in the public's mind-set. Rather than parroting a narrative of othering and enmity, it can play a role in mobilizing masses against psychological othering. There is an urgent need in this respect to discourage rigid narratives by disengaging in rhetoric. Instead of promoting a narrative of "winning" wars, it should promote a narrative of war-as-tragedy in which everyone loses. Violent punitive responses to perceived injustices may bring short-term victory for one side, but such actions merely perpetuate the cycle of othering and conflict that undermine sustainable peace. The media can effectively communicate this message. Instead of promoting propaganda and a counterproductive narrative of "teaching wrongdoers a lesson," the media should promote a narrative that discourages violence, showcases the destructive consequences of war, and encourages cultural belonging and peace. In the post-Pulwama period, #saynotowar tweets from both sides of the borders were noteworthy, suggesting that Gandhian voices exist on both sides of the border. These sane voices need to be supported, organized, and mobilized in a project of belonging and peace. They can become part of the Gandhian army, a "nonviolent army" fighting nonviolently for peace. This idea might sound contradictory or impractical, but it is possible. Though Gandhi coined this term in reference to nonviolent workers during the Indian freedom struggle, it is directly relevant for peace in South Asia. Gandhi celebrated: "A non-violent army acts unlike armed men. . . . Theirs will be the duty of seeking occasions for bringing warring communities together, carrying on peace propaganda."[63] The nonviolent army, in which we include all those people of South Asia who have concerns for peace and belonging, can swarm the landscape of South Asia and propagate belonging and peace through peaceful means.

India and Pakistan are bound by destiny. Many aspects of their society and culture converge, and economically they complement each other. Their leaders need to demonstrate the willingness, resolve, and requisite degree of sincerity to engage with each other nonviolently. To transcend the conflict, it is necessary to move beyond symbolism. There is a need to create and hold on to a new narrative that highlights a common past and a shared future. It is pertinent to explore all possible measures to generate trust. However, the engagements at all levels must be mutual. In a belonging project, both India and Pakistan must move forward together. The project will not be successful if one country and its leaders live in the past and the other side is ready to move on. If only one side is willing to pursue belonging nonviolently, the deep-seated cycle of mistrust and hostility is unlikely to end. Politics of self-righteous indignation or chauvinistic nationalism would, of course, undermine this project. The realization of peace and the steps forward must be appreciated and mutually reciprocated. Both sides must take trust-building measures and make peace their priority. The interplay of internal and external factors that fuel their rivalry can be addressed peacefully if its root cause, othering, is addressed. Gandhi argued that there is probably no incompatibility that cannot be addressed if genuine efforts are made. The vision of Jinnah that India and Pakistan could live peacefully like Britain and France will be possible only when the leaders of both the countries display strong optimism, demonstrate bold vision, and work accordingly.

As far as the future is concerned, there are not many options available except for either a shared peace or a shared disaster. In the case of a war, gains are uncertain, but losses are certain. Can the two estranged siblings remain engaged in violence infinitely? India aspires to be a global power. Will a violent and protracted engagement with its neighbor help fulfill this aspiration? Pakistan sees itself as a regional power. The question for Pakistan is how long it will, with a fragile economy and polity, be able to sustain its confrontation with India.[64] This rivalry is consuming resources that could be used for the welfare of its people. The resources that could be used for development are squandered in hoarding arms and armaments to generate a false promise of security. Rethinking conflict along Gandhian lines offers a way forward, an alternative to a hostile relationship. Gandhi would contend that peace is possible only when both countries come forward in a spirit of peace and give up the animosity and hatred of the past. Nayar reiterates this Gandhian optimism when he writes, "I hope that one day the high walls that fear and distrust have raised on the borders will crumble and the peoples of the subcontinent . . . will work together for the common good. . . . This is the faith . . . I have clung to in the sea of hatred and hostility that has for long engulfed the subcontinent."[65] In 2016, Colombian president Juan Manuel Santos, during his Nobel Peace Prize acceptance speech, said that it is "much harder to make peace than to wage war." India and Pakistan must opt for this harder option.

Conclusion

Beyond Othering

In this study we have explored how rigid othering shaped discourses on independence and division during the early decades of the twentieth century, in pre-partition British India, and how it continues to shape post-partition relations between India and Pakistan. The clash of visions on othering and belonging led to the clash of political plans of action, which subsequently engendered the violent partition. The proponents of othering argued that two separate territories for the two cultural systems would ensure enduring peace between the two communities. Gandhi offered an alternate vision and opposed the geographical partition of British India. He attempted to address its othering through his nonviolent method. He would insist that it was the psychology of othering that engendered partition and that persists in multiple forms and places. Following the Gandhian perspective, we argued othering did not lead to one partition, but instead engendered multiple partitions in the South Asian landscape and mindscape. The geographical partition that aimed to address communal differences has, in fact, largely failed to usher in peace in the region. That geographical partition happened and erected the border is a foregone conclusion, but we argue that within a Gandhian conflict resolution framework, the psychological partition that persists needs to be addressed.

The larger question is as follows: Is partition a viable solution to conflicts? There is significant literature on both sides of the spectrum on this issue, exploring its sanguine effects and deleterious effects. An analysis of the partition does not present a very peaceful picture. Our task in this study is not to question the geographical partition, but to emphasize that the psychological othering that led to partition has persisted and manifested in multiple unsavory forms. There is a need to ameliorate its effects by promoting belonging via the application of Gandhian methods. Projected as a viable political option, the partition brought short and long-term consequences. It prompted one of the largest forced migrations in human history, the massacre of about a million people, and the displacement of millions. The post-partition situation is equally dismal, as India and Pakistan have carried the legacy of psychological othering—a spiritual mirror to physical partition—like a sacred legacy. The estranged siblings have engaged in a seemingly never-ending rivalry for the past seven decades. The costs have been enormous and multifaceted, leaving no aspect of life untouched. It is necessary, therefore, to sincerely address the reality of othering for peace and development in South Asia.

The clash of visions that guided high politics before independence and led to partition needs to be critically reexamined, as this clash was not just confined to the remote past. Such critical reflection would clarify, in novel ways, the persistent nature of the historic animosity that shapes the politics of the subcontinent. Major leaders, particularly Gandhi on one side, argued in favor of accommodating difference through belonging, while Iqbal and Jinnah, on the other side, argued in favor of addressing othering through geographical division. These leaders are long dead, but their ideas are still alive. It appears that the othering ideas of Jinnah and Iqbal succeeded, resulted in partition, and are still guiding the South Asian politics, while the ideas of Gandhi failed to persist. An analysis of the developments over more than seven decades suggests that othering-inspired partition did not foster peace, as envisaged by Iqbal and Jinnah. Using Comtean logic, we argue that the present generation of political leaders and people of South Asia are still living the ideas that shaped the past. Considering this background, we have argued that Gandhian principles remain relevant, and South Asians need to cultivate Gandhian belonging in order to resolve the India-Pakistan conflict. We have made a forward-looking argument in this book and have made a case to accept a belonging-inspired vision, beyond othering and partition, to promote pathways toward overcoming deep-seated hatred and animosity. There is an urgent need to address othering, psychological and cultural, which thrives in the South Asian psyche, by adopting the Gandhian way of belonging. Its leaders must be visionary and genuinely interested in taking their respective states forward in this direction, rather than grounding their policies in mistrust and hatred. There are some positive developments, among which we count the opening of the Kartarpur corridor in 2019 as a step toward accepting a shared cultural legacy, but such steps should not be ad hoc.

Wars and other violent means have not succeeded in securing peace, so it is necessary to put alternate means into practice. Nuclear weapons may have generated a tenuous sense of temporary security, but their use would of course be catastrophic, and a post-nuclear-conflagration South Asia would be a proverbial Einsteinian battleground where any future war would be fought with "sticks and stones." Martin Luther King, Jr. wrote, "History's most devastating war (Second World War) has swept the globe, and new weapons of terrifying dimensions have made it more clear than ever that war and civilization cannot both continue into man's future. New ways of solving conflicts, without violence, must be discovered and put into operation."[1] The hope of King, who was influenced by Gandhi, must be reflected in the context of national security. India and Pakistan are neighbors; they cannot move away from each other even if they want to. In this era of globalization, multiculturalism, and pluralism, which spread through popular communication, information technology, and social media, the time is ripe to embrace Gandhi's conception of belonging. We do not argue that othering will recede completely and promptly, and also, we do not argue that differences will be diminished completely either, as peaceful and nonviolent differences are hallmarks of healthy cultural relativism, but differences do not necessitate distancing, wars, and violence. India and Pakistan are bound by geography, and while a border separates them, it also joins them. This shared border should promote joint initiatives and an impetus toward belonging. Toward this end, Gandhian ideas are relevant.

The Man and the Mission

Gandhi remains inscrutable to many, and many still "scarce believe that such a man of flesh and blood walked upon earth," wondering how "a half-naked fakir" changed the course of history and unleashed tremendous energy for nonviolent praxis. Gandhi shaped the freedom struggle of India, and his followers, such as Martin Luther King Jr., shaped race relations in America, and Nelson Mandela and Nkrumah shaped the struggles in Africa. These are but a few examples. Gandhism is not a speculative philosophy; it is a guide for individuals, states, and global society living in harmony. *Gandhi*, in that sense, is not a proper noun, but a common noun, or rather a verb—as he does not represent a man from Porbandar—but a force, a soul force, with the ability to penetrate the minds and hearts of individuals and groups in nonviolent transformation. He is a continuum, a force, of peace. He is an embodiment of *satyagraha*, who lived and died for peace and harmony. South Asia desperately needs Gandhians in this age who could revive the Gandhian legacy of belonging and pluralism.

Johansen writes, "Probably there will never be anyone who can match Gandhi, but there are many who can follow the same path and do "experiments with the truth." To use creativity and empathy to develop new nonviolent tools; test them in conflict situations and build up a record of well documented experiences is the most important job for those interested in nonviolence in the years to come. In this work there are tasks for academics and activists from all parts of human activities."[2] For South Asia to resolve its India-Pakistan conflict, the legacy of othering must be overcome. Gandhi repeatedly argued that fuller implications and potentials of nonviolence have yet to be conceived and realized. For peace to materialize, it is necessary, first, to understand the significance of Gandhian ideas for the contemporary world and, second, to incorporate those ideas in creative policymaking. While acknowledging that Gandhian principles have limitations, we argue that it would be useful to reevaluate current dominant policy postulations, which are quite favorable to violence—toward embracing nonviolent ideas for enriching the literature and for offering policy makers suggestions regarding pursuing policy interests without engaging in violent methods. Peace efforts, to be effective and sustainable, must go beyond the dominant realpolitik thinking, and Gandhi would not object to creative experimentation for ending rigid othering. A creative conflict resolution policy, originating from a broader Gandhian conflict resolution framework and grounded in the realities of South Asia, would help address the conflict in South Asia.

To understand Gandhian belonging, one needs to fathom his world-view, which is essentially nonviolent and inclusive. For Gandhi, individuals, irrespective of their identities, are the universe in miniature—part and parcel of their ubiquitous source. In the Gandhian world, there is no dualism, no exclusiveness. He famously proclaimed that life is an integrated whole, and if one is not honest and truthful in one aspect of life, he or she cannot be honest and truthful in any other aspect. Truth, in that sense, is the very core of Gandhian belonging, and in this core nonviolence is the imperative working principle. Truth (with a capital *T*) comprises many truths in life and action, and this Truth is absolute and universal—transcending all divisions of identity, including religious and cultural ones. Simply put, Truth is absolute Truth; there is no Hindu Truth, or Islamic Truth, or Christian Truth (Gandhi uses *God* and *Truth* interchangeably as, for him, Truth is God and God is Truth). Gandhi's philosophy of Sarva Dharma Sambhava (all religions are possible, or all religions are equally potent to empower individuals for noble deeds) contended that a syncretic pluralist culture, embracing all religions and cultures, could develop within a united India. McDaniel writes: "In the past one hundred years, the most visible advocate of a non-violent blossoming of many religions was Mahatma Gandhi. His passion in life was to help build multi-religious, self-reliant communities that were socially just, ecologically wise, and spiritually satisfying for all. This passion prefigured the hopes that many people rightly have for the world today."[3]

With world affairs becoming more complex, diverse, and often divisive, there is a compelling need to advocate human harmony. Dismissing the Gandhian worldview as utopian can be done only at the risk of making humanity vulnerable to violence. Jahanbegloo argues: "We need to look at Gandhi's legacy not only as a political strategy for civil resistance, but as a broader emancipatory praxis that is creative and constructive."[4] Gandhi's inclusive vision helped him to appreciate humanity beyond constructed divisions of race, class, religion, and culture. He summoned the potential of his nonviolent force, and work for peace through nonviolence, in all possible places. It does not matter to what group, religion, identity, or ideology the subject belongs; the Gandhian nonviolence imperative effortlessly directs him to embrace all humanity in a spirit of nonviolent transformation. The Gandhian soul force is there to heal, and it is context free, as he would argue that if it can work in one place, it could work everywhere. In a Gandhian world, there is no enemy, but there are differences of opinions and values that, nonetheless, should not undermine the inner nonviolent core of the individual. For Gandhi, conflicts are a reality, differences exist, and these differences need to be resolved through nonviolent engagement. This vision guided Gandhi's opposition to partition as he "saw a solution for Hindu-Muslim national hostilities within the context of what he called 'a true civilization.'" Gandhi was a die-hard optimist and strongly believed that nonviolent belonging is possible. Even after the partition and ensuing Hindu-Muslim violence, he did not lose faith in nonviolence. He wrote in November 1947, after a few months of the partition: "'Hope for the future' I have never lost and never will, because it is embedded in my undying faith in nonviolence. What has, however, clearly happened in my case is the discovery that in all probability there is a vital defect in my technique of the working of nonviolence. . . . [F]ailure of my technique of nonviolence causes no loss of faith in nonviolence itself. On the contrary, that faith is, if possible, strengthened by the discovery of a possible flaw in the technique."[5]

Gandhi had his own set of contradictions and share of failures and successes. His nonviolent struggle against the British could be termed a success and his nonviolent struggle against the partition movement a failure. But they should not be the criteria to measure his relevance. Gandhi's vision and practice are what give his principles enduring significance. Despite any contradictions that Gandhi embodied, he was a visionary of extraordinary depth and breadth, whose monumental vision for the brotherhood of humanity makes him relevant beyond the local circumstances in which he lived and worked. Judith Brown explains:

> Gandhi was no plaster saint. Nor did he find lasting and real solutions to many of the problems he encountered. Possibly he did not even see the implications of some of them. He was a man of his time and place, with a particular philosophical and religious background, facing a specific

political and social situation. He was also deeply human, capable of heights and depths of sensation and vision, of great enlightenment and dire doubt, and the roots of his attitudes and actions were deep and tangled, as are most people's. He made good and bad choices. He hurt some, yet consoled and sustained many. He was caught in compromises inevitable in public life. But fundamentally he was a man of vision and action, who asked many of the profoundest questions that face human kind as it struggles to live in community. It was this confrontation out of a real humanity which marks his true stature and which makes his struggles and glimpses of truth of enduring significance. As a man of his time who asked the deepest questions, even though he could not answer them, he became a man for all times and all places.[6]

Gandhi's relevance should not be assessed in terms of select historic successes or failures but should be judged by virtue of its inclusive vision, which is relevant for South Asia and, indeed, a world devastated by violent othering. Gandhi's emphasis on a common civilizational bond between Muslims and Hindus offers a vision upon which a narrative of universal belonging and peace could be founded. We use the term *universal* since Gandhi would argue that peace and belonging at various levels, local, regional, and international, are connected and operate in the same social milieu.

Othering and Belonging

Broadly, there are two arguments related to religion-based nationalism. First, religious nationalism, or Islamic nationalism, is congruent with the idea of nation-states. Second, universal brotherhood, Islamic brotherhood, or *ummah*, does not recognize the borders of nation-states, as it encompasses the whole world. The second argument as articulated by Iqbal is essentially based on the assumption that a brotherhood based on Islamic tenets is the exclusive substratum of justice and equality. In his early career Iqbal wrote *Sare Jahan Se Accha Hindustan Hamara*, but his later writings witnessed a shift in philosophical temperament. His visits to the Middle East, to Egypt, Iran, and Turkey, changed his worldview. He came to view the idea of church-state separation established by the Treaty of Westphalia as an anathema, or what he would call the "biggest blunder" (among many) made by Europe. He argued that nationalism without religion is akin to a body without life, or body without soul. Religious nationalism is true nationalism, as it upholds the foundational principles of life upon which sustain social cohesion. He sought to correct the "mistake" made by Europe, by advocating for a religious, or an Islamic, state. His argument culminates in ethnocentric absolutism when he argues that only an Islamic state can provide true justice, equality, and democracy. Nationalism and religion go hand in hand, and secular nationalism, predicated on a materialist, naturalistic worldview, is bound to fail. Indeed, its failure led to two world wars. Ultimately, a religious nation, for Iqbal, is only "for facility of reference," as the supreme goal is Islamic brotherhood, which does not recognize national borders. If Islamic brotherhood is the only genuine kind of brotherhood, and the Islamic justice system is the only true justice system, it should be expected that the whole sociopolitical system in British India would be geared toward partition as an evolutionary step toward Muslim nationalism and eventual universal brotherhood.

Gandhi did not offer a sophisticated vision of nationalism. He remained an activist for most of his life, and his philosophical theories emerged from his activism. At the very outset, violence was pariah to him. He preferred an alternative to bloodshed. When Nehru was making his "tryst with destiny" speech, Gandhi was touring areas affected by communal riots to stop the violence. Gandhi constantly stressed themes involving belonging among Hindus and Muslims. What one is emphasizing in their cultural systems would depend on what kind of nationalism one is espousing, and in this emphasis, the ideas of othering and belonging would draw sustenance. For Gandhi, belonging was a unifying factor for all India's citizens irrespective of their cultural identities, but for Iqbal and Jinnah, othering was a unifying factor among Muslims and made them distinct from other groups, including Hindus. But not all Muslims rallied behind Jinnah and Iqbal. While Iqbal and Jinnah emphasized othering, leaders like Maulana Azad and Abdul Ghaffar Khan advocated belonging and believed that a united India was possible. Kuldip Nayar in *Tales of Two Cities* narrates his meeting with Azad in a Lahore college, in which Azad argued that if someone could prove that a two-nation theory is beneficial to the subcontinent, he would accept it.

Both Gandhi and Iqbal championed brotherhood but conceived of it in significantly different ways—for Iqbal it was a brotherhood of religion, while for Gandhi it was a brotherhood of humanity. While for Iqbal its distinguishing element was Islam, for Gandhi it was common culture, language, identity, and what he called "common ancestry." Iqbal's argument was compelling by virtue of its simplicity, as he appealed to a single, identifiable, factor—religion. This argument is fraught with sectarian danger: religion can be the cause of territorial division in one place, language in another place, and ethnicity in another place—hardly an inducement for peace in a pluralistic society. Gandhi disagreed with Iqbal's view and argued that the two-nation theory, and psychological othering that gave rise to this theory, would not stop at one division, but would inevitably galvanize further divisions. The eventual separation of Bangladesh from Pakistan challenges Iqbal's two-nation vision. Gandhi could foresee this regression and therefore pleaded for unity.

Gandhi staunchly opposed the partition of British India. He did not, of course, want British India to remain united at the cost of the marginalization of minorities, since it would contradict the realization of belonging which was his primary goal. His struggle was directed not only toward independence, but also for intercultural belonging: "Whatever one may be tempted to believe about Gandhi as a political leader or religious character, it is clear that for him the goal of the struggle for freedom was not only to achieve political independence, but also to establish intercultural and interfaith dialogue among different religious traditions."[7] The larger question the Gandhian approach to partition poses is as follows: Can there be a nation-state in which individuals and groups will be in equal numbers to balance out each other? The numerical equality of identity groups is an impossibility. It did not exist in British India, and the supporters of othering-based partition were very aware of the fact that even after the creation of a separate homeland for Muslims, numerical equality or homogeneity would not be a possibility in a secular India or even in an Islamic Pakistan. Both India and Pakistan were expected to have significant minority groups within their territories. In fact, no modern state has social groups with equal membership. Modern states are pluralistic, and modernization, industrialization, and globalization have aided this process. Gandhi, while aware of Iqbal-Jinnah's fears, some of which were not unfounded, was trying to hold on to the inevitable and more practical idea of a multiethnic and pluralistic Indian state.

There are multiple theories of nationalism and nation-states. Broadly, the kind of nationalism that gained ground in the nineteenth and twentieth centuries saw an increasing separation of state and religion, or secular nationalism, accommodating multiple identities within territorial states. In that sense, there are nation-states consisting of multiple identities of religion, language, race, and history. Instead of valorizing traditional identities such as religion or race, modern states have embraced secular symbols such as national flags and national anthems as markers of common national identity. In the postmodern milieu, it is difficult to find any state consisting of a single traditional identity. While religious nationalist frameworks emphasize religious othering and a single traditional identity, the framework of secular, multiethnic, and pluralistic nationalism emphasizes the principle of belonging and argues that people living in a single territory with a shared heritage—or what Gandhi called "common ancestry"—belong to one nation. Since numerical equality of religious groups in secular states is not possible, there are two major options: either promoting unity in diversity or promoting othering by providing separate homelands to conflicting identity groups. Is it a feasible idea to continue dividing a state until all identity groups have their own homelands? Do these identity-based divisions stop at some point or continue indefinitely? Does such an arrangement usher in sustainable peace? Did it happen in the case of India and Pakistan? These questions require reflection not only from those who focus on India-Pakistan relations but also from those who believe in a world of nonviolence and belonging. Gandhi was not as much worried about the "territorial shrinkage" of India as he was concerned primarily about violent othering. He strongly objected to the idea that Hindus and Muslims cannot coexist because they belonged to different cultural systems. Gandhi did not deny that cultural differences existed among Hindus and Muslims. He refused to buy the argument that these differences are irreconcilable. For him, differences between groups do not provide enough rationale for a territorial partition. Recognition of difference and peaceful coexistence do not necessitate separation but mutual appreciation and belonging.

Several factors, including the policy of divide and rule, the anxiety of marginalization of minorities by the majority, the political ambitions, the rise of extremist groups on both sides, and the vision of a religious state, contributed to psychosocial othering in South Asia. It was not that Gandhi was not cognizant of these factors, but he reverted to his core argument or first principle, evident in his letter exchanges with Jinnah, that though differences between Hindus and Muslims existed, more important commonalities existed. On this basis, he argued that in an independent India, Hindu-Muslim peaceful coexistence could be a reality. Jinnah countered this Gandhian vision and argued that the differences between Islam and Hinduism were so acute that only a geographical partition would ensure peace. Their dissimilarities are so severe that it is simply impossible to forge them into one single national identity. This endeavor, Jinnah argued, would lead to destruction. What would have happened had united India become a reality? Would it have led to destruction, as Jinnah argued, or coexistence, as Gandhi argued? This is a hypothetical question. Interestingly, with confirmation that Pakistan would be carved out of British India as a state for Muslims, Jinnah changed his stance and seemed to move closer to Gandhi. Days before Pakistan became a reality, Jinnah argued that in an independent Pakistan, all ethnic communities— Muslims, Hindus, Parsis, Christians, and majority and minority groups— would remain united and prosper. In this Jinnah revealed an inherent contradiction: arguing for the possibility of a secular pluralistic Pakistan, despite the impossibility of secular pluralism in India. Was this a break from the philosophical vision of Iqbal? Only further research can clarify this. The point is as follows: Was not Gandhi making the same argument in the Indian context as Jinnah was in the context of Pakistan? Did not he argue that the coexistence of cultural groups is possible? The difference appears to be that Gandhi was interested in applying this principle to the Indian subcontinent, and Jinnah wanted to apply it to Islamic Pakistan.

Gandhi was bothered more by the psychology of othering than by actual territorial partition. The "partition of the hearts," as Gandhi averred, personally hurt him the most. It hurt him when Jinnah claimed that Gandhi represented only Hindus. Gandhi's entire agenda revolved around his being a representative of all humanity, not of a religion. He did not represent the Hindus, as Jinnah argued, and in his "tenacious quest for Hindu-Muslim unity," he would go to the extent of supporting the Khilafat Movement to encourage Jinnah to change his mind, even to the chagrin of some of his congressional colleagues. Once partition happened, Gandhi decided to visit Pakistan in a display of cultural unity. He was assassinated before it could materialize. To argue that Gandhi represented one community, or one identity, would be utterly antithetical to the Gandhian principle. It would nullify the very principle that Gandhi espoused so dearly and for which he died.

Gandhi resisted partition and even called the idea "evil" and "sinful." He tried to engage Jinnah and the Muslim League to stop it, and he pleaded with Congress to accommodate Jinnah's demands, but once realizing the inevitability of partition he accepted it geographically, not psychologically. He believed that geographical partition is essentially the partition between brothers of a family, as he considered the whole of India to be part of a traditional joint family. Even when members of joint family are separated, their brotherhood does not end. He claimed repeatedly that, even if the land is partitioned, the people of India and Pakistan should behave as if their hearts are joined.

Gandhi mourned the partition; the nonviolent worker in him mourned the defeat of his ideal. More important, he was worried that partition would not resolve the real separation it involved, since its mainspring, the psychology of othering, would persist and violence would continue. This fear was not unfounded. Gandhian skepticism that othering would persist proved true. His wish that India and Pakistan would live and thrive as friendly neighbors did not materialize. Gandhi had argued that unless othering at the psychological level is addressed, unless the deep-seated violence in the minds and hearts is dealt with, it is unlikely that geographical partition will bring peace in the region. It will persist and manifest in multiple ways. That the India-Pakistan hostility has not ended even after seven decades corroborates how this Gandhian fear was substantial. India and Pakistan expend huge resources to support this hostility—to supporting war, war machines, and nationalist propaganda, while people suffer from underdevelopment and poverty.

The book is not about dissecting the past or pronouncing judgments; rather, it is about learning from the past and moving forward toward a future of belonging. We have not claimed that one culture or cultural value, whether Hindu or Islam, is superior or inferior to other in achieving this. Following the cultural relativist approach of French anthropologist Claude Lévi-Strauss, we believe that "one culture has no absolute criteria for judging the activities of another culture as 'low' or 'noble.'"[8] What we have attempted to show instead is that cultural understanding and belonging are an essential requirement for peace in South Asia, and in this direction, Gandhi's ideas are relevant. For Gandhi, othering is essentially violent. It entails psychological violence and takes material forms. For him, nonviolence is an absolute value; it is not something contingent or conditional. The individual practicing nonviolence must be an embodiment of belonging; their whole being must reflect the connection with others. Despite opposition from his colleagues in the Congress, Gandhi suspended the Non-Cooperation Movement, which he had initiated against the British rule, when it incited an incident of violence. Nonviolence is not an instrument of weak or coward, or for someone who perceives it as a onetime opportunity, and then relinquishes it when the occasion demands. British rule itself was a manifestation of othering and violence, but he would not use violent means to fight the British or Jinnah. Jinnah's call for Direct Action aggrieved Gandhi, and instead of getting involved in a cycle of recrimination, he traveled across the length and breadth of India to douse the communal fire that the call generated. Nonviolence for Gandhi is a supreme virtue, and he would risk failure before violating it. Even when nonviolent methods failed to change Jinnah's mind, Gandhi would not resort to violence.

Gandhian passion to be a nonviolent worker had, as Bertrand Russell wrote, the "smell" of Saint Francis. In Gandhi's worldview there is no place for violence or its myriad overt and covert manifestations, including war, revenge, politicking, exploitation of minorities by the majority, subterfuge, and showmanship. When Congress hesitated to give the newly created Pakistan its due share of financial revenues, Gandhi resorted to fasting in protest, and Congress had to comply. Can this nonviolence principle of Gandhi become the norm for politics in South Asia? Such a vision may not appear plausible in the near future. But then, should violence be accepted as the normal method of political engagement in South Asia? How effective has the coercive method been in the past to bring peace? The answer, as we know, does not evoke hope. With all its limitations, there are elements in Gandhian thought that are relevant for conflict resolution in South Asia. Gandhi's argument that communities and individuals must learn to understand and respond to the complex set of factors that initiate and sustain violence needs serious reflection. If the root causes of violence, othering being the major one, are not addressed, peace will remain a chimera.

Transcending Othering

Gandhian conflict resolution has three broad elements: first, conflict is an unavoidable reality of human life; second, the inevitability of conflict must be acknowledged; and third, conflict must be addressed nonviolently so that it can be transcended. Conflict, for Gandhi, has an ontological value to human life; they are inseparable. Conflicts are everywhere: individuals, groups, larger societies, nations, and the world. The Gandhian conflict lexicon would include all the levels of conflicts and neglect none of these in the nonviolent conflict resolution process, which emphasizes the recognition of a fundamental factor—disharmony in our perception about ourselves and others—in the making of a conflict and then explores peaceful pathways to address that disharmony. Gandhi would apply the logic of disharmony to all levels of conflicts, though he would readily accept that operationality or degree of disharmony would vary from level to level. This disharmony led othering and its various manifestations, including, but not limited to, greed, hatred, and selfishness lead to violent conflicts, and until they are addressed nonviolently, such conflicts would continue to exist with varying intensities.

Broadly, there are two ways—violent and nonviolent—to address a conflict. For Gandhi, violent means are immoral and evil, and nonviolent means are moral and preferred as they are based on soul force. Gandhi never claimed that he is the discoverer of the principle of nonviolence or the first person to apply it; he often admitted that nonviolence is "as old as the hills." He traced the origin of nonviolence to ancient times and called the discoverers "greater geniuses than Newton." This epithet might sound exaggerated but not without its Gandhian logic; even with the means of violence at their command, these discoverers followed the path of nonviolence. Gandhi reasoned, if the nonviolent method fails, the fault is not with the method but with the practitioner. He had an unwavering conviction in the nonviolent method to bring desired change, and he put that conviction into practice despite all the hardships in his struggles against injustice in South Africa in his early career and then in India. When a colleague doubted the efficacy of the nonviolent method to fight the mighty British colonial power and argued that history does not offer a successful freedom struggle through nonviolence, Gandhi responded with his usual humor, without compromising the essence of his argument, saying that the history book is not yet complete as there are many pages to be written. This conviction had a deluge effect on Gandhi's followers as they followed their leader to fight the British might with weapons of courage and nonviolence and did not waver from the nonviolent path despite untold atrocities. American journalist Webb Miller described vividly how the Gandhian protesters unwaveringly practiced nonviolence during Salt Satyagraha despite police brutality and provocation.

Nonviolent transcendence does not imply the victory of one party to a conflict at the cost of the other. Gandhi would abhor such a goal. Conflict transcendence for him is not to view a solution through the binaries of winning or losing, victory or defeat, or even win-win. It is more than that. It is not something to be realized through superficial negotiations, arbitrations, agreements, or dialogues. Transcendence involves not only resolution of the conflict but also dissolution of violence in the mind and, by extension, also in the collective mind of communities. Unless agreements, negotiations, and declarations are genuinely aimed at belonging, the results will not be lasting.

In what ways is Gandhi relevant to South Asia? Can his thoughts be productively used to promote belonging without compromising diverse cultural values of the communities? All these crucial questions we have explored in this book. We have argued that there are multiple pathways that emerge from Gandhian nonviolent praxis—some of them perhaps are yet to be discovered as they demand ingenuity, contextualization, and a deeper understanding of the evolving dynamics in the South Asian region—but they all need visionary political leadership and a national commitment to peace. Dialogues, summits, negotiations, talks, meetings, and political ceremonies have their own value, but they will not address the conflict unless they emerge from a deeper psychology of nonviolent belonging. A Gandhian would point to the failure of past summits and agreements and make a case for enabling peace emerging out of empathy and deeper understanding of each other's positions. The past seven decades amply demonstrate that words and deeds, shaped by the psychology of othering, failed to bring desired outcome—peace. Policy makers must internalize the core message of Gandhi and accordingly craft policies. This remains an arduous task, though; it would require audacity, passion, and perseverance. Did not Gandhi say, it takes courage to follow the path of nonviolence and work for peace?

Emphasizing policies to promote belonging, we have argued that psychological engagement is the fulcrum of enabling peace. The argument of Jinnah in the context of partition—one culture's hero is another culture's villain—might appear true, but, at the same time, it cannot be denied that there are elements common to both Hindu and Muslim cultural systems that need recognition, to be cultivated to promote belonging. We have explored the India-Pakistan conflict in this book, but we argue that our emphasis on commonalities and their exploration is salient for conflictual relations emerging from othering at other places, between the states and within the states. Instead of promoting othering, as reflected in rambunctious ceremonies like those at the Wagah border—characterized as "carefully choreographed contempt"—it is necessary to craft ways to cultivate belonging between the cultures, reflected in language, dance, drama, music, food, and dress. In this endeavor, the people who witnessed partition could play a prominent and inspiring role. Their heartrending stories could effectively recall the pain of othering and generate catharsis in the present generation—motivating them to think in novel ways and inaugurating a mass campaign to end violent othering. The campaign could

also focus on documenting and promoting narratives of care, cooperation, and compassion. It could generate hope in younger generations for a
new South Asia. Gandhi hoped students will be harbingers of belonging
and wrote on August 18, 1947, just after a few days of partition, "Students
are the makers of the future. They cannot be partitioned."[9] He urged the
youth "to shed your indifference, inertia and sloth and throw yourselves
into constructive work with all your heart and soul."[10]

Both countries have enough potential to cooperate economically, but
there is hardly any such cooperation. South Asia is one of the least integrated regions economically, despite the efforts of organizations like the
South Asian Association for Regional Cooperation, whereas other culturally diverse regions like East Asia and Europe are well integrated. During
our research in the border areas of Jammu and Kashmir, we documented
the desperation of local people who have family members on the other
side of the border, along with their longing to open the border. The Silk
Road, which crisscrossed the subcontinent and connected the Indian subcontinent, Central Asia, China, and beyond, could be employed in this
belonging project. It would be in the interest of both India and Pakistan to
engage in road-revival efforts.

Political engagements need to be buttressed. A common destiny binds
India and Pakistan; a border separates them but also connects them. They
share nature's bounties in the form of rivers, flora, fauna and mountains,
and nature's fury, such as landslides, fires, and earthquakes. It is not that
there has been a dearth of visionary leaders in the two countries, but it
seems that the cloud of othering is so dark that the sky of opportunities is
hidden from their view. The heavy historical baggage of othering pervad-
ing the cultural ethos is powerful. In the past, leaders from both countries
attempted to promote peace, but many of those attempts were marred
by othering. For example, Vajpayee-Musharraf dialogue was spoiled by
the Indian Parliament attack, and Singh-Zardari peace moves initiatives
were undermined by the Mumbai terror attack. Spoilers, the radical constituencies that do not want peace to dawn in South Asia, play a part in
thwarting peace attempts. Only a vital and bold new vision and political
will can thwart the trajectory set by these spoilers and prioritize a project
of belonging via genuine nonviolent engagements at multiple levels. As

Gandhi argued, halfhearted attempts to maximize one's gains at the cost of exploiting the other cannot lead to conflict transcendence. And genuine engagement is possible only when political leaders act as statesmen rising above political gamesmanship and genuinely prioritize belonging in their policies.

In the twenty-first-century world, where the idea of a borderless world is increasingly accepted and cultivated, India and Pakistan need to galvanize their apparatuses to promote belonging. In this direction the Gandhian conviction that violence is a failed method to resolve the conflict must take deep roots. The past attempts to build peace were either symbolic or halfhearted as they lacked political vision. The spoilers on both sides of the border profit from the conflictual relationship. They invest heavily in the continuation of the conflict and attempt to create and stabilize a situation in which the conflict continues to boil, and the political and defense machineries continue to waste scarce resources and legitimize their othering agenda. The question is as follows: Can othering thrive infinitely? If othering continues, as history stands witness, the conflict will not end, though it might see periods of stagnation. There is an increasing possibility of escalation, exacting further psychological, cultural, political, and economic costs. The political leaders, media, corporate houses, think tanks, civil society, and nonstate organizations from both sides of the border must come together to play their part in promoting engagement and belonging. Such a mission, undertaken by all with a spirit of belonging, Gandhi would argue, is not an extravagance but a necessity. It will be a gradual process, but it will bring desired results if engineered with the right intention. The Gandhian vision of nonviolent conflict transcendence, in which othering is relegated to the dustbin of history and belonging becomes the future, when realized, will transform a violent present via a field of nonviolent praxis. While the past witnessed othering and partition and the present carries the legacy of the past, it is not necessary that the future resembles the past or the present.

Revolutionary Pakistani poet Faiz Ahmed Faiz, who called Gandhi a "true servant of humanity," wrote a poem, "The Dawn of Freedom," in August 1947. The poem evokes pangs of partition and longing for belonging:

This is not that Dawn for which . . .
we had set out in sheer longing . . .
Did the morning breeze ever come? . . .
Night weighs us down, it still weighs us down.
Friends, come away from this false light. Come, we must
search for that promised Dawn.[11]

Did not Gandhi say, "If our hearts are true, we should behave as if they (the hearts) had not been partitioned"? It is time that India and Pakistan heed Gandhi and work together for a peaceful South Asia.

Notes

Bibliography

Index

Notes

Introduction: Partition, South Asian Conflict, and Gandhi

1. "Othering" has negative and positive dimensions. In its positive dimension, well captured by the term "unity in diversity," it recognizes different ideas and identities in society and encourages mutual understanding and belonging. Multicultural societies thrive as different social groups live in harmony and do not perceive each other in hostile terms. The differences do not lead to violence, per se. In its negative dimension, "othering" adopts an essentialist view of culture, seeing cultures as separate and rigid. This view leads to the creating of the other, clash of identities, and violence. In this study, we focus on this negative dimension of "othering." There is a rich literature on the subject. See, for example, G. Baumann, *Contesting Culture*; G. Hofstede, G. J. Hofstede, and M. Minkov, *Culture and Organizations: Software of the Mind*; A. I. Alami, *Mutual Othering: Islam, Modernity, and the Politics of Cross-Cultural Encounters in Pre-colonial Moroccan and European Travel Writing*; T. D. Boyce and W. M. Chunnu, *Historicizing Fear: Ignorance, Vilification, and Othering*; Zachary Smith, *Age of Fear: Othering and American Identity during World War I*; Emmanuel Levinas, *Le temps et l'autre (Time and the Other): Lectures in Paris at the College Philosophique, 1946–1947*; Emmanuel Levinas, *Totalité et infini (Totality and Infinity)*; and Martine Abdallah-Pretceille, "Interculturalism as a Paradigm for Thinking about Diversity."

2. Quoted in Jawaharlal Nehru, *The Discovery of India*, 20. Nehru wrote, "We live, as Auguste Comte said, dead men's lives, encased in our pasts, but this is especially so in prison where we try to find some sustenance for our starved and locked-up emotions in memory of the past or fancies of the future." Nehru wrote this famous book while in prison in the 1940s.

3. For example, see Phillips Talbot, *An American Witness to India's Partition*; Pippa Virdee, *From the Ashes of 1947: Reimagining Punjab*; Gyanendra Pandey, *Remembering Partition: Violence, Nationalism and History in India*; Yasmin Khan, *The Great Partition: The Making of India and Pakistan*; Suvir Kaul, ed., *The Partitions of Memory: The Afterlife of the Division of India*; Ian Talbot and Gurharpal Singh, *The Partition of India*; B. R. Ambedkar, *Pakistan; or, The Partition of India*; Joya Chatterji, *The Spoils of*

Partition: Bengal and India, 1947–1967; Ishtiaq Ahmed, *The Punjab Bloodied, Partitioned and Cleansed*; Jaswant Singh, *Jinnah: India—Partition—Independence*; C. H. Philips and M. D. Wainwright, eds., *The Partition of India: Policies and Perspectives, 1935–1947*; Ayesha Jalal, *The Sole Spokesman: Jinnah, the Muslim League, and the Demand for Pakistan*; Sukeshi Kamra, *Bearing Witness: Partition, Independence, End of the Raj*; Ritu Menon and Kamla Bhasin, *Borders and Boundaries: How Women Experienced the Partition of India*; and Vazira Zamindar, *The Long Partition and the Making of Modern South Asia: Refugees, Boundaries, Histories*.

4. David Gilmartin, "Partition, Pakistan, and South Asian History: In Search of a Narrative."

5. Walker Connor, "Nation-Building or Nation-Destroying?," 320.

6. In the French Revolution, Durkheim found the historical moment when new sacred forms of modernity appeared as "things purely laical in nature were transformed . . . into sacred things: the Fatherland, Liberty and Reason." Emile Durkheim, *The Elementary Forms of the Religious Life*, 214. Robert Bellah in his study "Civil Religion in America," draws on the work of Durkheim and argues that the civil religion in America was not linked to a particular church or supernatural religion, but to a collection of beliefs, symbols, and rituals that sanctified the national community. From this perspective, the American flag and the national anthem can be considered sacred symbols of the state. According to Bellah, Durkheim "believed that traditional religion was on its way out, essentially because it conflicts with science. But the concept of the sacred would remain: without this basis of moral respect society itself is impossible. But what would be the referent to which sacred symbols refer? Durkheim replied 'society,' and as the most comprehensive functioning society the 'nation'" (47). For a fuller exposition of Bellah's argument, see Robert Bellah, "Durkheim and History."

7. Stanley Waterman, "Partitioned States"; Brendan O'Leary, Ian Lustick, and Thomas Callaghy, *Right-Sizing the State: The Politics of Moving Borders*; Nicholas Sambanis, "Partition as a Solution to Ethnic War: An Empirical Critique of the Theoretical Literature"; Liam Anderson, *Federal Solutions to Ethnic Problems: Accommodating Diversity*; Daniel Byman, *Keeping the Peace: Lasting Solutions to Ethnic Conflicts*; Thomas Chapman and Philip Roeder, "Partition as a Solution to Wars of Nationalism: The Importance of Institutions"; Carter Johnson, "Keeping the Peace after Partition: Ethnic Minorities, Civil Wars, and the Third Generation Ethnic Security Dilemma"; Chaim Kaufmann, "Possible and Impossible Solutions to Ethnic Civil Wars."

8. J. C. Turner and R. Y. Bourhis, "Social Identity, Interdependence and the Social Groups: A Reply to Rabbie et al.," 51.

9. John Burton, *Resolving Deep-Rooted Conflict: A Handbook*, 3.

10. Burton, *Resolving Deep-Rooted Conflict*, 3.

11. J. P. Lederach, *Preparing for Peace: Conflict Transformation across Cultures*, 8.

12. John Agnew, "Beyond Reason: Spatial and Temporal Sources of Ethnic Conflicts," 42.

13. Debidatta Aurobinda Mahapatra, *Conflict Management in Kashmir: State-People Relations and Peace*.

14. Annemarie Schimmel, *Gabriel's Wing: A Study into the Religious Ideas of Sir Muhammad Iqbal*, 84. Here is the full quote: "I had seen in a dream that a black dressed army was riding on Arab horses; I felt that they were angels. As to me the explanation of this dream is that in the near future a new movement will appear in Islamic countries. The meaning of Arab horses is the spirit of Islam."

15. Schimmel, *Gabriel's Wing*, 19.

16. Muhammad Iqbal, *Reconstruction of Religious Thought in Islam*.

17. Bhikhu Parekh, *Rethinking Multiculturalim: Cultural Diversity and Political Theory*, 16.

18. For the full text of the speech, see http://www.columbia.edu/itc/mealac/pritchett/00islamlinks/txt_iqbal_1930.html.

19. P. Talbot, *American Witness*, 45.

20. H. Kulke and D. Rothermund, *A History of India*, 232.

21. P. Talbot, *American Witness*, 102.

22. Kulke and Rothermund, *A History of India*, 235.

23. Quoted in W. David McIntyre, *The Commonwealth of Nations: Origins and Impact, 1869–1971*, 227.

24. Presidential address by Muhammad Ali Jinnah to the Muslim League, Lahore, 1940, http://www.columbia.edu/itc/mealac/pritchett/00islamlinks/txt_jinnah_lahore_1940.html.

25. Ambedkar, *Pakistan*, http://www.columbia.edu/itc/mealac/pritchett/00ambedkar/ambedkar_partition/index.html#contents.

26. Nehru, *The Discovery of India*, 59.

27. The commission was created by the United Nations in 1948 to "investigate and mediate" India-Pakistan conflict. The two newly independent states waged a war over Kashmir after a few months of their independence. The UN-mediated cease-fire ended this war.

28. Josef Korbel, *Danger in Kashmir*.

29. Sisir Gupta, *Kashmir: A Study in India-Pakistan Relations*.

30. For example, while the World Bank and the regional organization South Asian Association for Regional Cooperation include eight countries—India, Pakistan, Bangladesh, Nepal, Bhutan, Sri Lanka, Maldives, and Afghanistan—in their definition of South Asia, the United Nations adds Iran in its definition. Myanmar, a part of British India until 1937, was earlier included in the definition of South Asia, though it has now become a part of the Southeast Asian region and a full member of Association of Southeast Asian

Nations. In his 1969 study of ethnolinguistic composition of South Asia and its political implications, Connor includes the following states: "Afghanistan, Burma (Myanmar), Cambodia, India, Laos, Mainland Malaysia, Nepal, Pakistan, Singapore, Thailand, Vietnam North, and Vietnam South." See Walker Connor, "Ethnology and the Peace of South Asia."

31. L. van de Goor, K. Rupesinghe, and P. Sciarone, eds., *Between Development and Destruction: An Enquiry into the Causes of Conflict in Post-colonial States*, 7.

32. Connor, "Ethnology and the Peace of South Asia," 55.

33. S. P. Cohen, *Shooting for a Century: The India-Pakistan Conundrum*.

34. T. V. Paul, ed., *The India-Pakistan Conflict: An Enduring Rivalry*.

35. For example, see Ashok Kapur, "Major Powers and the Persistence of the India–Pakistan Conflict"; R. C. Tremblay and J. Schofield, "Institutional Causes of the India–Pakistan Rivalry"; R. J. Leng, "Realpolitik and Learning in the India–Pakistan Rivalry"; and R. M. Burke, *Mainsprings of Indian and Pakistani Foreign Policies*.

36. Burke, *Mainsprings of Indian and Pakistani Foreign Policies*.

37. Sumit Ganguly, *Conflict Unending: India-Pakistan Tensions since 1947*, 1.

38. Virdee, *From the Ashes of 1947*, 3.

39. For example, see Foster Klug, "Pakistan PM Warns of War with India over Disputed Kashmir," Associated Press, Sept. 24, 2019, https://apnews.com/f6c5960c3a9a48 c2a98508081271c55e; and Julian Borger and Azhar Farooq, "Imran Khan Warns UN of Potential Nuclear War in Kashmir," *Guardian*, Sept. 26, 2019, https://www.theguardian .com/world/2019/sep/26/imran-khan-warns-un-of-potential-nuclear-war-in-kashmir.

40. O. B. Toon et al., "Rapidly Expanding Nuclear Arsenals in Pakistan and India Portend Regional and Global Catastrophe."

41. Stanley Wolpert, *India and Pakistan: Continued Conflict or Cooperation?*, 2.

42. Peter Popham, "'The World's Most Dangerous Place' Is Already at War," *Independent*, Mar. 18, 2000, https://www.independent.co.uk/news/world/asia/the-worlds-most -dangerous-place-is-already-at-war-282458.html.

43. George Orwell, "Reflections on Gandhi," 85.

44. John Lewis, *The Case against Pacifism*.

45. U. S. Mehta, "Gandhi and the Common Logic of War and Peace," 156.

46. M. K. Gandhi, *The Collected Works of Mahatma Gandhi*, 87:432–33, 88:341, 130, 125.

47. In 1946, to one of his colleague's complaint that he was busy most of the time, Gandhi quipped, "Unless I did that I would have to give up the desire to live up to the age of 125 which I must not do, if my dream of nonviolence as a world-conquering force is to be realized." See Gandhi, *Collected Works of Gandhi*, 84:20.

48. Thomas Weber, "Gandhian Philosophy, Conflict Resolution Theory and Practical Approaches to Negotiation," 493. In another important work, Weber focuses on the organization Shanti Sena, which, influenced by Gandhi, used nonviolent methods in

postindependent India. See Thomas Weber, *Gandhi's Peace Army: The Shanti Sena and Unarmed Peacekeeping*.

49. M. K. Gandhi, *Autobiography: The Story of my Experiments with Truth*.

50. Douglas Allen, "Mahatma Gandhi on Violence and Peace Education," 294.

51. Ashutosh Varshney, *Ethnic Conflict and Civic Life: Hindus and Muslims in India*, 237.

52. Gandhi, *Collected Works of Gandhi*, 84:127.

53. Kenneth Boulding, *Conflict and Defense: A General Theory*, 324.

54. Mark Juergensmeyer, "Gandhi vs. Terrorism," 30.

55. Gene Sharp, "Gandhi's Political Significance Today," 169.

56. Amartya Sen, "Gandhi Values and Terrorism," 76.

57. Gandhi, *Collected Works of Gandhi*, 28:305.

1. Gandhian Conflict Resolution

1. "Pelosi Remarks at Embassy of India MLK and Gandhi Reception," press release, Oct. 3, 2019, https://www.speaker.gov/newsroom/10319-0.

2. Secretary-general's remarks at the event: "Leadership Matters: Relevance of Mahatma Gandhi in the Contemporary World," Sept. 24, 2019, https://www.un.org/sg/en/content/sg/statement/2019-09-24/secretary-generals-remarks-the-event-leadership-matters-relevance-of-mahatma-gandhi-the-contemporary-world-delivered.

3. Quoted in Matthew Stabley, "Obama's Ideal Dinner Guest: Gandhi, President Talks to Group of Wakefield Freshman before National Address," Sept. 8, 2009, https://www.nbcwashington.com/news/local/obama-would-love-to-host-gandhi-for-a-small-meal/1879875/.

4. Quoted in Paul Vale, "Mahatma Gandhi Statue Unveiled by David Cameron in London's Parliament Square," Mar. 14, 2015, https://www.huffingtonpost.co.uk/2015/03/14/gandhi-statue-unveiled-by-david-cameron-outside-parliament-in-london_n_6869536.html.

5. Weber, "Gandhian Philosophy," 493.

6. For instance, see Joan V. Bondurant, *Conquest of Violence: The Gandhian Philosophy of Conflict*; Arne Naess, *Gandhi and Group Conflict: An Exploration of Satyagraha*; Johan Galtung, *The Way Is the Goal: Gandhi Today*; and Georg Sorensen, "Utopianism in Peace Research: The Gandhian Heritage."

7. Robert E. Klitgaard, "Gandhi's Non-violence as a Tactic," 143.

8. Veena R. Howard, *Gandhi's Ascetic Activism: Renunciation and Social Action*.

9. See, for instance, Michael Brown, ed., *Ethnic Conflict and International Security*; Michael Brown, ed., *The International Dimensions of Internal Conflict*; R. Stavenhagen, *Ethnic Conflicts and the Nation-State*; Kalevi Holsti, *The State, War, and the State of War*; and Goor, Rupesinghe, and Sciarone, *Between Development and Destruction*.

10. To understand the complexity, see Anthony D. Smith, "Conflict and Collective Identity: Class, Ethnie and Nation"; Burton, *Resolving Deep-Rooted Conflict*; Louis Kriesberg, Terrell Northrup, and S. Thorson, eds., *Intractable Conflicts and Their Transformation*; and Edward Rice, *Wars of the Third Kind: Conflict in Underdeveloped Countries*.

11. Dave Mosher, "If India and Pakistan Have a 'Limited' Nuclear War, Scientists Say It Could Wreck Earth's Climate and Trigger Global Famine," *Business Insider*, Feb. 28, 2019, https://www.businessinsider.com/india-pakistan-kashmir-nuclear-weapons-climate-cooling.

12. Anima Bose, "A Gandhian Perspective on Peace," 163.

13. Gerald H. Shure, Robert J. Meeker, and Earle A. Hansford, "The Effectiveness of Pacifist Strategies in Bargaining Games."

14. Morton Deutsch et al., "Strategies of Inducing Cooperation: An Experimental Study."

15. Gandhi, *Collected Works of Gandhi*, 28:305.

16. Nehru once said Gandhi "was no dreamer living in some fantasy of his own creation, cut off from life and its problems." Jawaharlal Nehru, *Nehru on Gandhi*, 83.

17. G. Sharp, "The Role of Power in Nonviolent Struggle," 18.

18. Quoted in Polly Toynbee, "Now We Know: Conventional Campaigning Won't Prevent Our Extinction," *Guardian*, May 1, 2019, https://www.theguardian.com/comment isfree/2019/may/01/extinction-rebellion-non-violent-civil-disobedience. See also Sean Scalmer, *Gandhi in the West: The Mahatma and the Rise of Radical Protest*. In this study, Scalmer presents cases of protests that were influenced by Gandhi.

19. Jørgen Johansen, "Nonviolence: More than the Absence of Violence," 152.

20. The interesting literature includes Erica Chenoweth and Maria Stephan, "Why Civil Resistance Works: The Strategic Logic of Nonviolent Conflict"; Sharon E. Nepstad, *Nonviolent Revolutions: Civil Resistance in the Late 20th Century*; Renat Shaykhutdinov, "Give Peace a Chance: Nonviolent Protest and the Creation of Territorial Autonomy Arrangements"; Isak Svensson and Mathilda Lindgren, "From Bombs to Banners? The Decline of Wars and the Rise of Unarmed Uprisings in East Asia"; Brian Martin, *Uprooting War*; Gene Sharp, *The Politics of Nonviolent Action*; Peter Ackerman and Jack DuVall, *A Force More Powerful: A Century of Nonviolent Conflict*; Doug McAdam and Sidney Tarrow, "Nonviolence as Contentious Interaction"; and Robert L. Holmes and Barry L. Gan, *Nonviolence in Theory and Practice*.

21. Erica Chenoweth and Kathleen Gallagher Cunningham, "Understanding Nonviolent Resistance: An Introduction," 273.

22. Ramin Jahanbegloo, *The Gandhian Moment*, 157.

23. Johan Galtung, "On the Meaning of Nonviolence," 228.

24. Johansen, "Nonviolence," 143.

25. Steven Pinker, *The Better Angels of Our Nature: Why Violence Has Declined*; Joshua Goldstein, *Winning the War on War: The Decline of Armed Conflict Worldwide*.

26. David Hardiman, *Gandhi in His Time and Ours: The Global Legacy of His Ideas*; Michael J. Nojeim, *Gandhi and King: The Power of Non-violent Resistance*.

27. Johansen, "Nonviolence," 143.

28. Robert L. Holmes, *On War and Morality*, 276.

29. Gandhi, *Collected Works of Gandhi*, 84:440–41.

30. Gandhi, *Collected Works of Gandhi*, 43:268–69.

31. Gandhi wrote a letter to Adolf Hitler on December 24, 1940, appealing him to adopt a nonviolent method against the Allied powers. He wrote: "Dear Friend, that I address you as a friend is no formality. I own no foes. My business in life has been for the past 33 years to enlist the friendship of the whole of humanity by befriending mankind, irrespective of race, color or creed. I hope you will have the time and desire to know how a good portion of humanity who have been living under the influence of that doctrine of universal friendship view your action. . . . Is it too much to ask you to make an effort for peace during a time which may mean nothing to you personally but which must mean much to the millions of Europeans whose dumb cry for peace I hear, for my ears are attended to hearing the dumb millions?" Gandhi, *Collected Works of Gandhi*, 73:253. He appealed Hitler "in the name of humanity" to stop the war: "You will lose nothing by referring all the matters of dispute between you and Great Britain to an international tribunal of your joint choice. If you attain success in the war, it will not prove that you were in the right. It will only prove that your power of destruction was greater. Whereas an award by an impartial tribunal will show as far as it is humanly possible which party was in the right" (255).

32. Gandhi, *Collected Works of Gandhi*, 68:57.

33. Johansen, "Nonviolence," 147.

34. Holmes, *On War and Morality*, 276.

35. Sharp, "Gandhi's Political Significance Today," 169.

36. Juergensmeyer, "Gandhi vs. Terrorism," 30.

37. Juergensmeyer, "Gandhi vs. Terrorism," 30.

38. Paul F. Power, "A Gandhian Model for World Politics," 295.

39. Power, "Gandhian Model for World Politics," 295.

40. Douglas Allen, *Gandhi after 9/11: Creative Nonviolence and Sustainability*.

41. Johansen, "Nonviolence," 143.

42. Dean G. Pruitt and Jeffrey Z. Rubin, *Social Conflict: Escalation, Stalemate and Settlement*.

43. Lewis A. Coser, *The Functions of Social Conflict*.

44. Burton, *Resolving Deep-Rooted Conflict*.

45. Johan Galtung, "Introduction: Peace by Peaceful Conflict Transformation—the TRANSCEND Approach," 22.

46. Hugh Miall, *The Peacemakers*. For an interesting account of conflict and peace paradox, see also Hugh Miall, Oliver Ramsbotham, and Tom Woodhouse, *Contemporary Conflict Resolution: The Prevention, Management and Transformation of Deadly Conflicts*.

47. Holsti, *State, War, and the State of War,* 123.

48. Lester Kurtz, "Gandhi and His Legacies," 840.

49. Galtung, "Introduction," 8.

50. Gandhi, *Collected Works of Gandhi,* 42:452–53.

51. Mohandas K. Gandhi, *Hind Swaraj, and Other Writings,* 81.

52. Joan V. Bondurant, "Satyagraha versus Duragraha: The Limits of Symbolic Violence," 107.

53. Gandhi, *Collected Works of Gandhi,* 28:305.

54. John Sifton, *Violence All Around,* 192.

55. Gandhi, *Collected Works of Gandhi,* 83:279.

56. Scalmer, *Gandhi in the West.*

57. Sankar Ghose, *Mahatma Gandhi.* See esp. chap. 27, "INA, Cabinet Mission and Independence," 321–45.

58. M. K. Gandhi, *All Men Are Brothers: Autobiographical Reflections,* vii.

59. Gandhi, *Collected Works of Gandhi,* 73:253, 31:142, 67:437.

60. Gandhi, *Collected Works of Gandhi,* 9:471.

61. Rabindranath Tagore, *Home and the World,* 25–26.

62. Johan Galtung, "Violence, Peace, and Peace Research," 183.

63. Galtung, "Violence, Peace, and Peace Research," 183.

64. Mehta, "Gandhi and the Common Logic of War and Peace."

65. Mehta, "Gandhi and the Common Logic of War and Peace," 134.

66. Gandhi, *Collected Works of Gandhi,* 27:133–34.

67. Raymond Aron, *Peace and War: A Theory of International Relations.*

68. Gandhi, *Collected Works of Gandhi,* 84:127.

69. Boulding, *Conflict and Defense,* 324.

70. Gandhi, *Collected Works of Gandhi,* 40:365.

71. See, for instance, Edward Azar, *The Management of Protracted Social Conflict: Theory and Causes.*

72. R. Raj Singh, "Gandhi and the Fundamentals of World Peace."

73. Roy J. Eidelson and Judy I. Eidelson, "Dangerous Ideas: Five Beliefs That Propel Groups toward Conflict."

74. A. H. Maslow, "A Theory of Human Motivation."

75. For instance, see John Burton, *Violence Explained.*

76. Gandhi, *Collected Works of Gandhi,* 73:253.

77. Morton Deutsch, "A Theoretical Perspective on Conflict and Conflict Resolution," 48.

78. Michael Brown and Richard Rosecrance, eds., *The Costs of Conflict: Prevention and Cure in the Global Arena*; Paul Collier and Anke Hoeffler, "Conflicts"; Paul Collier and Anke Hoeffler, "Greed and Grievance in Civil War"; Paul Collier, *Wars, Guns, and*

Votes: Democracy in Dangerous Places; Paul Collier, *Economic Causes of Civil Conflict and Their Implications for Policy*; Paul Collier, Anke Hoeffler, and Dominic Rohner, "Beyond Greed and Grievance: Feasibility and Civil War."

79. Barbara Walter, "Does Conflict Beget Conflict? Explaining Recurring Civil War."

80. B. R. Nanda, *Gandhi and Non-violence*, https://www.mkgandhi.org/nonviolence /g_non.htm.

81. Johansen, "Nonviolence," 149.

82. Gandhi, *Collected Works of Gandhi*, 23:197.

83. Quoted in Richard B. Gregg, *The Power of Nonviolence*, 25–26.

84. Gandhi, *Collected Works of Gandhi*, 66:416.

85. Terry Beitzel, "Virtue in the Nonviolence of William James and Gandhi."

86. The speech is available at http://www.constitution.org/wj/meow.htm.

87. Beitzel, "Virtue in the Nonviolence of James and Gandhi."

88. Gandhi, *Collected Works of Gandhi*, 72:450, 24:142, 69:313–16, 61:265–66.

89. Gandhi, *Collected Works of Gandhi*, 85:53, 18:132, 76:95.

90. Ken Booth, "Navigating the 'Absolute Novum': John H. Herz's Political Realism and Political Idealism," 517.

91. A. Bose, "Gandhian Perspective on Peace."

92. Judith Stiehm, "Nonviolence Is Two."

93. Robert J. Burrowes, *The Strategy of Nonviolent Defense: A Gandhian Approach*, 98–101.

94. Gandhi, *Collected Works of Gandhi*, 42:452–53, 68:29, 48:224.

95. M. K. Gandhi, *Harijan*, Nov. 5, 1936.

96. For an overview and definition of these terms, see Hugh Miall, "Conflict Transformation: A Multi-dimensional Task."

97. John P. Lederach, *The Little Book of Conflict Transformation*, 3.

98. See Johan Galtung, *Peace by Peaceful Means*; and Johan Galtung and Carl Jacobsen, *Searching for Peace*.

99. Lederach, *Preparing for Peace*, 212.

100. Kurtz, "Gandhi and His Legacies," 840.

101. Joan V. Bondurant, *Conquest of Violence*, 195.

102. Alan C. Tidwell, *Conflict Resolved? A Critical Assessment of Conflict Resolution*, 10–17.

103. Dean G. Pruitt, "Creative Approaches to Negotiation," 69.

104. Jeffrey Z. Rubin and Bert R. Brown, *The Social Psychology of Bargaining and Negotiation*, 202–6.

105. Weber, "Gandhian Philosophy."

106. Kurtz, "Gandhi and His Legacies," 847.

107. Pruitt and Rubin, *Social Conflict.*

108. R. R. Diwakar, *Saga of Satyagraha*, 25.

109. Kurtz, "Gandhi and His Legacies," 840, 841.

110. Considerable literature focuses on the role that humiliation plays in fueling violence, including the works of Evelin G. Lindner and her Human Dignity and Humiliation Studies network. For instance, see Evelin G. Lindner, *Making Enemies: Humiliation and International Conflict.*

111. Michael N. Nagler, "Peacemaking through Nonviolence."

112. Morton Deutsch and Robert M. Krauss, "Effect of Threat on Interpersonal Bargaining."

113. Stephen Weiss-Wik, "Enhancing Negotiators' Successfulness: Self-Help Books and Related Empirical Research," 728.

114. Kellog V. Wilson and V. Edwin Bixenstine, "Forms of Social Control in Two-Person Two-Choice Games."

115. Sidney Siegel and Lawrence E. Fouraker, *Bargaining and Group Decision Making*, 100.

116. Otomar J. Bartos, "Simple Model of Negotiation: A Sociological Point of View."

117. Power, "Gandhian Model for World Politics," 295.

118. "U.N. Chief: World Should Be Ashamed at Failure to End Syria Conflict," *New York Times*, June 30, 2015. http://www.nytimes.com/aponline/2015/06/30/world/middleeast/ap-un-united-nations-syria.html.

119. Jahanbegloo, *The Gandhian Moment*, 40.

120. Naess, *Gandhi and Group Conflict*, 60–84.

121. Gandhi, *Collected Works of Gandhi*, 69:69.

122. Paul Diesing, "Bargaining Strategy and Union-Management Relationships," 369.

123. M. Deutsch, "Theoretical Perspective," 48.

124. Galtung, "Introduction," 14.

125. Johansen, "Nonviolence," 143.

126. Johansen, "Nonviolence," 143.

127. This Gandhian understanding of many-sidedness of truth is partly shaped by the Jain concept of Anekantavada (truth has many sides). In a letter to his son Devdas, Gandhi, on March 5, 1922, wrote, "I am an *anekantavadi*. I can see many sides of a question." Gandhi, *Collected Works of Gandhi*, 23:18.

128. Holmes, *On War and Morality*, 288, 287, 291.

129. Holmes, *On War and Morality*, 291.

130. Johan Galtung, "Two Worlds: Gandhi and the Modern World," 2.

131. Power, "Gandhian Model for World Politics."

132. Gandhi, *Collected Works of Gandhi*, 41:203.

133. Kurtz, "Gandhi and His Legacies," 841.

2. Othering, Clash of Visions, and Partition

1. Pandey, *Remembering Partition*.

2. Edward Said, *Orientalism*, 9.

3. John E. Mack, "The Psychodynamics of Victimization among National Groups in Conflict," 123.

4. For a connection between deprivation of nonmaterial needs and conflict, see Azar, *Management of Protracted Social Conflict*.

5. Kevin Avruch, *Culture and Conflict Resolution*, 5–6.

6. Hofstede, Hofstede, and Minkov, *Culture and Organizations*, 23.

7. George Devereux, *From Anxiety to Method in the Behavioral Sciences, Etc.*

8. Avruch, *Culture and Conflict Resolution*, 10.

9. Quoted in Judith B. Asuni, "Culture and Conflict," 2.

10. Lederach, *Preparing for Peace*, 4.

11. For example, see Hofstede, Hofstede, and Minkov, *Culture and Organizations*; Arjun Appadurai, *Modernity at Large: Cultural Dimensions of Globalization*; Baumann, *Contesting Culture*; Z. Bauman, *Liquid Modernity*; E. T. Hall, *The Silent Language*; and Martine Abdallah-Pretceille, "Interculturalism as a Paradigm for Thinking about Diversity."

12. Baumann, *Contesting Culture*.

13. Darren Kew, *Civil Society, Conflict Resolution, and Democracy in Nigeria*.

14. Avruch, *Culture and Conflict Resolution*, 5–6.

15. Abdallah-Pretceille, "Interculturalism as a Paradigm," 477.

16. Hofstede, Hofstede, and Minkov, *Culture and Organizations*, 26.

17. Connor, "Nation-Building or Nation-Destroying?," 349.

18. Alami, *Mutual Othering*, 25.

19. Alami, *Mutual Othering*, 25.

20. Levinas, *Le temps et l'autre* and *Totalité et infini*.

21. Boyce and Chunnu, *Historicizing Fear*.

22. For instance, see Denise Herd, "On George Floyd and the Struggle to Belong," Othering and Belonging Institute, University of California–Berkeley, May 29, 2020, https://belonging.berkeley.edu/george-floyd-and-struggle-belong. The University of California–Berkeley's Othering and Belonging Institute provide useful resources on othering and belonging. Most of those resources focus on the American context.

23. E. J. Hobsbawm, *Nations and Nationalism Since 1870: Programme, Myth, Reality*, 5.

24. Benedict Anderson, *Imagined Communities: Reflections on the Origin and Spread of Nationalism*, 6.

25. For an elaboration of Bauer's idea on nationalism, see Otto Bauer, *The Question of Nationalities and Social Democracy*.

26. E. H. Carr, *Nationalism and After*.

27. A. Smith, "Conflict and Collective Identity," 70.

28. A. Smith, "Conflict and Collective Identity," 63.

29. Connor, "Nation-Building or Nation-Destroying?," 319, 321.

30. Mohammed Ayoob, *The Third World Security Predicament: State Making, Regional Conflict, and the International System*.

31. Connor, "Nation-Building or Nation-Destroying?," 320.

32. Durkheim, *Elementary Forms of the Religious Life*.

33. Bellah, "Durkheim and History."

34. Karl Deutsch, *Nationalism and Social Communication: An Inquiry into the Foundations of Nationality*, 126.

35. Karl Deutsch, "Social Mobilization and Political Development," 501.

36. Ernest Gellner, *Nations and Nationalism*, 39.

37. Elie Kedourie, *Nationalism*.

38. Elie Kedourie, *Nationalism in Asia and Africa*.

39. Iqbal, *Reconstruction of Religious Thought in Islam*.

40. Schimmel, *Gabriel's Wing*, 84.

41. Iqbal, *Reconstruction of Religious Thought in Islam*.

42. Fred Halliday, "The Politics of the Umma: States and Community in Islamic Movements," 23.

43. For a useful discussion on *ummah* and its origins and contestation between the terms of nation-state and *ummah*, see Abdullah Al-Ahsan, *Ummah or Nation? Identity Crisis in Contemporary Muslim Society*.

44. Halliday, "Politics of the Umma," 22.

45. Elisabeth Özdalga, "Islamism and Nationalism as Sister Ideologies: Reflections on the Politicization of Islam in a Longue Durée Perspective," 421.

46. James G. Mellon, "Pan-Arabism, Pan-Islamism and Inter-state Relations in the Arab World."

47. Mehdi Mozaffari, "What Is Islamism? History and Definition of a Concept." See also, by the same author, *Islamism: A New Totalitarianism*.

48. Mozaffari, "What Is Islamism?," 29.

49. Iqbal, *Reconstruction of Religious Thought in Islam*.

50. For a detail analysis of this confusion—whether to follow a liberal democratic system or an Islamic system—among the Pakistani intellectuals, see Al-Ahsan, *Ummah or Nation?*, 88–95.

51. Al-Ahsan, *Ummah or Nation?*, 95.

52. Benazir Bhutto, *Reconciliation: Islam, Democracy, and the West*, 2–3.

53. Farahnaz Ispahani, "Cleansing Pakistan of Minorities," Hudson Institute, July 31, 2013, https://www.hudson.org/research/9781-cleansing-pakistan-of-minorities#:~:text=At%20the%20time%20of%20partition,more%20accentuated%20over%20the%20years.

54. Gregg, *The Power of Nonviolence*, 157.

55. Bertrand Russell, "Mahatma Gandhi."

56. Russell, "Mahatma Gandhi."

57. Ambedkar, *Pakistan* (emphasis added). The book is available at http://www
.columbia.edu/itc/mealac/pritchett/00ambedkar/ambedkar_partition/index.html#
contents. Chapter 2 of the book is titled "A Nation Calling for a Home."

58. We have not elaborated these developments as they are not necessary for the
purpose of the book, but Gandhi's role in these movements demonstrates his eagerness
to promote Hindu-Muslim unity even at the risk of being perceived as soft on Muslims
and rough on Hindus.

59. Ambedkar, *Pakistan*. For this argument, chap. 7 of the book, "Hindu Alternative
to Pakistan," is crucial. In this chapter, there is a section titled "Mr. Gandhi's Tenacious
Quest for Hindu-Muslim Unity."

60. Ambedkar, *Pakistan*.

61. Gandhi, *Collected Works of Gandhi*, 85:366–67.

62. P. Talbot, *American Witness*, 154.

63. Gandhi, *Collected Works of Gandhi*, 86:294.

64. Gandhi, *Collected Works of Gandhi*, 76:434.

65. Lahore Resolution, https://historypak.com/lahore-resolution-1940/.

66. Lahore Resolution.

67. Gandhi, *Collected Works of Gandhi*, 78:407, 408.

68. B. Anderson, *Imagined Communities*. Anderson in this book makes a forceful
case that it is not necessary to have clear, distinct marks to have a national identity; it can
be imagined as well. Here psychology comes to play. There are a lot of studies and experiments on this. The blue eye and brown eye experiment, in the context of the United
States, is relevant in this context: https://www.youtube.com/watch?v=oGvoXeXCoUY.
And this identity can shift. This identity assertion became more prominent after the end
of colonialism in the twentieth century. Kedourie referred to this identity assertion as a
new form of "millennial religion." See Kedourie, *Nationalism* and *Nationalism in Asia
and Africa*.

69. Gandhi, *Collected Works of Gandhi*, 78:410, 412.

70. Ramachandra Guha, *India after Gandhi: The History of the World's Largest Democracy*, 48.

71. P. Talbot, *American Witness*, 165, 166.

72. Jalal, *Sole Spokesman*.

73. Gilmartin, "Partition, Pakistan, and South Asian History," 1071.

74. M. A. Jinnah, First Presidential Address to the Constituent Assembly of Pakistan.

75. Stephen Cohen, *Idea of Pakistan*, 43–44 (emphasis in the original).

76. Bhikhu Parekh, *Gandhi*, 32.

77. Gregg, *The Power of Nonviolence*, 9.

78. Gregg, *The Power of Nonviolence*, 119.

79. Gandhi, *Collected Works of Gandhi*, 78:412.

80. Parekh, *Gandhi*, 34.

81. Gandhi, *Collected Works of Gandhi*, 85:10.

82. Aurobindo Ghose, *The Complete Works of Sri Aurobindo*, 1050. *The Complete Works of Sri Aurobindo* are also available at https://www.sriaurobindoashram.org/sri aurobindo/writings.php.

83. A. Ghose, *Complete Works of Sri Aurobindo*, 216.

84. Gilmartin, "Partition, Pakistan, and South Asian History," 1078.

85. Guha, *India after Gandhi*.

86. Ambedkar, *Pakistan*. Chapter 1 of the book, "What Does the League Demand?," elaborates the politics of the league.

87. Ambedkar, *Pakistan*.

88. Parekh, *Gandhi*, 33–34.

89. Virdee, *From the Ashes of 1947*, 35–36.

90. Parekh, *Gandhi*, 32–33.

91. Jawaharlal Nehru, *Soviet Russia: Some Random Sketches and Impressions*. In the first chapter, "The Fascination of Russia," Nehru wrote, "No one can deny the fascination of this strange Eurasian country of the hammer and sickle, where workers and peasants sit on the thrones of the mighty and upset the best-laid schemes of mice and men. . . . For us in India the fascination is even greater and even our self-interest compels us to understand the vast forces which have upset the old order of things and brought a new world into existence, where values have changed utterly and old standards have given place to new" (4).

92. "Two Letters from Iqbal to Jinnah (1937)," http://www.columbia.edu/itc/meal ac/pritchett/00islamlinks/txt_iqbal_tojinnah_1937.html.

93. Ambedkar, *Pakistan*.

94. Ambedkar, *Pakistan*.

95. Larry Collins and Dominique Lapierre, *Freedom at Midnight*, 7.

96. Prithwindra Mukherjee, "Had Bagha Jatin Succeeded! A Nationalist Revolt in Colonial India during World War I."

97. P. Talbot, *American Witness*, 166.

98. Kulke and Rothermund, *A History of India*, 232.

99. Khushwant Singh, *Train to Pakistan*, 1–2.

100. Guha, *India after Gandhi*.

101. For instance, see Nurit Kilot and David Newman, eds., *Geopolitics at the End of the Twentieth Century: The Changing World Political Map*; Thomas M. Wilson and Hastings Donnan, eds., *Border Identities: Nation and State at International Frontiers*; Barry Buzan, *People, States and Fear: An Agenda for International Security Studies in*

the Post–Cold War Era; and Edward Newman and Joanne van Selm, eds., *Refugee and Forced Displacement: International Security, Human Vulnerability and the State*.

102. Zamindar, *Long Partition*.

3. Post-partition South Asia

1. Kuldip Nayar, "From Sialkot to Delhi," in *Tales of Two Cities*, Kuldip Nayar and Asif Noorani, 65. Nayar observes, "I found to my horror that beyond the broad objective to separate Muslim areas from non-Muslim ones, Radcliffe had not set of rules or guidelines to go by when he drew the boundaries" (64).

2. Seema Shekhawat and Debidatta Aurobinda Mahapatra, *Contested Borders and Division of Families in Kashmir: Contextualizing the Ordeal of the Kargil Women*.

3. Thomas M. Wilson and Hastings Donnan, "Nation, State and Identity at International Borders," 10.

4. Burton, *Resolving Deep-Rooted Conflict*, 3.

5. A. Smith, "Conflict and Collective Identity," 70.

6. Berto J. Jongman, "Mapping the Dimensions of Contemporary Conflicts and Human Rights Violations," 19.

7. For an overview of conflict and peace in Afghanistan, see Debidatta Aurobinda Mahapatra, "Prospects of Inclusive Peace, Perception of Players and Stakes Involved in Post-9/11 Afghanistan."

8. Myron Weiner, *The Politics of Scarcity*, 9.

9. Taya Zinkin, "The Background of Indo-Pakistani Relations," 31.

10. Ayesha Jalal, *The Pity of Partition: Manto's Life, Times, and Work across the India-Pakistan Divide*, 4.

11. Andrew Whitehead, "Partition 70 Years On: The Turmoil, Trauma—and Legacy," BBC News, July 27, 2017, https://www.bbc.com/news/world-asia-40643413.

12. Edward E. Azar and Nadia Farah, "The Structure of Inequality and Protracted Social Conflicts: A Theoretical Framework," 320.

13. Edward E. Azar, Paul Jureidini, and Ronald McLaurin, "Protracted Social Conflict: Theory and Practice in the Middle East," 53.

14. Edward E. Azar and Chung-in Moon, "Towards an Alternative Conceptualization," 288.

15. See, for instance, Paul Diehl and Gary Goertz, *War and Peace in International Rivalry*; William R. Thompson, "Identifying Rivals and Rivalries in World Politics"; Paul F. Diehl, ed., *The Dynamics of Enduring Rivalries*; William R. Thompson, "Principal Rivalries"; Frank W. Wayman, "Rivalries: Recurrent Disputes and Explaining War"; Scott D. Bennett, "The Dynamics of Enduring Rivalries"; and Brandon Valeriano, *Becoming Rivals: The Process of Interstate Rivalry Development*.

16. Zeev Maoz and Ben D. Mor, *Bound by Struggle: The Strategic Evolution of Enduring International Rivalries*, 5.

17. How and why of this war have been subject of several scholarly works. See, for instance, Gupta, *Kashmir*; Prem Shankar Jha, *Kashmir, 1947: Rival Versions of History*; Lars Blinkenberg, *India-Pakistan: The History of Unresolved Conflicts*; S. K. Sinha, *Operation Rescue: Military Operations in Jammu and Kashmir, 1947–49*; L. P. Sen, *Slender Was the Thread: Kashmir Confrontation, 1947–48*; and Akbar Khan, *Raiders in Kashmir*.

18. A. Khan, *Raiders in Kashmir*.

19. Korbel, *Danger in Kashmir*; Pauline Dawson, *The Peacekeepers of Kashmir: The UN Military Observer Group in India and Pakistan*.

20. See chapters in Paul, *India-Pakistan Conflict*; Lawrence Ziring, "The Geopolitics of the Asian Subcontinent: Pakistan's Security Environment"; and Cohen, *Shooting for a Century*.

21. Jaroslav Tir and Paul F. Diehl, "Geographic Dimensions of Enduring Rivalries."

22. Russell Brines, *The Indo-Pakistani Conflict*, 7.

23. Zinkin, "Background of Indo-Pakistani Relations," 38.

24. Devin T. Hagerty, *The Consequences of Nuclear Proliferation: Lessons from South Asia*, 67.

25. Wolpert, *India and Pakistan*, 2.

26. See, for instance, Hagerty, *Consequences of Nuclear Proliferation*; Ashley Tellis, *India's Emerging Nuclear Posture*; Scott D. Sagan, ed., *Inside Nuclear South Asia*; W. P. S. Sidhu, "India's Nuclear Use Doctrine"; Zafar I. Cheema, "Pakistan's Nuclear Use Doctrine and Command and Control"; and R. Chengappa, *Weapons of Peace: The Secret Story of India's Quest to Be a Nuclear Power*.

27. S. Paul Kapur, *Dangerous Deterrent: Nuclear Weapons Proliferation and Conflict in South Asia*; Michael Krepon, *The Stability-Instability Paradox, Misperception, and Escalation Control in South Asia*; Dinshaw Mistry, "Tempering Optimism about Nuclear Deterrence in South Asia."

28. Sumit Ganguly and D. Hagerty, *Fearful Symmetry: India-Pakistan Crises in the Shadow of Nuclear Weapons*, 2.

29. Rajesh Basrur, *Minimum Deterrence and India's Nuclear Security*.

30. John A. Vasquez, "The India–Pakistan Conflict in Light of General Theories of War, Rivalry, and Deterrence."

31. Saira Khan, "Nuclear Weapons and the Prolongation of the India–Pakistan Rivalry," 158.

32. Russell J. Leng, *Bargaining and Learning in Recurring Crises*, 270.

33. Azar, Jureidini, and McLaurin, "Protracted Social Conflict," 51, 55.

34. Anit Mukherjee, "A Brand New Day or Back to the Future? The Dynamics of India-Pakistan Relations," 404.

35. Oscar Martinez, *Border People: Life and Society in the US–Mexico Borderlands*, 2. See Also Debidatta Aurobinda Mahapatra, "From Alienation to Co-existence and Beyond: Examining the Evolution of the Borderland in Kashmir."

36. Ravina Aggarwal, *Beyond Lines of Control: Performance and Politics on the Disputed Borders of Ladakh, India*, 1.

37. For a detailed study on the border and border tensions, see Debidatta Aurobinda Mahapatra, *Making Kashmir Borderless*.

38. John Mitton, "The India-Pakistan Rivalry and Failure in Afghanistan," 353.

39. Michael G. Findley, James Piazza, and Joseph Young, "Games Rivals Play: Terrorism in International Rivalries."

40. See J. David Singer, Stuart Bremer, and John Stuckey, "Capability Distribution, Uncertainty, and Major Power War, 1820–1965"; Thompson, "Principal Rivalries"; and John A. Vasquez, *The War Puzzle*.

41. For an account of Pakistan's internal politics, see Husain Haqqani, *Pakistan: Between Mosque and Military*.

42. "Kashmir: Confrontation and Miscalculation," *International Crisis Group: Asia Report No. 35* (2002), 6, https://www.files.ethz.ch/isn/28348/035_kashmir_confrontation _miscalculation.pdf.

43. For a study of the internal dimension of the Kashmir conflict, see Balraj Puri, *Kashmir: Towards Insurgency*; Robert G. Wirsing, *Kashmir: In the Shadow of War*; Sumantra Bose, *The Challenge in Kashmir: Democracy, Self-Determination and a Just Peace*; Navnita Behera, *Demystifying Kashmir*; Sumit Ganguly, *The Crisis in Kashmir: Portents of War, Hopes of Peace*; Sten Widmalm, *Kashmir in Comparative Perspective: Democracy and Violent Separatism in India*; Victoria Schofield, *Kashmir in Conflict: India, Pakistan and the Unfinished War*; Seema Shekhawat, *Gender, Conflict and Peace in Kashmir: Invisible Stakeholders*; and Mahapatra, *Conflict Management in Kashmir*.

44. "Kashmir: The View from Islamabad," *International Crisis Group: Asia Report No. 68* (2003), https://d2071andvip0wj.cloudfront.net/68-kashmir-the-view-from-islamabad.pdf.

45. For an assessment of Pakistan's identity and its role in Kashmir, see Cohen, *The Idea of Pakistan*.

46. Stephen P. Cohen, *India: Emerging Power*, 217.

47. J. N. Dixit, *India-Pakistan in War and Peace*; Rajat Ganguly, *Kin State Intervention in Ethnic Conflicts: Lessons from South Asia*; Praveen Swami, *India, Pakistan and the Secret Jihad: The Covert War in Kashmir, 1947–2004*.

48. Paul Staniland, "Organizing Insurgency: Networks, Resources, and Rebellion in South Asia," 156.

49. Dipanjan Roy Chaudhury, "PoK Belongs to India, Will Have Jurisdiction over That Area One Day: Foreign Minister S Jaishankar," *Economic Times*, Sept. 18, 2019, https://

economictimes.indiatimes.com/news/politics-and-nation/pok-belongs-to-india-will-have
-jurisdiction-over-that-area-one-day-foreign-minister-s-jaishankar/articleshow/71169028
.cms?utm_source=contentofinterest&utm_medium=text&utm_campaign=cppst.

50. John A. Vasquez, "Distinguishing Rivals That Go to War from Those That Do
Not: A Quantitative Comparative Case Study of the Two Paths to War," 532.

51. William R. Thompson and David Dreyer, *Handbook of International Rivalries,
1494–2010*, 2.

52. Gandhi, *Collected Works of Gandhi*, 42:452–53.

53. Shishir Gupta, "Imran Khan to Join Xi Jinping to Shore Up Nepal's PM Oli
against India," *Hindustan Times*, July 1, 2020, https://www.hindustantimes.com/india
-news/imran-khan-to-join-xi-jinping-to-shore-up-nepal-s-pm-oli-against-india/story-oOn
bE0uSw9LKi8cYmPYrBK.html.

54. "'No Takers for Your Malware': India Hits Out at Pakistan at UN, Says It 'Epitomises Dark Arts,'" *Scroll.in*, Jan. 10, 2020, https://scroll.in/latest/949393/india-hits-out-at
-pakistan-at-un-says-it-epitomises-dark-arts-no-takers-for-your-malware.

55. George Fernandes, "India Could Take a Strike and Survive, Pakistan Won't,"
Hindustan Times, Dec. 30, 2001.

56. "Indian Army Is Ready to Attack PoK If Ordered, New Chief MM Naravane
Tells NDTV," *Scroll.in*, Jan. 2, 2020, https://scroll.in/latest/948619/indian-army-is-ready
-to-attack-pok-if-ordered-new-chief-mm-naravane-tells-ndtv.

57. "Full Text: 'Non-military Preemptive Strike' on Biggest JeM Camp Was Absolutely Necessary, Says India," *Scroll.in*, Feb. 26, 2019, https://scroll.in/latest/914642/full
-text-non-military-preemptive-strike-on-biggest-jaish-camp-was-absolutely-necessary-says
-india.

58. "Indian Army Is Ready to Attack PoK If Ordered."

59. Azar, Jureidini, and McLaurin, "Protracted Social Conflict," 50.

60. Strategic Foresight Group, "Cost of Conflict between India and Pakistan," 2004,
https://www.strategicforesight.com/publication_pdf/91581Cost%20of%20Conflict%20
Between%20India%20and%20Pakistan.pdf.

61. See, for instance, "India and Pakistan: How the War Was Fought in TV Studios,"
BBC News, Mar. 10, 2019, https://www.bbc.com/news/world-asia-47481757; "Indo-Pak
Conflict: Media Endorsing Jingoism Did More Harm than Good, Editor Says," Mar. 1,
2019, https://sputniknews.com/asia/201903011072872939-india-pakistan-conflict-media/.

62. Sankalp Phartiyal, "Social Media Fake News Fans Tension between India and
Pakistan," Reuters, Feb. 28, 2019, https://www.reuters.com/article/us-india-kashmir-social
media-idUSKCN1QH1NY; Anumeha Chaturvedi, "Fake News & Misinformation on Indo-
Pak Tension Flood the Social Media," *Economic Times*, Feb. 28, 2019, https://economic
times.indiatimes.com/tech/internet/fake-news-misinformation-on-indo-pak-tension-flood
-the-social-media/articleshow/68194093.cms.

63. Vignesh Radhakrishnan, "Indian Hackers Bring Down Pak Websites on Independence Day," *Hindustan Times*, Aug. 15, 2015, https://www.hindustantimes.com/india/indian-hackers-bring-down-pak-websites-on-independence-day/story-8lJr9kpGMzu5irk62SImyH.html; and, Gwyn D'Mello, "A Pakistani Group Hacked into 10 Indian University Websites as Revenge against Indian Hackers," *India Times*, Apr. 26, 2017, https://www.indiatimes.com/technology/news/a-pakistani-group-hacked-defaced-10-indian-university-websites-as-retaliation-against-indian-hackers-276456.html.

64. "Watch: Twitter Is Not Pleased with This Pakistani Video of Children Calling for India's Destruction," *Scroll.in*, Oct. 14, 2019, https://scroll.in/video/940417/watch-twitter-is-not-pleased-with-this-pakistani-video-of-children-calling-for-indias-destruction%20October%2014.

65. Tim Wigmore, "Why India vs Pakistan Is the Biggest Game in All Sport: When Politics, Passion and National Identity Collide," *Telegraph*, June 16, 2019, https://www.telegraph.co.uk/cricket/2019/06/15/india-vs-pakistan-biggest-game-sport-politics-passion-national/.

66. Sean Ingle, "Not Just Cricket: India and Pakistan Prepare to Renew Rivalry at World Cup," *Guardian*, June 14, 2019, https://www.theguardian.com/sport/2019/jun/14/india-pakistan-cricket-rivalry-world-cup-old-trafford.

67. Whitehead, "Partition 70 Years On."

68. "India: Karan Johar Pledge Not to Use Pakistan Actors Goes Viral," BBC News, Oct. 19, 2016, https://www.bbc.com/news/world-asia-india-37701024.

69. Ilmas Futehally and Semu Bhatt, "Cost of Conflict between India and Pakistan."

70. Mahmud Ali Durrani, *India and Pakistan: The Cost of Conflict and the Benefits of Peace.*

71. Durrani, *India and Pakistan*, 4, xii.

72. Newman and Selm, *Refugee and Forced Displacement*, 8.

73. For instance, see Lloyd Axworthy, "Human Security and Global Governance: Putting People First"; Edward Newman, "Human Security and Constructivism"; Barry Buzan, "A Reductionist, Idealistic Notion That Adds Little Analytical Value"; and Andrew Mack, "A Signifier of Shared Values."

74. Debidatta Aurobinda Mahapatra, "Negotiating Space in the Conflict Zone of Kashmir"; Debidatta Aurobinda Mahapatra, "Positioning the People in the Contested Borders of Kashmir"; Seema Shekhawat and D. A. Mahapatra, *Kargil Displaced of Akhnoor in Jammu and Kashmir: Enduring Ordeal and Bleak Future*; Shekhawat and Mahapatra, *Contested Border and Division of Families in Kashmir.*

75. Futehally and Bhatt, "Cost of Conflict between India and Pakistan."

76. Shrikant Rao, "The Price of War," *Sunday Mid-Day*, July 4, 1999, http://www.sacw.net/kargil/price.html.

77. Futehally and Bhatt, "Cost of Conflict between India and Pakistan."

78. "Pakistan Reopens Airspace after India Standoff," BBC News, July 16, 2019, https://www.bbc.com/news/world-asia-india-48999736.

79. Rezaul Laskar, "Pakistan Airspace Closure Affects 400 Flights a Day, Costs Islamabad $100 mn," *Hindustan Times*, July 3, 2019, https://www.hindustantimes.com /india-news/pakistan-airspace-closure-hits-flights-a-day-as-costs-escalate/story-xa4do2 LQD6vEDzk6uOTNrI.html.

80. Parvez Hasan, *My Life, My Country: Memoirs of a Pakistani Economist*, 262.

81. "Status Paper on India-Pakistan Economic Relations," Federation of Indian Chambers of Commerce and Industry, Feb. 2012, http://ficci.in/spdocument/20183/status paperonindiapakistan.pdf.

82. Jayshree Sengupta, "Economic Burdens of War on India and Pakistan," Observer Research Foundation, Mar. 14, 2019, https://www.orfonline.org/expert-speak/economic -burdens-war-india-pakistan-48991/.

83. Shuja Nawaz and Mohan Guruswamy, "India and Pakistan: The Opportunity Cost of Conflict."

84. For details, see https://hdr.undp.org/data-center/human-development-index# /indicies/HDI.

85. Nawaz and Guruswamy, "India and Pakistan."

86. Dwight D. Eisenhower, "Chance for Peace," address delivered to the American Society of Newspaper Editors, Washington, DC, Apr. 16, 1953, https://www.presidency .ucsb.edu/documents/address-the-chance-for-peace-delivered-before-the-american-society -newspaper-editors.

87. Brahma Chellaney, "Keep Up the Pressure on Pakistan," *Hindustan Times*, Feb. 28, 2019, https://www.hindustantimes.com/columns/keep-up-the-pressure-on-pakistan /story-JRQqaEexMalNiTexahVohI.html.

4. Promoting Belonging

1. For the full text of the joint statement, see https://www.stimson.org/1999/lahore -summit/.

2. Celia W. Dugger, "India's Premier Invites Pakistani Leader to Talks," *Chicago Tribune*, May 26, 2001, https://www.chicagotribune.com/news/ct-xpm-2001-05-26-01052 60095-story.html.

3. V. Mohan Narayan, "Musharraf Pakistan's Biggest Leader: Vajpayee," Jan. 3, 2004, https://www.rediff.com/news/2004/jan/03saarc6.htm.

4. V. Mohan Narayan, "Musharraf Pakistan's Biggest Leader: Vajpayee."

5. Thorsten Wojczewski, "The Persistency of the India–Pakistan Conflict: Chances and Obstacles of the Bilateral Composite Dialogue," 322.

6. G. Sudhakar Nair, "India, Pak to Be 'Severe' on Terror," *Hindustan Times*, Sept. 25, 2008, https://www.hindustantimes.com/world/india-pak-to-be-severe-on-terror/story -UXClS7djIkwrwgEg4L5qRK.html.

7. Mukhtar Ahmad, "India PM Inaugurates Kashmir Train amid Curfew," CNN, Oct. 11, 2008, http://www.cnn.com/2008/WORLD/asiapcf/10/11/india.kashmir/index .html.

8. "Turn LoC into Line of Peace: PM," *Indian Express*, July 16, 2007, http://archive .indianexpress.com/news/turn-loc-into-line-of-peace-pm/205085/2.

9. "Sushma Swaraj Rules Out Talks with Pakistan, John Kerry Says No Good or Bad Terrorist," *Indian Express*, Aug. 31, 2016, https://indianexpress.com/article/india /india-news-india/sushma-swaraj-pakistan-terrorism-john-kerry-india-visit-3004565/.

10. Ankit Panda, "Gurdaspur, Pathankot, and Now Uri: What Are India's Options?," *Diplomat*, Sept. 19, 2016, https://thediplomat.com/2016/09/gurdaspur-pathankot-and-now -uri-what-are-indias-options/.

11. For details on spoilers and how they play a role in conflict, see, for instance, Tamir Sheafer and Shira Dvir-Gvirsman, "The Spoiler Effect: Framing Attitudes and Expectations toward Peace"; Matthew Hoddie and Caroline A. Hartzell, *Strengthening Peace in Post–Civil War States: Transforming Spoilers into Stakeholders*; and Kelly M. Greenhill and Solomon Major, "The Perils of Profiling: Civil War Spoilers and the Collapse of Intrastate Peace Accords."

12. Azar, *Management of Protracted Social Conflict*.

13. Stephen J. Stedman, "Spoiler Problems in Peace Processes," 5.

14. Azar, Jureidini, and McLaurin, "Protracted Social Conflict," 43.

15. For details, see Diehl and Goertz, *War and Peace in International Rivalry*.

16. See Richard Ned Lebow, *Between Peace and War*; and Stephen Rock, *Why Peace Breaks Out*.

17. For example, see Tony Armstrong, *Breaking the Ice*.

18. For example, see Kuldip Nayar, *Wall at Wagah: India-Pakistan Relations*; Wajahat Habibullah, *My Kashmir: Conflict and the Prospects for Enduring Peace*; Sumantra Bose, *Kashmir: Roots of Conflict, Paths to Peace*; Dixit, *India-Pakistan in War and Peace*; and Verghese Koithara, *Crafting Peace in Kashmir*.

19. See, for instance, Nasreen Akhtar, "Composite Dialogues Between India and Pakistan: Challenges and Impediments"; Umbreen Javaid, "Urgency for Inter-state Dialogue for Fighting Terrorism in South Asia"; C. Raja Mohan, *How Prime Minister Modi Can Sustain India's Pakistan Dialogue*; and Sajad Padder, "Beginning a Conversation," *Indian Express*, Sept. 13, 2016, https://indianexpress.com/article/opinion/columns/kashmir -unrest-all-party-delegation-meet-pdp-bjp-alliance-jammu-curfew-violence-eid-omar -abdullah-hurriyat-conference-3028012/.

20. Ashley J. Tellis, *Are India-Pakistan Peace Talks Worth a Damn?*, 64.

21. See, for details, L. Diamond and J. McDonald, *Multi-track Diplomacy*; Hussein Agha et al., *Track II Diplomacy: Lessons from the Middle East*; W. D. Ziegler, *War, Peace, and International Politics*; C. J. Magalhaēs, *The Pure Concept of Diplomacy*; J. Montville, "Track Two Diplomacy: The Arrow and the Olive Branch, a Case for Track Two Diplomacy"; and C. Landsberg, *The Quiet Diplomacy of Liberation: International Politics and South Africa's Transition*.

22. Dwight D. Eisenhower, "Chance for Peace," address delivered to the American Society of Newspaper Editors, Washington, DC, Apr. 16, 1953, https://www.presidency.ucsb.edu/documents/address-the-chance-for-peace-delivered-before-the-american-society-newspaper-editors.

23. Quoted in Sascha Lohmann, "Diplomats and the Use of Economic Sanctions."

24. For an overview of how interdependence and conflict reduction are linked, see Edward D. Mansfield and Brian M. Pollins, eds., *Economic Interdependence and International Conflict: New Perspectives on an Enduring Debate*.

25. Immanuel Kant, *Perpetual Peace: A Philosophical Essay*.

26. Norman Angell, *The Great Illusion: A Study of the Relation of Military Power to National Advantage*.

27. See Jerry Brotton, *The Renaissance Bazaar: From the Silk Road to Michelangelo*; Richard Foltz, *Religions of the Silk Road: Overland Trade and Cultural Exchange from Antiquity to the Fifteenth Century*; Xinru Liu, *Silk and Religion: An Exploration of Material Life and the Thought of People*, AD 600–1200; Kenneth Nebenzahl, *Mapping the Silk Road and Beyond: 2000 Years of Exploring the East*; and Frances Wood, *The Silk Road: Two Thousand Years in the Heart of Asia*. Gandhi did not use the term *Silk Road*, though he talked much about silk in contrast to cotton. We did not find a mention of Silk Road in his one-hundred-volume collected writings, but there are numerous references to the word *silk*. Gandhi was against silk and promoted homemade cotton. He also thought that production of silk is a violent process, as it involved insects. While promoting khadi and the spinning wheel, referring to Kaka Kalelkar, a freedom fighter and Gandhian, he wrote, "Kalelkar had made the further point that our ancestors were not unaware of silk though he held that originally there was no silk in India. As the people did not know that it came from China and was produced from the body of insects, they must have welcomed it. Once the people liked a thing, it was difficult to discard it. However, the moment this fact became known, they gave it up" (Gandhi, *Collected Works of Gandhi*, 37:82). However, it would be in the Gandhian nonviolent spirit to open the ancient trade routes if the initiative helped address the conflict among the countries and their peoples.

28. For a description of this road, see Debidatta Aurobinda Mahapatra, *Central Eurasia: Geopolitics, Compulsions and Connections*.

29. The findings of our visit to the museum and the survey of the Kargil-Skardu branch of the Silk Road were published in Debidatta Aurobinda Mahapatra, "The Silk Route in Kashmir: Preliminary Research Findings."

30. For our primary research in the Kargil region, see Shekhawat and Mahapatra, *Contested Borders and Division of Families in Kashmir.*

31. See Debidatta Aurobinda Mahapatra, "Disasters Defy Border," *Peace, Democracy and Development Blog*, University of Massachusetts–Boston, Apr. 28, 2013, http://blogs.umb.edu/paxblog/2013/04/28/disasters-defy-borders/. For a detailed report on 2005 earthquake, see D. A. Mahapatra, "Earthquake in Jammu and Kashmir: A Report."

32. For an extensive discussion on this issue, see Michael Kugelman and Robert M. Hathaway, *Pakistan-India Trade: What Needs to Be Done? What Does It Matter?*

33. Sanjay Kathuria, "A Glass Half Full: The Promise of Regional Trade in South Asia."

34. Riya Sinha and Niara Sareen, "India's Limited Trade Connectivity with South Asia."

35. Nawaz and Guruswamy, *India and Pakistan*, iv.

36. Nawaz and Guruswamy, *India and Pakistan*.

37. Nayar and Noorani, *Tales of Two Cities*, 14.

38. Nayar and Noorani, *Tales of Two Cities*, 37.

39. Nayar and Noorani, *Tales of Two Cities*, 18.

40. KumKum Dasgupta, "Respect Our Soldiers, Stop Parading Them at Wagah," *Hindustan Times*, Nov. 4, 2004, https://www.hindustantimes.com/ht-view/respect-our-soldiers-stop-parading-them-at-wagah/story-4duYvHdzCBqhHYsaQ7dLMP.html. Debidatta Aurobinda Mahapatra had a similar experience when he visited the border at Wagah in 2006 and watched the parades, while the audience from Indian side were shouting pro-India slogans, the audience from Pakistan side were shouting pro-Pakistan slogans. The atmosphere was charged; it was a warlike atmosphere without actual war. We consider this a manifestation of the othering by the two countries.

41. See Mahapatra, *Making Kashmir Borderless*; Shekhawat and Mahapatra, *Contested Border and Division of Families in Kashmir*; Debidatta Aurobinda Mahapatra, "Mapping Transitional Justice in Kashmir: Drivers, Initiatives, and Challenges"; and Mahapatra, "Positioning the People in the Contested Borders of Kashmir."

42. "1947 Archive," https://www.1947partitionarchive.org/mission.

43. Krishnendu Bandyopadhyay, "With Tram Ride, Pakistan Students Enjoy Old-World Charm of Kolkata," *Times of India*, June 12, 2018, https://timesofindia.indiatimes.com/city/kolkata/with-tram-ride-pakistan-students-enjoy-old-world-charm-of-kolkata/articleshow/64550845.cms.

44. Shah Meer Baloch, "Global Hit Pasoori Opens Doors for Pakistani Pop," *Guardian*, May 13, 2022, https://www.theguardian.com/world/2022/may/13/global-hit-pasoori-opens-doors-for-pakistani-pop.

45. Debidatta Aurobinda Mahapatra, "Music as a Tool of Conflict Transformation," *Peace, Democracy and Development Blog*, University of Massachusetts–Boston, Sept. 29, 2013, http://blogs.umb.edu/paxblog/2013/09/29/music-as-a-tool-of-conflict-transformation/.

46. Nayar and Noorani, *Tales of Two Cities*, 63.

47. Niha Masih, "In Goodwill Gesture, Pakistan Opens Corridor to Sikh Shrine for Indian Pilgrims amid Wider Tensions," *Washington Post*, Nov. 9, 2019, https://www.washingtonpost.com/world/asia-pacific/in-pakistan-a-sikh-shrine-opens-to-indian-pilgrims-as-goodwill-gesture-amid-wider-tensions/2019/11/09/de1443f8-01a7-11ea-8341-cc3dce52e7de_story.html.

48. Greek philosopher Plato in a philosophical context famously argues, "People imagine that they know about the nature of things, when they don't know about them, and, not having come to an understanding at first because they think that they know, they end, as might be expected, in contradicting one another." Plato, *Phaedrus*. Interestingly, Gandhi, in 1933, recommended to Annapurnanand, who was seriously ill, to read, among others, another Plato dialogue, *Phaedo*, which focuses on the immortality of the soul (Gandhi, *Collected Works of Gandhi*, 53:469). At another place, he wrote, "I have referred to Socrates and Plato, to Christ and to modern morality" (Gandhi, *Collected Works of Gandhi*, 8:497). Though Gandhi did not refer to Plato in his writings and speeches frequently, it seems that he was aware of Plato's works.

49. Evan Bissel, *Notes on a Cultural Strategy for Belonging*, 8.

50. Gandhi, *Collected Works of Gandhi*, 97:453–54.

51. Gregg, *The Power of Nonviolence*, 25.

52. Joshua Clark, ed., *Civic Engagement for Empowerment and Belonging*, 4.

53. Aasim S. Akhtar, "Even in These Dark Times, Indians and Pakistanis Can Undo Colonialism's Legacy of Distrust," *Scroll.in*, Feb. 25, 2020, https://scroll.in/article/953891/even-in-these-dark-times-indians-and-pakistanis-can-undo-colonialisms-legacy-of-distrust.

54. Holmes, *On War and Morality*, 267.

55. Quoted in M. P. Mathai, *Mahatma Gandhi's World-View*, 144.

56. According to a recent study, a nuclear war between India and Pakistan would likely kill 50 to 125 million lives besides causing an environmental disaster. For details, see Toon et al., "Rapidly Expanding Nuclear Arsenals in Pakistan and India."

57. Russell J. Leng, "Realpolitik and Learning in the India–Pakistan Rivalry," 126.

58. Hofstede, Hofstede, and Minkov, *Culture and Organizations*, 19.

59. Varshney, *Ethnic Conflict and Civic Life*.

60. Nawaz and Guruswamy, *India and Pakistan*, iv.

61. Leng, "Realpolitik and Learning in the India–Pakistan Rivalry," 127.

62. Bissel, *Notes on a Cultural Strategy for Belonging*.

63. Gandhi, *Collected Works of Gandhi*, 66:407.

64. "There is already a vast body of evidence suggesting that the Pakistan Army's strategy of fighting India either through conventional war or incessant jihad has taken a huge toll on Pakistan's fortunes as a state, its ability to improve the livelihood of its people, and its reputation as a responsible actor in the international system," notes Tellis. Tellis,

Are India-Pakistan Peace Talks Worth a Damn?, 49. See also Ahmad Faruqui, *Rethinking the National Security of Pakistan: The Price of Strategic Myopia.*

65. Nayar and Noorani, *Tales of Two Cities*, 70.

Conclusion: Beyond Othering

1. Martin Luther King Jr., foreword to *The Power of Nonviolence*, by Gregg, 9.

2. Johansen, "Nonviolence, 158.

3. Jay McDaniel, *Gandhi's Hope: Learning from Other Religions as a Path to Peace*, 18.

4. Jahanbegloo, *The Gandhian Moment*, 156.

5. Gandhi, *Collected Works of Gandhi*, 90:2–3.

6. Judith M. Brown, *Gandhi: Prisoner of Hope*, 394.

7. Jahanbegloo, *The Gandhian Moment*, 10.

8. Quoted in Hofstede, Hofstede, and Minkov, *Culture and Organizations*, 25.

9. Gandhi, *Collected Works of Gandhi*, 96:200.

10. Gandhi, *Collected Works of Gandhi*, 96:249.

11. Faiz Ahmed Faiz, "The Dawn of Freedom," Aug. 1947, https://mronline.org/2010/07/17/the-dawn-of-freedom-august-1947/.

Bibliography

Primary Sources

Gandhi, M. K. *The Collected Works of Mahatma Gandhi.* 100 vols. New Delhi: Publications Division Government of India, 2015.
Iqbal, Muhammad. *The Reconstruction of Religious Thought in Islam.* http://www.allamaiqbal.com/.
Jinnah, M. A. First Presidential Address to the Constituent Assembly of Pakistan, Aug. 11, 1947. http://www.columbia.edu/itc/mealac/pritchett/00islamlinks/txt_jinnah_assembly_1947.html.
———. Presidential Address to the Muslim League, Lahore, 1940. http://www.columbia.edu/itc/mealac/pritchett/00islamlinks/txt_jinnah_lahore_1940.html.
"Two Letters from Iqbal to Jinnah (1937)." http://www.columbia.edu/itc/mealac/pritchett/00islamlinks/txt_iqbal_tojinnah_1937.html.

Secondary and Published Works

Abdallah-Pretceille, Martine. "Interculturalism as a Paradigm for Thinking about Diversity." *Intercultural Education* 17, no. 5 (2006): 475–83. https://doi.org/10.1080/14675980601065764.
Ackerman, Peter, and Jack DuVall. *A Force More Powerful: A Century of Nonviolent Conflict.* New York: Palgrave-Macmillan, 2000.
Aggarwal, Ravina. *Beyond Lines of Control: Performance and Politics on the Disputed Borders of Ladakh, India.* Durham, NC: Duke Univ. Press, 2004.
Agha, Hussein, Shai Feldman, Ahmad Khalidi, and Zeev Schiff. *Track II Diplomacy: Lessons from the Middle East.* Cambridge, MA: MIT Press, 2004.
Agnew, John. "Beyond Reason: Spatial and Temporal Sources of Ethnic Conflicts." In *Intractable Conflicts and Their Transformation*, edited by Louis

Kriesberg, T. A. Northrup, and S. J. Thorson, 41–52. Syracuse, NY: Syracuse Univ. Press, 1989.

Ahmed, Ishtiaq. *The Punjab Bloodied, Partitioned and Cleansed*. Oxford: Oxford Univ. Press, 2012).

Akhtar, Nasreen. "Composite Dialogues between India and Pakistan: Challenges and Impediments." *International Journal on World Peace* 32, no. 3 (2015): 49–74.

Al-Ahsan, Abdullah. *Ummah or Nation? Identity Crisis in Contemporary Muslim Society*. Leicester: Islamic Foundation, 1992.

Alami, A. I. *Mutual Othering: Islam, Modernity, and the Politics of Cross-Cultural Encounters in Pre-colonial Moroccan and European Travel Writing*. Albany: State Univ. of New York Press, 2013.

Allen, Douglas. *Gandhi after 9/11: Creative Nonviolence and Sustainability*. Oxford: Oxford Univ. Press, 2019.

————. "Mahatma Gandhi on Violence and Peace Education." *Philosophy East and West* 57, no. 3 (2007): 290–310.

Ambedkar, B. R. *Pakistan; or, The Partition of India*. Bombay: Thackers, 1946.

Anderson, Benedict. *Imagined Communities: Reflections on the Origin and Spread of Nationalism*. London: Verso, 1991.

Anderson, Liam. *Federal Solutions to Ethnic Problems: Accommodating Diversity*. Oxon: Routledge, 2013.

Angell, Norman. *The Great Illusion: A Study of the Relation of Military Power to National Advantage*. New York: G. P. Putnam and Sons, 1913.

Appadurai, Arjun. *Modernity at Large: Cultural Dimensions of Globalization*. Minneapolis: Univ. of Minnesota Press, 1996.

Armstrong, Tony. *Breaking the Ice*. Washington, DC: United States Institute of Peace, 1993.

Aron, Raymond. *Peace and War: A Theory of International Relations*. New York: Doubleday, 1966.

Asuni, Judith B. "Culture and Conflict." Paper presented at the NOIC conference for NGOs in Kano, Aug. 2002. Abuja: Academic Associates Peaceworks.

Avruch, Kevin. *Culture and Conflict Resolution*. Washington, DC: United States Institute of Peace Press, 1998.

Axworthy, Lloyd. "Human Security and Global Governance: Putting People First." *Global Governance* 7, no. 1 (2001): 19–23.

Ayoob, Mohammed. *The Third World Security Predicament: State Making, Regional Conflict, and the International System*. Boulder, CO: Lynne Rienner, 1995.

Azar, Edward. *The Management of Protracted Social Conflict: Theory and Causes*. Dartmouth: Aldershot, 1990.

Azar, Edward E., and Nadia Farah. "The Structure of Inequality and Protracted Social Conflicts: A Theoretical Framework." *International Interactions* 7, no. 4 (1981): 317–35. https://doi.org/10.1080/03050628108434558.

Azar, Edward E., Paul Jureidini, and Ronald McLaurin. "Protracted Social Conflict: Theory and Practice in the Middle East." *Journal of Palestine Studies* 8, no. 1 (1978): 41–60.

Azar, Edward E., and Chung-in Moon. "Towards an Alternative Conceptualization." In *National Security in the Third World*, edited by Edward E. Azar and Chung-in Moon, 277–98. Aldershot: Edward Elgar, 1988.

Bartos, Otomar J. "Simple Model of Negotiation: A Sociological Point of View." *Journal of Conflict Resolution* 21, no. 4 (1977): 565–79.

Basrur, Rajesh. *Minimum Deterrence and India's Nuclear Security*. Stanford, CA: Stanford Univ. Press, 2006.

Bauer, Otto. *The Question of Nationalities and Social Democracy*. Translated by Joseph O'Donnell. Minneapolis: Univ. of Minnesota Press, 2000.

Bauman, Z. *Liquid Modernity*. Cambridge: Polity Press, 2000.

Baumann, G. *Contesting Culture*. Cambridge: Cambridge Univ. Press, 1996.

Behera, Navnita C. *Demystifying Kashmir*. Washington, DC: Brookings Institution Press, 2006.

Beitzel, Terry. "Virtue in the Nonviolence of William James and Gandhi." *International Journal on World Peace* 30, no. 3 (2013): 55–81.

Bellah, Robert. "Durkheim and History." In *Emile Durkheim: Critical Assessments*, edited by Peter Hamilton, 36–56. London: Routledge, 1995.

Bennett, Scott D. "The Dynamics of Enduring Rivalries." *American Political Science Review* 93, no. 3 (1999): 749–50.

Bhutto, Benazir. *Reconciliation: Islam, Democracy, and the West*. New York: Harper Luxe, 2008.

Bissel, Evan. *Notes on a Cultural Strategy for Belonging*. Berkeley: Haas Institute, Univ. of California, Oct. 2019.

Blinkenberg, Lars. *India-Pakistan: The History of Unresolved Conflicts*. Vol. 2. Odense: Odense Univ. Press, 1998.

Bondurant, Joan V. *Conquest of Violence: The Gandhian Philosophy of Conflict.* Berkeley: Univ. of California Press, 1965.

———. "Satyagraha versus Duragraha: The Limits of Symbolic Violence." In *Gandhi: His Relevance for Our Times,* edited by G. Ramachandran and T. K. Mahadevan, 99–120. Berkeley: World without War Council, 1967.

Booth, Ken. "Navigating the 'Absolute Novum': John H. Herz's Political Realism and Political Idealism." *International Relations* 22, no. 4 (2008): 510–26.

Bose, Anima. "A Gandhian Perspective on Peace." *Journal of Peace Research* 18, no. 2 (1981): 159–64.

Bose, Sumantra. *The Challenge in Kashmir: Democracy, Self-Determination and a Just Peace.* London: Sage, 1997.

———. *Kashmir: Roots of Conflict, Paths to Peace.* Cambridge, MA: Harvard Univ. Press, 2003.

Boulding, Kenneth. *Conflict and Defense: A General Theory.* New York: Harper & Brothers, 1962.

Boyce, T. D., and W. M. Chunnu. *Historicizing Fear: Ignorance, Vilification, and Othering.* Boulder: Univ. Press of Colorado, 2020.

Brines, Russell. *The Indo-Pakistani Conflict.* New York: Pall Mall Press, 1968.

Brotton, Jerry. *The Renaissance Bazaar: From the Silk Road to Michelangelo.* Oxford: Oxford Univ. Press, 2003.

Brown, Judith M. *Gandhi: Prisoner of Hope.* New Haven, CT: Yale Univ. Press, 1989.

Brown, Michael, ed. *Ethnic Conflict and International Security.* Princeton, NJ: Princeton Univ. Press, 1993.

———, ed. *The International Dimensions of Internal Conflict.* Cambridge, MA: MIT Press, 1996.

Brown, Michael, and Richard Rosecrance, eds. *The Costs of Conflict: Prevention and Cure in the Global Arena.* Lanham, MD: Rowman and Littlefield, 1999.

Burke, R. M. *Mainsprings of Indian and Pakistani Foreign Policies.* Minneapolis: Univ. of Minnesota Press, 1974.

Burrowes, Robert J. *The Strategy of Nonviolent Defense: A Gandhian Approach.* Albany: State Univ. of New York Press, 1996.

Burton, John. *Resolving Deep-Rooted Conflict: A Handbook.* Lanham, MD: Univ. Press of America, 1987.

———. *Violence Explained.* Manchester: Manchester Univ. Press, 1997.

Buzan, Barry. *People, States and Fear: An Agenda for International Security Studies in the Post–Cold War Era.* New York: Harvester Wheatsheaf, 1992.

———. "A Reductionist, Idealistic Notion That Adds Little Analytical Value." *Security Dialogue* 35, no. 3 (2004): 369–70.

Byman, Daniel. *Keeping the Peace: Lasting Solutions to Ethnic Conflicts.* Baltimore: Johns Hopkins Univ. Press, 2002.

Carr, E. H. *Nationalism and After.* London: Macmillan, 1945.

Chapman, Thomas, and Philip Roeder. "Partition as a Solution to Wars of Nationalism: The Importance of Institutions." *American Political Science Review* 101, no. 4 (2007): 677–91.

Chatterji, Joya. *The Spoils of Partition: Bengal and India, 1947–1967.* Cambridge: Cambridge Univ. Press, 2007.

Cheema, Zafar I. "Pakistan's Nuclear Use Doctrine and Command and Control." In *Planning the Unthinkable: How New Powers Will Use Nuclear, Biological, and Chemical Weapons,* edited by Peter R. Lavoy, Scott D. Sagan, and James J. Wirtz, 158–81. Ithaca, NY: Cornell Univ. Press.

Chengappa, R. *Weapons of Peace: The Secret Story of India's Quest to Be a Nuclear Power.* New Delhi: HarperCollins, 2001.

Chenoweth, Erica, and Kathleen Gallagher Cunningham. "Understanding Nonviolent Resistance: An Introduction." *Journal of Peace Research* 50, no. 3 (2013): 271–76.

Chenoweth, Erica, and Maria Stephan. "Why Civil Resistance Works: The Strategic Logic of Nonviolent Conflict." *International Security* 33, no. 1 (2008): 7–44.

Clark, Joshua, ed. *Civic Engagement for Empowerment and Belonging.* Berkeley: Othering and Belonging Institute, Univ. of California, Mar. 2020.

Cohen, Stephen P. *The Idea of Pakistan.* Washington, DC: Brookings Institution Press, 2004.

———. *India: Emerging Power.* Washington, DC: Brookings Institution Press, 2001.

———. *Shooting for a Century: The India-Pakistan Conundrum.* Washington, DC: Brookings Institution Press, 2013.

Collier, Paul. *Economic Causes of Civil Conflict and Their Implications for Policy.* Washington, DC: World Bank, 2000.

———. *Wars, Guns, and Votes: Democracy in Dangerous Places.* New York: Harper Perennial, 2010.

Collier, Paul, and Anke Hoeffler. "Conflicts." In *Global Crises: Global Solutions*, edited by B. Lomborg, 129–74. Cambridge: Cambridge Univ. Press, 2004.

———. "Greed and Grievance in Civil War." *Oxford Economic Papers* 56, no. 4 (2004): 563–95.

Collier, Paul, Anke Hoeffler, and Dominic Rohner. "Beyond Greed and Grievance: Feasibility and Civil War." *Oxford Economic Papers* 61, no. 1 (2009): 1–27.

Collins, Larry, and Dominique Lapierre. *Freedom at Midnight*. New York: Simon and Schuster, 1975.

Connor, Walker. "Ethnology and the Peace of South Asia." *World Politics* 22, no. 1 (1969): 51–86.

———. "Nation-Building or Nation-Destroying?" *World Politics* 24, no. 3 (1972): 319–55.

Coser, Lewis A. *The Functions of Social Conflict*. New York: Free Press, 1956.

Dawson, Pauline. *The Peacekeepers of Kashmir: The UN Military Observer Group in India and Pakistan*. New York: St. Martin's Press, 1994.

Deutsch, Karl. *Nationalism and Social Communication: An Inquiry into the Foundations of Nationality*. Cambridge, MA: MIT Press, 1966.

———. "Social Mobilization and Political Development." *American Political Science Review* 55, no. 3 (1961): 493–514.

Deutsch, Morton. "A Theoretical Perspective on Conflict and Conflict Resolution." In *Conflict Management and Problem Solving: Interpersonal to International Applications*, edited by Dennis J. D. Sandole and Ingrid Sandole-Staroste, 38–49. New York: New York Univ. Press, 1987.

Deutsch, Morton, Yakov Epstein, Donnah Canavan, and Peter Gumpert. "Strategies of Inducing Cooperation: An Experimental Study." *Journal of Conflict Resolution* 11, no. 3 (1967): 345–60.

Deutsch, Morton, and Robert M. Krauss. "Effect of Threat on Interpersonal Bargaining." *Journal of Abnormal and Social Psychology* 61 no. 2 (1960): 181–89.

Devereux, George. *From Anxiety to Method in the Behavioral Sciences, Etc.* Paris: Mouton, 1967.

Diamond, L., and J. McDonald. *Multi-track Diplomacy*. West Hartford, CT: Kumarian Press, 1996.

Diehl, Paul F., ed. *The Dynamics of Enduring Rivalries*. Urbana: Univ. of Illinois Press, 1998.

Diehl, Paul, and Gary Goertz. *War and Peace in International Rivalry*. Ann Arbor: Univ. of Michigan Press, 2000.

Diesing, Paul. "Bargaining Strategy and Union-Management Relationships." *Journal of Conflict Resolution* 5, no. 4 (1961): 369–78.

Diwakar, R. R. *Saga of Satyagraha*. New Delhi: Gandhi Peace Foundation, 1969.

Dixit, J. N. *India-Pakistan in War and Peace*. London: Routledge, 2002.

Durkheim, Emile. *The Elementary Forms of the Religious Life*. London: Allen and Unwin, 1964.

Durrani, Mahmud Ali. *India and Pakistan: The Cost of Conflict and the Benefits of Peace*. Karachi: Oxford Univ. Press, 2001.

Eidelson, Roy J., and Judy I. Eidelson. "Dangerous Ideas: Five Beliefs That Propel Groups toward Conflict." *American Psychologist* 58, no. 3 (2003): 182–92.

Faruqui, Ahmad. *Rethinking the National Security of Pakistan: The Price of Strategic Myopia*. Aldershot: Ashgate, 2003.

Findley, Michael G., James Piazza, and Joseph Young. "Games Rivals Play: Terrorism in International Rivalries." *Journal of Politics* 74, no. 1 (2012): 235–48.

Foltz, Richard. *Religions of the Silk Road: Overland Trade and Cultural Exchange from Antiquity to the Fifteenth Century*. New York: St. Martin's Press, 1999.

Futehally, Ilmas, and Semu Bhatt. "Cost of Conflict between India and Pakistan." Strategic Foresight Group, 2004.

Galtung, Johan. "Introduction: Peace by Peaceful Conflict Transformation—the TRANSCEND Approach." In *Handbook of Peace and Conflict Studies*, edited by Charles Webel and Johan Galtung, 14–32. Routledge: London & New York, 2007.

———. "On the Meaning of Nonviolence." *Journal of Peace Research* 2, no. 3 (1965): 228–57.

———. *Peace by Peaceful Means*. London: Sage, 1996.

———. "Two Worlds: Gandhi and the Modern World." In *Gandhi and the Modern World*, edited by Debidatta Aurobinda Mahapatra and Yashwant Pathak, 1–12. New York: Lexington, 2018.

———. "Violence, Peace, and Peace Research." *Journal of Peace Research* 6, no. 3 (1969): 167–91.

———. *The Way Is the Goal: Gandhi Today*. Ahmedabad: Gujarat Vidyapith Peace Research Centre, 1992.

Galtung, Johan, and Carl Jacobsen. *Searching for Peace*. London: Pluto, 2000.

Gandhi, M. K. *All Men Are Brothers: Autobiographical Reflections*. Edited by Krishna Kripalani. New York: Continuum, 1990.

———. *Autobiography: The Story of My Experiments with Truth*. Translated by Mahadev Desai. New York: Dover, 1983.

———. *Hind Swaraj, and Other Writings.* Edited by Anthony Parel. Cambridge: Cambridge Univ. Press, 1997.

Ganguly, Rajat. *Kin State Intervention in Ethnic Conflicts: Lessons from South Asia.* New Delhi: Sage, 1998.

Ganguly, Sumit. *Conflict Unending: India-Pakistan Tensions since 1947.* New Delhi: Oxford Univ. Press, 2002.

———. *The Crisis in Kashmir: Portents of War, Hopes of Peace.* Cambridge: Cambridge Univ. Press, 1999.

Ganguly, Sumit, and D. Hagerty. *Fearful Symmetry: India-Pakistan Crises in the Shadow of Nuclear Weapons.* Seattle: Univ. of Washington Press, 2005.

Gellner, Ernest. *Nations and Nationalism.* Ithaca, NY: Cornell Univ. Press, 1983.

Ghose, Aurobindo. *The Complete Works of Sri Aurobindo.* Vols. 6–7. Pondicherry: Sri Aurobindo Ashram, 2002.

Ghose, Sankar. *Mahatma Gandhi.* Bombay: Allied, 1991.

Gilmartin, David. "Partition, Pakistan, and South Asian History: In Search of a Narrative." *Journal of Asian Studies* 57, no. 4 (1998): 1068–95.

Goldstein, Joshua. *Winning the War on War: The Decline of Armed Conflict Worldwide.* New York: Plume, 2011.

Goor, L. van de, K. Rupesinghe, and P. Sciarone, eds. *Between Development and Destruction: An Enquiry into the Causes of Conflict in Post-colonial States.* New York: St. Martin's Press, 1996.

Greenhill, Kelly M., and Solomon Major. "The Perils of Profiling: Civil War Spoilers and the Collapse of Intrastate Peace Accords." *International Security* 31, no. 3 (2006–7): 7–40.

Gregg, Richard B. *The Power of Nonviolence.* Canton, ME: Greenleaf Books, 1960.

Guha, Ramachandra. *India after Gandhi: The History of the World's Largest Democracy.* New York: HarperCollins, 2007.

Gupta, Sisir. *Kashmir: A Study in India-Pakistan Relations.* Bombay: Asia, 1966.

Habibullah, Wajahat. *My Kashmir: Conflict and the Prospects for Enduring Peace.* Washington, DC: United States Institute of Peace Press, 2008.

Hagerty, Devin T. *The Consequences of Nuclear Proliferation: Lessons from South Asia.* Cambridge, MA: MIT Press, 1998.

Hall, E. T. *The Silent Language.* New York: Doubleday, 1981.

Halliday, Fred. "The Politics of the Umma: States and Community in Islamic Movements." *Mediterranean Politics* 7, no. 3 (2002): 20–41.

Haqqani, Husain. *Pakistan: Between Mosque and Military*. Washington, DC: Carnegie Endowment for International Peace, 2005.

Hardiman, David. *Gandhi in His Time and Ours: The Global Legacy of His Ideas*. New York: Columbia Univ. Press, 2003.

Hasan, Parvez. *My Life, My Country: Memoirs of a Pakistani Economist*. Lahore: Ferozsons, 2011.

Hobsbawm, E. J. *Nations and Nationalism since 1870: Programme, Myth, Reality*. Cambridge: Cambridge Univ. Press, 1993.

Hoddie, Matthew, and Caroline A. Hartzell. *Strengthening Peace in Post–Civil War States: Transforming Spoilers into Stakeholders*. Chicago: Univ. of Chicago Press, 2011.

Hofstede, G., G. J. Hofstede, and M. Minkov. *Culture and Organizations: Software of the Mind*. New York: McGraw-Hill, 2010.

Holmes, Robert L. *On War and Morality*. Princeton, NJ: Princeton Univ. Press, 1989.

Holmes, Robert L., and Barry L. Gan. *Nonviolence in Theory and Practice*. Long Grove, IL: Waveland, 2004.

Holsti, Kalevi. *The State, War, and the State of War*. Cambridge: Cambridge Univ. Press, 1996.

Howard, Veena R. *Gandhi's Ascetic Activism: Renunciation and Social Action*. Albany: State Univ. of New York Press, 2013.

Jahanbegloo, Ramin. *The Gandhian Moment*. Cambridge, MA: Harvard Univ. Press, 2013.

Jalal, Ayesha. *The Pity of Partition: Manto's Life, Times, and Work across the India-Pakistan Divide*. Princeton, NJ: Princeton Univ. Press, 2013.

———. *The Sole Spokesman: Jinnah, the Muslim League and the Demand for Pakistan*. Cambridge: Cambridge Univ. Press, 1985.

Javaid, Umbreen. "Urgency for Inter-state Dialogue for Fighting Terrorism in South Asia." *Journal of Political Studies* 18, no. 1 (2011): 1–14.

Jha, Prem Shankar. *Kashmir, 1947: Rival Versions of History*. New Delhi: Oxford Univ. Press, 1996.

Johansen, Jørgen. "Nonviolence: More than the Absence of Violence." In *Handbook of Peace and Conflict Studies*, edited by Charles Webel and Johan Galtung, 143–59. London: Routledge, 2007.

Johnson, Carter. "Keeping the Peace after Partition: Ethnic Minorities, Civil Wars, and the Third Generation Ethnic Security Dilemma." *Civil Wars* 17, no. 1 (2015): 25–50.

Jongman, Berto J. "Mapping the Dimensions of Contemporary Conflicts and Human Rights Violations." In *Searching for Peace in Central and South Asia: An Overview of Conflict Prevention and Peacebuilding Activities*, edited by Monique Mekenkamp, Paul van Tongreen, and Hans van de Veen, 17–27. Boulder, CO: Lynne Rienner, 2003.

Juergensmeyer, Mark. "Gandhi vs. Terrorism." *Daedalus* 136, no. 1 (2007): 30–39.

Kamra, Sukeshi. *Bearing Witness: Partition, Independence, End of the Raj*. Calgary: Univ. of Calgary Press, 2002.

Kant, Immanuel. *Perpetual Peace: A Philosophical Essay*. London: George Allen & Unwin, 1917.

Kapur, Ashok. "Major Powers and the Persistence of the India–Pakistan Conflict." In *The India-Pakistan Conflict: An Enduring Rivalry*, edited by T. V. Paul, 131–55. New York: Cambridge Univ. Press, 2005.

Kapur, S. Paul. *Dangerous Deterrent: Nuclear Weapons Proliferation and Conflict in South Asia*. Stanford, CA: Stanford Univ. Press, 2007.

Kathuria, Sanjay. "A Glass Half Full: The Promise of Regional Trade in South Asia." South Asia Development Forum, World Bank, 2018. https://open knowledge.worldbank.org/bitstream/handle/10986/30246/9781464812941 .pdf?sequence=8&isAllowed=y.

Kaufmann, Chaim. "Possible and Impossible Solutions to Ethnic Civil Wars." *International Security* 20, no. 4 (1996): 136–75.

Kaul, Suvir, ed. *The Partitions of Memory: The Afterlife of the Division of India*. Bloomington: Indiana Univ. Press, 2002.

Kedourie, Elie. *Nationalism*. London: Hutchinson, 1960.

———. *Nationalism in Asia and Africa*. London: Weidenfeld & Nicolson, 1971.

Kew, Darren. *Civil Society, Conflict Resolution, and Democracy in Nigeria*. Syracuse, NY: Syracuse Univ. Press, 2016.

Khan, Akbar. *Raiders in Kashmir*. Karachi: Pak, 1970.

Khan, Saira. "Nuclear Weapons and the Prolongation of the India–Pakistan Rivalry." In *The India-Pakistan Conflict: An Enduring Rivalry*, edited by T. V. Paul, 156–77. New York: Cambridge Univ. Press, 2005.

Khan, Yasmin. *The Great Partition: The Making of India and Pakistan*. New Haven, CT: Yale Univ. Press, 2007.

Kilot, Nurit, and David Newman, eds. *Geopolitics at the End of the Twentieth Century: The Changing World Political Map*. London: Frank Cass, 2000.

Klitgaard, Robert E. "Gandhi's Non-violence as a Tactic." *Journal of Peace Research* 8, no. 2 (1971): 143–53.

Kohn, Hans. *The Idea of Nationalism: A Study in Its Origins and Background.* 1944. Reprint, New Brunswick, NJ: Transaction, 2008.

Koithara, Verghese. *Crafting Peace in Kashmir.* New Delhi: Sage, 2004.

Korbel, Josef. *Danger in Kashmir.* Princeton, NJ: Princeton Univ. Press, 1954.

Krepon, Michael. *The Stability-Instability Paradox, Misperception, and Escalation Control in South Asia.* Washington, DC: Henry L. Stimson Center, 2003. http://www.stimson.org/southasia/pdtykreponmay03.pdf.

Kriesberg, Louis, Terrell Northrup, and S. Thorson, eds. *Intractable Conflicts and Their Transformation.* Syracuse, NY: Syracuse Univ. Press, 1989.

Kugelman, Michael, and Robert M. Hathaway. *Pakistan-India Trade: What Needs to Be Done? What Does It Matter?* Washington, DC: Wilson Center, 2013. https://www.wilsoncenter.org/sites/default/files/media/documents/publication/ASIA_121219_Pakistn%20India%20Trade%20rptFINAL.pdf.

Kulke, H., and D. Rothermund. *A History of India.* New York: Routledge, 2016.

Kurtz, Lester. "Gandhi and His Legacies." In *Encyclopedia of Violence, Peace, & Conflict,* edited by Lester Kurtz, 2:837–51. Oxford: Elsevier, 2008.

Landsberg, C. *The Quiet Diplomacy of Liberation: International Politics and South Africa's Transition.* Johannesburg: Jacana Media, 2004.

Lebow, Richard Ned. *Between Peace and War.* Baltimore: Johns Hopkins Univ. Press, 1984.

Lederach, J. P. *The Little Book of Conflict Transformation.* Intercourse, PA: Good Books, 2003.

———. *Preparing for Peace: Conflict Transformation across Cultures.* Syracuse, NY: Syracuse Univ. Press, 1995.

Leng, Russell J. *Bargaining and Learning in Recurring Crises.* Ann Arbor: Univ. of Michigan Press, 2000.

———. "Realpolitik and Learning in the India–Pakistan Rivalry." In *The India Pakistan Conflict: An Enduring Rivalry,* edited by T. V. Paul, 103–27. Cambridge: Cambridge Univ. Press, 2005.

Levinas, Emmanuel. *Le temps et l'autre (Time and the Other): Lectures in Paris at the College Philosophique, 1946–1947.* Translated by Richard A. Cohen. Pittsburgh: Duquesne Univ. Press, 1990.

———. *Totalité et infini (Totality and Infinity).* Translated by Alphonso Lingis. Pittsburgh: Duquesne Univ. Press, 1969.

Lewis, John. *The Case against Pacifism.* London: Allen and Unwin, 1937.

Lindner, Evelin G. *Making Enemies: Humiliation and International Conflict.* Greenwood, CT: Praeger Security International, 2006.

Liu, Xinru. *Silk and Religion: An Exploration of Material Life and the Thought of People, AD 600–1200.* Delhi: Oxford Univ. Press, 1996.

Lohmann, Sascha. "Diplomats and the Use of Economic Sanctions." In *New Realities in Foreign Affairs: Diplomacy in the 21st Century,* edited by Volker Stanzel. Berlin: German Institute for International and Security Affairs, 2018. https://www.swp-berlin.org/fileadmin/contents/products/research_papers/2018RP11_sze.pdf.

Mack, Andrew. "A Signifier of Shared Values." *Security Dialogue* 35, no. 3 (2004): 366–67.

Mack, John E. "The Psychodynamics of Victimization among National Groups in Conflict." In *The Psychodynamics of International Relationships.* Vol. 1, *Concepts and Theories,* edited by Vamik Volkan, Demetrios Julius, and Joseph Montville. Lanham, MD: Lexington Books, 1990.

Magalhaēs, C. J. *The Pure Concept of Diplomacy.* New York: Greenwood Press, 1988.

Mahapatra, D. A. *Central Eurasia: Geopolitics, Compulsions and Connections.* New Delhi: Lancers, 2008.

———. *Conflict Management in Kashmir: State-People Relations and Peace.* Cambridge: Cambridge Univ. Press, 2018.

———. "Earthquake in Jammu and Kashmir: A Report." *Himalayan and Central Asian Studies* 9, no. 4 (2005): 37–46.

———. "From Alienation to Co-existence and Beyond: Examining the Evolution of the Borderland in Kashmir." *Journal of Borderland Studies* 33, no. 1 (2016): 141–55.

———. *Making Kashmir Borderless.* New Delhi: Manohar, 2012.

———. "Mapping Transitional Justice in Kashmir: Drivers, Initiatives, and Challenges." Working paper, Oxford Transitional Justice Research, Oxford Univ., 2010.

———. "Negotiating Space in the Conflict Zone of Kashmir." In *Spaces of Conflict in Everyday Life,* edited by Martin Sokefeld, 163–85. Bielefeld, Germany: Transcript.

———. "Positioning the People in the Contested Borders of Kashmir." *Center for International Border Research.* Working paper 21, Queen's Univ., UK, 2011. https://www.qub.ac.uk/research-centres/CentreforInternationalBorders Research/Publications/WorkingPapers/CIBRWorkingPapers/Filetoupload,219140,en.pdf.

———. "Prospects of Inclusive Peace, Perception of Players and Stakes Involved in Post-9/11 Afghanistan." In *Conflict and Peace in Eurasia,* edited by D. A. Mahapatra, 159–75. New York: Routledge, 2013.

———. "The Silk Route in Kashmir: Preliminary Research Findings." *Central Eurasian Studies Review* 8, no. 1 (2009): 13–15.

———. "Two Cities, Shared History." *Transcend Media Weekly,* May 12–18, 2014. https://www.transcend.org/tms/2014/05/two-cities-shared-history/.

Mansfield, Edward D., and Brian M. Pollins, eds. *Economic Interdependence and International Conflict: New Perspectives on an Enduring Debate.* Ann Arbor: Univ. of Michigan Press, 2003.

Maoz, Zeev, and Ben D. Mor. *Bound by Struggle: The Strategic Evolution of Enduring International Rivalries.* Ann Arbor: Univ. of Michigan Press, 2002.

Martin, Brian. *Uprooting War.* London: Freedom, 1984.

Martinez, Oscar. *Border People: Life and Society in the US–Mexico Borderlands.* Tucson: Univ. of Arizona Press, 1994.

Maslow, A. H. "A Theory of Human Motivation." *Psychological Review* 50, no. 4 (1943): 370–96.

Mathai, M. P. *Mahatma Gandhi's World-View.* New Delhi: Gandhi Peace Foundation, 2000.

McAdam, Doug, and Sidney Tarrow. "Nonviolence as Contentious Interaction." *PS: Political Science & Politics* 33, no. 2 (2000): 149–54.

McDaniel, Jay. *Gandhi's Hope: Learning from Other Religions as a Path to Peace.* New York: Orbis Books, 2005.

McIntyre, W. David. *The Commonwealth of Nations: Origins and Impact, 1869–1971.* Minneapolis: Univ. of Minnesota Press, 1977.

Mehta, U. S. "Gandhi and the Common Logic of War and Peace." *Raritan: A Quarterly Review* 30, no. 1 (2010): 134–56.

Mellon, James G. "Pan-Arabism, Pan-Islamism and Inter-state Relations in the Arab World." *Nationalism and Ethnic Politics* 8, no. 4 (2002): 1–15.

Menon, Ritu, and Kamla Bhasin. *Borders and Boundaries: How Women Experienced the Partition of India.* New Brunswick, NJ: Rutgers Univ. Press, 1998.

Miall, Hugh. "Conflict Transformation: A Multi-dimensional Task." Berlin: Berghof Research Center for Constructive Conflict Management, 2004. https://www.berghof-foundation.org/fileadmin/redaktion/Publications/Handbook/Articles/miall_handbook.pdf.

———. *The Peacemakers.* London: Palgrave Macmillan, 1992.

Miall, Hugh, Oliver Ramsbotham, and Tom Woodhouse. *Contemporary Conflict Resolution: The Prevention, Management and Transformation of Deadly Conflicts*. Cambridge: Polity Press, 1999.

Mistry, D. "Tempering Optimism about Nuclear Deterrence in South Asia." *Security Studies* 18, no. 1 (2009): 148–82.

Mitton, John. "The India-Pakistan Rivalry and Failure in Afghanistan." *International Journal* 69, no. 3 (2014): 353–76.

Mohan, C. Raja. *How Prime Minister Modi Can Sustain India's Pakistan Dialogue*. Washington, DC: Carnegie Endowment for International Peace, 2016.

Montville, J. "Track Two Diplomacy: The Arrow and the Olive Branch, a Case for Track Two Diplomacy." In *The Psychodynamics of International Relations*. Vol. 2, *Unofficial Diplomacy at Work*, edited by V. D. Volkan, M. D. J. Montville, and D. A. Julius, 161–75. Lexington, MA: Lexington Books, 1991.

Mozaffari, Mehdi. *Islamism: A New Totalitarianism*. Boulder, CO: Lynne Rienner, 2017.

———. "What Is Islamism? History and Definition of a Concept." *Totalitarian Movements and Political Religions* 8, no. 1 (2007): 17–33.

Mukherjee, Anit. "A Brand New Day or Back to the Future? The Dynamics of India-Pakistan Relations." *India Review* 8, no. 4 (2009): 404–45.

Mukherjee, Prithwindra. "Had Bagha Jatin Succeeded! A Nationalist Revolt in Colonial India during World War I." *Selections from the Radical Humanist* 2 (2006–18): 81–93.

Naess, Arne. *Gandhi and Group Conflict: An Exploration of Satyagraha*. Oslo: Universitetsforlaget, 1974.

Nagler, Michael N. "Peacemaking through Nonviolence." *Peace and Conflict Studies* 4, no. 2 (1997). http://www.gmu.edu/programs/icar/pcs/nagler.html.

Nawaz, Shuja, and Mohan Guruswamy. "India and Pakistan: The Opportunity Cost of Conflict." *Atlantic Council* (Apr. 2014). https://www.files.ethz.ch/isn/182161/India_and_Pakistan_Opportunity_Cost_of_Conflict_web.pdf.

Nayar, Kuldip. *Wall at Wagah: India-Pakistan Relations*. New Delhi: Gyan Publishing House, 2003.

Nayar, Kuldip, and Asif Noorani. *Tales of Two Cities*. New Delhi: Roli Books, 2008.

Nebenzahl, Kenneth. *Mapping the Silk Road and Beyond: 2000 Years of Exploring the East*. New York: Phaidon Press, 2004.

Nehru, Jawaharlal. *The Discovery of India*. Delhi: Oxford Univ. Press, 1985.

———. *Nehru on Gandhi*. New York: John Day, 1948.

———. *Soviet Russia: Some Random Sketches and Impressions*. Allahabad: Allahabad Law Journal Press, 1928.

Nepstad, Sharon Erickson. *Nonviolent Revolutions: Civil Resistance in the Late 20th Century*. New York: Oxford Univ. Press, 2011.

Newman, Edward. "Human Security and Constructivism." *International Studies Perspectives* 2, no. 3 (2001): 239–51.

Newman, Edward, and Joanne van Selm, eds. *Refugee and Forced Displacement: International Security, Human Vulnerability and the State*. Tokyo: United Nations Univ. Press, 2003.

Nojeim, Michael J. *Gandhi and King: The Power of Non-violent Resistance*. Westport, CT: Praeger, 2004.

O'Leary, Brendan, Ian Lustick, and Thomas Callaghy. *Right-Sizing the State: The Politics of Moving Borders*. New York: Oxford Univ. Press, 2001.

Orwell, George. "Reflections on Gandhi." *Partisan Review* 16, no. 1 (1949): 85–92.

Özdalga, Elisabeth. "Islamism and Nationalism as Sister Ideologies: Reflections on the Politicization of Islam in a Longue Durée Perspective." *Middle Eastern Studies* 45, no. 3 (2009): 407–23.

Pandey, Gyanendra. *Remembering Partition: Violence, Nationalism and History in India*. Cambridge: Cambridge Univ. Press, 2001.

Parekh, Bhikhu. *Gandhi*. New York: Sterling, 2010.

———. *Rethinking Multiculturalism: Cultural Diversity and Political Theory*. Cambridge, MA: Harvard Univ. Press, 2000.

Paul, T. V., ed. *The India-Pakistan Conflict: An Enduring Rivalry*. New York: Cambridge Univ. Press, 2005.

Philips, C. H., and M. D. Wainwright, eds. *The Partition of India: Policies and Perspectives, 1935–1947*. Cambridge, MA: MIT Press, 1970.

Pinker, Steven. *The Better Angels of Our Nature: Why Violence Has Declined*. New York: Viking, 2011.

Plato. *Phaedrus*. Translated by Benjamin Jowett. http://classics.mit.edu/Plato/phaedrus.html.

Power, Paul F. "A Gandhian Model for World Politics." In *Gandhi: His Relevance For Our Times*, edited by G. Ramachandran and T. K. Mahadevan. New Delhi: Gandhi Peace Foundation, 1967.

Pruitt, Dean G. "Creative Approaches to Negotiation." In *Conflict Management and Problem Solving: Interpersonal to International Applications*, edited by Dennis J. D. Sandole and Ingrid Sandole-Staroste. New York: New York Univ. Press, 1987.

Pruitt, Dean G., and Jeffrey Z. Rubin. *Social Conflict: Escalation, Stalemate and Settlement*. New York: Random House, 1986.

Puri, Balraj. *Kashmir: Towards Insurgency*. New Delhi: Orient Longman, 1993.

Rice, Edward. *Wars of the Third Kind: Conflict in Underdeveloped Countries*. Berkeley: Univ. of California Press, 1988.

Rock, Stephen. *Why Peace Breaks Out*. Chapel Hill: Univ. of North Carolina Press, 1989.

Rubin, Jeffrey Z., and Bert R. Brown. *The Social Psychology of Bargaining and Negotiation*. New York: Academic Press, 1975.

Russell, Bertrand. "Mahatma Gandhi." *Atlantic Monthly*, Dec. 1952. https://www.mkgandhi.org/articles/about_gandhi.htm.

Sagan, Scott D., ed. *Inside Nuclear South Asia*. Stanford, CA: Stanford Univ. Press.

Said, Edward. *Orientalism*. London: Routledge and Kegan Paul, 1978.

Sambanis, Nicholas. "Partition as a Solution to Ethnic War: An Empirical Critique of the Theoretical Literature." *World Politics* 52, no. 4 (2000): 437–83.

Scalmer, Sean. *Gandhi in the West: The Mahatma and the Rise of Radical Protest*. Cambridge: Cambridge Univ. Press, 2011.

Schimmel, Annemarie. *Gabriel's Wing: A Study into the Religious Ideas of Sir Muhammad Iqbal*. Leiden: E. J. Brill, 1963.

Schofield, Victoria. *Kashmir in Conflict: India, Pakistan and the Unfinished War*. London: I. B. Tauris, 2002.

Sen, Amartya. "Gandhi Values and Terrorism." *ETC: A Review of General Semantics* 65, no. 1 (2008): 76–79.

Sen, L. P. *Slender Was the Thread: Kashmir Confrontation, 1947–48*. New Delhi: Orient Longman, 1969.

Sharp, Gene. "Gandhi's Political Significance Today." In *Gandhi: His Relevance for Our Times*, edited by G. Ramachandran and T. K. Mahadevan. New Delhi: Gandhi Peace Foundation, 1967.

———. *The Politics of Nonviolent Action*. Boston: Porter-Sargent, 1973.

———. "The Role of Power in Nonviolent Struggle." Monograph Series, no. 3. Albert Einstein Institution, 1990.

Shaykhutdinov, Renat. "Give Peace a Chance: Nonviolent Protest and the Creation of Territorial Autonomy Arrangements." *Journal of Peace Research* 47, no. 2 (2010): 179–91.

Sheafer, Tamir, and Shira Dvir-Gvirsman. "The Spoiler Effect: Framing Attitudes and Expectations toward Peace." *Journal of Peace Research* 47, no. 2 (2010): 205–15.

Shekhawat, Seema. *Gender, Conflict and Peace in Kashmir: Invisible Stakehold-ers*. Cambridge: Cambridge Univ. Press, 2014.

Shekhawat, Seema, and D. A. Mahapatra. *Contested Borders and Division of Families in Kashmir: Contextualizing the Ordeal of the Kargil Women*. New Delhi: WISCOMP, 2009.

———. *Kargil Displaced of Akhnoor in Jammu and Kashmir: Enduring Ordeal and Bleak Future*. Geneva: Internal Displacement Monitoring Centre, 2006.

Shure, Gerald H., Robert J. Meeker, and Earle A. Hansford. "The Effectiveness of Pacifist Strategies in Bargaining Games." *Journal of Conflict Resolution* 9, no. 1 (1965): 106–17.

Sidhu, W. P. S. "India's Nuclear Use Doctrine." In *Planning the Unthinkable: How New Powers Will Use Nuclear, Biological, and Chemical Weapons*, ed-ited by Peter R. Lavoy, Scott D. Sagan, and James J. Wirtz, 125–57. Ithaca, NY: Cornell Univ. Press, 2000.

Siegel, Sidney, and Lawrence E. Fouraker. *Bargaining and Group Decision Mak-ing*. New York: McGraw-Hill, 1960.

Sifton, John. *Violence All Around*. Cambridge, MA: Harvard Univ. Press, 2015.

Singer, J. David, Stuart Bremer, and John Stuckey. "Capability Distribution, Un-certainty, and Major Power War, 1820–1965." In *Peace, War, and Numbers*, edited by Bruce Russett, 19–48. Beverly Hills: Sage, 1972.

Singh, Jaswant. *Jinnah: India—Partition—Independence*. Oxford: Oxford Univ. Press, 2010.

Singh, Khushwant. *Train to Pakistan*. New York: Grove Press, 1981.

Singh, R. Raj. "Gandhi and the Fundamentals of World Peace." *Peace Research* 30, no. 3 (1998): 96–102.

Sinha, Riya, and Niara Sareen. "India's Limited Trade Connectivity with South Asia." *Brooking Report*, May 26, 2020. https://www.brookings.edu/research/indias-limited-trade-connectivity-with-south-asia/.

Sinha, S. K. *Operation Rescue: Military Operations in Jammu and Kashmir, 1947–49*. New Delhi: Visions Books, 1977.

Smith, Anthony D. "Conflict and Collective Identity: Class, Ethnie and Nation." In *International Conflict Resolution: Theory and Practice*, edited by E. Azar and J. Burton, 63–84. Sussex: Wheatsheaf, 1986.

Smith, Zachary. *Age of Fear: Othering and American Identity during World War I*. Baltimore: Johns Hopkins Univ. Press, 2019.

Sorensen, Georg. "Utopianism in Peace Research: The Gandhian Heritage." *Journal of Peace Research* 29, no 2 (1992): 135–44.

Staniland, Paul. "Organizing Insurgency: Networks, Resources, and Rebellion in South Asia." *International Security* 37, no. 1 (2012): 142–77.

Stavenhagen, R. *Ethnic Conflicts and the Nation-State.* Basingstoke: Macmillan, 1996.

Stedman, Stephen J. "Spoiler Problems in Peace Processes." *International Security* 22, no. 2 (1997): 5–53.

Stiehm, Judith. "Nonviolence Is Two." *Social Inquiry* 38, no. 1 (1968): 23–30.

Svensson, Isak, and Mathilda Lindgren. "From Bombs to Banners? The Decline of Wars and the Rise of Unarmed Uprisings in East Asia." *Security Dialogue* 42, no. 3 (2011): 219–37.

Swami, Praveen. *India, Pakistan and the Secret Jihad: The Covert War in Kashmir, 1947–2004.* New Delhi: Routledge, 2006.

Tagore, Rabindranath. *Home and the World.* New Delhi: Macmillan India, 1919.

Talbot, Ian, and Gurharpal Singh. *The Partition of India.* Cambridge: Cambridge Univ. Press, 2009.

Talbot, Phillips. *An American Witness to India's Partition.* New Delhi: Sage, 2007.

Tellis, Ashley. *Are India-Pakistan Peace Talks Worth a Damn?* Washington, DC: Carnegie Endowment for International Peace, 2017. https://carnegie endowment.org/files/India-Pakistan_Peace_Talks_finall.pdf.

————. *India's Emerging Nuclear Posture.* Santa Monica: RAND, 2001.

Thompson, William R. "Identifying Rivals and Rivalries in World Politics." *International Studies Quarterly* 45, 4 (1995): 557–87.

————. "Principal Rivalries." *Journal of Conflict Resolution* 39, no. 2 (1995): 195–223.

Thompson, William R., and David Dreyer. *Handbook of International Rivalries, 1494–2010.* Washington, DC: CQ Press, 2011.

Tidwell, Alan C. *Conflict Resolved? A Critical Assessment of Conflict Resolution.* London: Pinter, 1998.

Tir, Jaroslav, and Paul F. Diehl. "Geographic Dimensions of Enduring Rivalries." *Political Geography* 21, 2 (2002): 263–86.

Toon, O. B., et al. "Rapidly Expanding Nuclear Arsenals in Pakistan and India Portend Regional and Global Catastrophe." *Science Advances* 5, no. 10 (2019). https://advances.sciencemag.org/content/5/10/eaay5478.

Tremblay, R. C., and J. Schofield. "Institutional Causes of the India–Pakistan Rivalry." In *The India-Pakistan Conflict: An Enduring Rivalry,* edited by T. V. Paul, 225–48. New York: Cambridge Univ. Press, 2005.

Turner, J. C., and R. Y. Bourhis. "Social Identity, Interdependence and the Social Groups: A Reply to Rabbie et al." In *Social Groups as Identities: Developing the Legacy of Henri Tajfel*, edited by W. P. Robinson. Oxford: Butterworth Heinemann, 1996.

Valeriano, Brandon. *Becoming Rivals: The Process of Interstate Rivalry Development*. New York: Routledge, 2013.

Varshney, Ashutosh. *Ethnic Conflict and Civic Life: Hindus and Muslims in India*. New Haven, CT: Yale Univ. Press, 2002.

Vasquez, John A. "Distinguishing Rivals That Go to War from Those That Do Not: A Quantitative Comparative Case Study of the Two Paths to War." *International Studies Quarterly* 40, no. 4 (1996): 531–58.

———. "The India–Pakistan Conflict in Light of General Theories of War, Rivalry, and Deterrence." In *The India-Pakistan Conflict: An Enduring Rivalry*, edited by T. V. Paul, 54–79. New York: Cambridge Univ. Press, 2005.

———. *The War Puzzle*. New York: Cambridge Univ. Press, 1993.

Virdee, Pippa. *From the Ashes of 1947: Reimagining Punjab*. Cambridge: Cambridge Univ. Press, 2018.

Walter, Barbara. "Does Conflict Beget Conflict? Explaining Recurring Civil War." *Journal of Peace Research* 41, no. 3 (2004): 371–88.

Waterman, Stanley. "Partitioned States." *Political Geography Quarterly* 6, no. 2 (1987): 151–70.

Wayman, Frank W. "Rivalries: Recurrent Disputes and Explaining War." In *What Do We Know about War?*, edited by John Vasquez, 219–34. Oxford: Rowman and Littlefield, 2000.

Weber, Thomas. "Gandhian Philosophy, Conflict Resolution Theory and Practical Approaches to Negotiation." *Journal of Peace Research* 38, no. 4 (2001): 493–513.

———. *Gandhi's Peace Army: The Shanti Sena and Unarmed Peacekeeping*. Syracuse, NY: Syracuse Univ. Press, 1996.

Weiner, Myron. *The Politics of Scarcity*. Chicago: Univ. of Chicago Press, 1962.

Weiss-Wik, Stephen. "Enhancing Negotiators' Successfulness: Self-Help Books and Related Empirical Research." *Journal of Conflict Resolution* 27, no. 4 (1983): 706–39.

Widmalm, Sten. *Kashmir in Comparative Perspective: Democracy and Violent Separatism in India*. London: Routledge Curzon, 2002.

Wilson, Kellog V., and V. Edwin Bixenstine. "Forms of Social Control in Two-Person Two-Choice Games." In *Games Theory and Related Approaches to Social Behavior*, edited by Martin Shubik, 338–58. New York: Wiley, 1964.

Wilson, Thomas M., and Hastings Donnan, eds. *Border Identities: Nation and State at International Frontiers.* Cambridge: Cambridge Univ. Press, 1998.

———. "Nation, State and Identity at International Borders." In *Border Identities: Nation and State at International Frontiers*, edited by Thomas M. Wilson and Hastings Donnan, 1–30. Cambridge: Cambridge Univ. Press, 1998.

Wirsing, Robert G. *Kashmir: In the Shadow of War.* New York: M. E. Sharpe, 2003.

Wojczewski, Thorsten. "The Persistency of the India–Pakistan Conflict: Chances and Obstacles of the Bilateral Composite Dialogue." *Journal of Asian Security and International Affairs* 1, no. 3 (2014): 319–45.

Wolpert, Stanley. *India and Pakistan: Continued Conflict or Cooperation?* Berkeley: Univ. of California Press, 2010.

———. *Jinnah of Pakistan.* Delhi: Oxford Univ. Press, 2005.

Wood, Frances. *The Silk Road: Two Thousand Years in the Heart of Asia.* London: British Library, 2003.

Zamindar, Vazira. *The Long Partition and the Making of Modern South Asia: Refugees, Boundaries, Histories.* New York: Columbia Univ. Press, 2007.

Ziegler, W. D. *War, Peace, and International Politics.* Boston: Little, Brown, 1984.

Zinkin, Taya. "The Background of Indo-Pakistani Relations." *International Relations* 9, no. 1 (1987): 31–38.

Ziring, Lawrence. "The Geopolitics of the Asian Subcontinent: Pakistan's Security Environment." In *Contemporary Problems of Pakistan*, edited by J. Henry Korson, 147–69. Boulder, CO: Westview Press, 1993.

Selected Online Sources

https://belonging.berkeley.edu
https://www.1947partitionarchive.org
https://www.crisisgroup.org
https://www.hudson.org
https://www.presidency.ucsb.edu
https://www.speaker.gov
https://www.stimson.org
https://www.un.org

Index

Debidatta Aurobinda Mahapatra is a professor of political science at the Florida State College at Jacksonville.

Seema Shekhawat teaches political science at the University of North Florida.

Printed in the USA
CPSIA information can be obtained
at www.ICGtesting.com
LVHW042025061023
758535LV00081B/537

9 780815 638100